GCSE
SOCIOLOGY

Stephen Moore
Reader in Social Policy
Anglia Polytechnic University

Letts

EDUCATIONAL

Every effort has been made to trace copyright holders and to obtain their
permission for the use of copyright material. The author and publishers will
gladly receive information enabling them to rectify any error or omission in
subsequent editions.

First published 1985
Revised 1989, 1992
Second edition 1997

Text: © Stephen Moore 1985, 1997
Design and illustrations: © BPP (Letts Educational) Ltd 1985, 1997

Letts Educational
Aldine House
Aldine Place
London W12 8AW
Tel: 0181 740 2266
Fax: 0181 743 8451
e-mail: mail@lettsed.co.uk

British Library Cataloguing in Publication Data
A CIP record for this book is available from the British Library.

ISBN 1 85758 593 3

Acknowledgements

I would like to acknowledge the invaluable work done by Simon Elliot on the sample answers and on the
chapter on the research project.

Stephen Moore

The author and publishers gratefully acknowledge the following for permission to use questions and
copyright material in this book:
Stimulus/structured-response and short-answer questions (Chapter 20) 1, 4, 5, 8, 12, 14 and 15:
Reproduced by kind permission of the Midland Examining Group. The University of Cambridge local
Examinations Syndicate/Midland Examining Group bears no responsibility for the example answers to
questions taken from its past question papers which are contained in this publication. Essay questions
(Chapter 20) 4d, 5b and d, 9c and 14a, b and c: Reproduced by kind permission of Northern Examinations
and Assessment Board. The author accepts responsibility for the answers provided, which may not
necessarily constitute the only possible solutions. Stimulus/structured-response and short-answer questions
(Chapter 20) 2, 3, 6, 10, 11, 13 and 16; essay questions 4e and 17c: Reproduced by kind permission of the
Southern Examining Group. Any answers or hints on answers are the sole responsibility of the author and
have not been provided or approved by the Board.
Figs. 3.1 (p. 20), 3.3 (p. 24), 5.4 (p. 55) and 17.1 (p. 161) Reproduced by courtesy of Stanley Thornes
Publishers; Figs. 3.2 (p. 21), 8.1 (p. 76), 11.1 (p. 103), 11.2 (p. 104), 11.5 (p. 106), 11.6 (p. 108), 16.1
(p.153) and the tables/illustrations/text extract on pp. 192, 197, 198, 201, 202, 204 and 206 Reproduced
by courtesy of the Office for National Statistics; Figs. 5.3A (p. 54) and 17.2 (p. 168) Reproduced by
courtesy of Guardian Newspapers Ltd; Fig. 5.3 B–D Reproduced by courtesy of Macmillan Publishers;
Figs. 13.2 (p. 122) and 13.4 (p. 124) Reproduced by courtesy of the Child Poverty Action Group; the
cartoons on pp. 193 and 195, the text extract on p. 199 and the table on p. 209 Reproduced by courtesy of
Blackwell Publishers; the advertisement on p. 197 Reproduced by courtesy of the Ramblers Association;
the table on p. 200 Reproduced by courtesy of the Sunday Times © Times Newspapers Limited, 1992.

Typesetting by KAI, Nottingham
Printed and bound in Great Britain by Progressive Printing (UK) Ltd, Leigh-on-Sea, Essex

Letts Educational is the trading name of BPP (Letts Educational) Ltd

Contents

Introduction

The GCSE examination requires you to know the subject matter of Sociology; to be able to analyse issues based on this information; and to be able to carry out an enquiry in the field of Sociology which shows you have mastered the research techniques of the subject.

This Study Guide contains all the information and coverage of issues necessary to gain your GCSE. There is all the information you need to plan and carry out an excellent piece of coursework, plus advice on what types of examination questions occur and practice in how best to answer them. There are also self-test questions which you can ask yourself at the end of each chapter to see if you have really understood what you have read.

Use the book carefully throughout your examination course and you will enter the examination well-prepared and with confidence, and also with the knowledge that you have completed a good piece of coursework.

How to use this book

1. First, check which Examining Group you are following. Ask your teacher or, if you are a private student, write to the Group for a copy of the syllabus. Incidentally, if you are a private student, you have to be registered and accepted by a recognised educational institution. Check with the Examining Group. The addresses of the Examining Groups are given below.

2. Look at the syllabus checklists below to find out which topics you need to study. As you complete each topic, tick it off in the column provided.

3. Work your way through all the relevant chapters. Try to do this at the same time as you are studying that particular subject at school, rather than in a panic at the end of your course!

4. At the end of each chapter you will find **self-test questions**. Answer these and then compare your answers with those provided at the back of the book. Do not worry if your answers are not always the same, though they should be similar.

5. After you have got some way through the book, turn to Chapter 19 on Types of GCSE examination questions. Find out the types of examination questions asked by your Examining Group and study the techniques which are suggested for answering them.

6. When you have finished all the chapters in the book, go through the examination questions (Chapter 20) and select relevant questions. Compare your answers with those given – again they need not be exactly the same, although they should be similar in both content and standard.

7. Your teacher will tell you when he/she wants to begin the project work. At this time, please turn to Chapter 21, where you will be provided with help and advice on coursework. In selecting topics for a possible project, flick through the book and tackle an issue that interests you.

Syllabus checklists

Midland Examining Group (MEG)

Address: 1 Hills Road, Cambridge CB1 2EU   Tel: 01223 553311

Sociology 2370

Syllabus topic	*Covered in Unit No:*	✓
Stratification		
Wealth and income	5.9, 13.6, 13.7, 13.8	
Social construction of age	7.1 – 7.4	
Ethnic groups	8.1 – 8.6	
Gender	6.1, 6.2, 6.3	
Social class	5.3, 5.4, 5.5, 5.6, 5.7, 5.8, 5.9	
Power and authority		
Forms of power and authority	14.1	
Influencing decision making	14.6	
Democracy in the UK	14.2, 14.3, 14.4, 14.5	
Family		
Why families?	3.5	
Roles in the family	3.6, 3.7	
Changing family patterns	3.1, 3.2, 3.3, 3.4	
Education		
What is education?	4.1, 4.3	
British educational system	4.2	
Variations within the educational process	4.4 – 4.5, 4.6	
Employment		
Meaning of work and non-work	9.1	
Structural organisation of work and the changing nature of technology	9.3, 10.1, 10.2, 10.4	
Changing work and employment	9.2, 10.3, 10.4	
Experience of work and non-work	9.4, 9.5, 9.6, 10.5, 10.6	
Methodology		
Main methods of investigation	2.1 – 2.10	
Presenting information	Chapter 21	
OPTIONS		
Crime and deviance		
Normal and deviant behaviour	15.1 – 15.5	
Explaining crime	16.4, 16.5, 16.6, 16.7	
Extent of crime	16.8, 16.9	
The Media		
Forms of media	17.1	
Impact of the media	17.2, 17.3, 17.4, 17.5, 17.6, 17.7	
Youth Culture and Social Movements		
Sub-cultures	7.3	
Development of subcultures	7.4, 7.5	

Examination breakdown

Foundation tier (G–C): Papers 1 and 2; coursework

Higher Tier (D–A★): Papers 3 and 4; coursework

Papers 1 and 3	2 hours	Consist of five structured questions based on stimulus material. Candidates to answer **all** questions, each based on one section of the Core.	40%
Papers 2 and 4	$1\frac{1}{2}$ hours	*Section A*: Consists of one compulsory exercise on Methodology based on source material on a theme drawn from the Core. Candidates to answer **all** questions.	40%
		Section B: Consists of three structured questions based on stimulus material. Candidates to answer **one** question, each based on the Options.	
Coursework	2000 words maximum	Candidates to complete a sociology Enquiry based on the syllabus content.	20%

Northern Examinations and Assessment Board

Devas Street, Manchester M15 6EX   Tel: 0161 953 1180

Sociology 1374

Syllabus topic	*Covered in Unit No:*	✓
A Methods of Investigation and Sources of Information		
Main methods used by sociologists	2.1, 2.2, 2.3, 2.4, 2.5, 2.6, 2.7, 2.10	
Official statistics	2.8, 2.9	
Presentation	Chapter 21	
B The Individual in Society		
Culture	1.7, 1.8, 1.9	
Socialisation	1.1, 1.2, 1.3, 1.4, 1.5, 1.6	
The family	3.1 – 3.7	
Education	4.1 – 4.7	
Work	9.1 – 9.6, 10.1 – 10.6	
Mass media	17.1 – 17.10	
C Society in the Individual		
Social Differentiation		
Stratification	5.1, 5.2	
Class, wealth and income	5.3 – 5.9, 13.1 – 13.8	
Age	7.1 – 7.5	
Gender	3.6, 4.5, 6.1, 6.2, 16.9, 17.3	
Race	8.1 – 8.6	
Power and Control		
Power and authority	14.1	
Political decision making	14.2, 14.3, 14.4, 1.5, 14.6, 14.7	
Social control, deviance and crime	15.1 – 15.5, 16.1 – 16.8	

Examination breakdown

Tier P (G–C)

Tier Q (D–A★)

Paper	$2\frac{1}{2}$ hours	Consists of stimulus questions.	80%
Coursework	3000 words approx.	Candidates to complete a sociological investigation based on a theme related to either sections B or C of the syllabus.	20%

Southern Examining Group

Stag Hill House, Guilford, Surrey GU 2 5XJ   Tel: 01483 506506

Sociology 1179

Syllabus topic	*Covered in Unit No:*	✓
1 What is Sociology?		
Sociological terms and concepts	1.1 – 1.8	
Some aspects of sociological methods	2.1 – 2.10	
2 The Sociology of the Family		
Development and characteristics of family forms in modern Britain	3.1, 3.2, 3.3, 3.4	
Changing role of the family	3.5	
Changing relationships within the family	3.6, 3.7	
3 The Sociology of Education		
Changes in the structure and functions	4.2, 4.3	
Ability and differential achievement	4.4, 4.5, 4.6	
Informal and formal education	4.1	
4 Social Differentiation		
Types of social stratification	5.1, 5.2	
Distribution of wealth, income, power and status	5.3, 5.4, 5.5, 5.6, 5.7, 5.8	
Social mobility	5.9	
5 The Welfare State and Poverty		
Provisions and problems of the Welfare State	13.9, 13.10, 13.11, 13.12	
Poverty	13.1 – 13.8	
6 The Sociology of Politics		
Power and decision making	14.1, 14.7	
Voting behaviour	14.2, 14.3, 14.4, 14.5	
Pressure and interest groups	14.6	
7 The Sociology of Work		
Meaning of work and relationship between work and non-work	9.1	
The effects of technological change	9.3, 9.4, 9.5	
Industrial relations	9.6	
Unemployment	10.1 – 10.5	
Age, gender and ethnic factors	9.2, 6.2, 8.5	
8 Social and Demographic Aspects of Population		
Causes and nature of population changes in Britain and the effect of these changes	11.1, 11.2, 11.3, 11.4, 11.5, 11.6, 11.7	
Process and implications of urbanisation	12.1 – 12.4	
9 Social Control and Deviance		
The nature of social order	1.1, 1.2, 1.3, 15.1	
Formal and informal agencies of social control	15.2, 15.3, 15.4	
Definition and interpretation of deviant behaviour	16.1 – 16.7	

Examination breakdown
Foundation Tier (C–G): Papers 1 and 3
Higher Tier (A★–D): Papers 2 and 3

Paper 1	2 hours	*Section A*: Consists of **one** compulsory structured question, based mainly on syllabus section 1.	80%
		Section B: Candidates to answer **four** out of eight structured questions, based on syllabus sections 2–9.	

Paper 2	$2\frac{1}{2}$ hours	*Section A*: consists of **one** compulsory structured question, based mainly on syllabus section 1.	80%
		Section B: candidates to answer **three** out of five structured questions, based on syllabus sections 2–9.	
		Section C: Candidates to answer **two** out of at least three free response questions, based on syllabus sections 2–9.	
Paper 3	Coursework	Candidates to complete a 1000–2500-word project on a topic related to the syllabus.	20%

Welsh Joint Education Committee (WJEC)

245 Western Avenue, Cardiff CF5 2YX   Tel: 01222 265000

Sociology

Syllabus topic	Covered in Unit No:	✓
Methods of Investigation	2.1–2.9	
The Individual in Society	1.1–1.9	
The Family	3.1–3.7	
Education	4.1–4.6	
Work	9.1–9.6, 10.1–10.6	
Mass Media	17.1–17.10	
Social Differentiation	5.1–5.9	
Age	7.1–7.5	
Ethnic Groups	8.1–8.6	
Power	14.1–14.7	
Control	15.1–15.5, 16.1–16.8	

Examination breakdown

Two tiers of assessment (C-G; D–A)

Tier Q (D–A★)

Paper	$2\frac{1}{2}$ hours	Consists of a variety of question types including those based on stimulus material. Structured questions 'provide opportunities for extended writing'.	80%
Coursework	2000 words	Candidates to complete a project **directly** related to the syllabus.	20%

Studying and revising

When you are studying and revising Sociology, here are some simple guidelines that will help you to get the most out of the book.

- Once you know what the relevant topics are, work through them steadily.
- Do not try to study in a room with the television on, but go somewhere where you can be alone, or at least fairly quiet, and really try to concentrate. A half hour of hard work is worth a whole evening of sitting with one eye on the television and one on your *GCSE Sociology Study Guide*.
- It is very useful to write on books and add in extra notes or underline/use marker pen on areas of special importance or difficulty. But only if you own the book. If it

is a library book, think of others.

- Everything in this book is written in the clearest way possible, but if anything confuses you or is difficult to understand ask your teacher.

- It is pointless trying to learn all the information in this book off by heart, and it is not what the examiners are looking for. You should aim to understand the material, and use this as a springboard for developing your ability to analyse problems through a sociological perspective.

- Use the self-test questions and the examination practice questions to the full. It is only by being forced to use your knowledge that you can see how much you know.

- Do not rush your revision at the last moment if you can help it. If your examination is in June, start your revision in April.

Chapter 1
Socialisation

1.1 The meaning of socialisation

At birth children have few of the qualities, apart from the physical ones, that we expect of human beings – they cannot walk or talk, they do not know how to eat and they have no opinions on religion, politics or sport.

Sociologists believe that human beings are not just created in a physical manner, but also in a social manner. If people were left on their own after birth, merely being fed and physically cared for, they would not develop into recognisable human beings. They would not be able to talk, perhaps even to walk, to laugh, or to understand others. In effect they would merely be animals.

As soon as a child is born the members of society begin to influence and mould the child's beliefs, personality and behaviour.

What changes human beings from animals into the **social actors** (a term to describe people living in society) whom we recognise as members of society, is the process of **socialisation**.

The learning process begins in childhood, but continues throughout life. The growing child, through contact with others of the society, gradually learns the language, beliefs and behaviour of the group in which he/she is brought up. The values and behaviour of groups vary, so that the socialisation process is different from one society to another.

1.2 Instinct or socialisation?

It is a basic belief of sociology that the major part of all human behaviour is learned and is not the result of some **biological drive**. For example, it is often claimed that women have a natural **mothering instinct**: sociologists firmly deny this, arguing that women are taught in our society that as they bear the children they ought to take the main responsibility for looking after them. The proof as far as sociologists understand it can be found by comparing patterns of behaviour across societies. The argument is that if certain forms of behaviour are *natural*, then all 'normal' people in all societies ought to show that particular form of behaviour. For example, it is natural to feel pain, to be able to walk, to eat (although even here people need to be shown how). However, if the patterns of action vary considerably, being absent in one society and present in another, it cannot be argued that that behaviour is 'natural' to human beings.

1.3 People without socialisation

To make the point quite clear concerning the power and importance of socialisation, it is worth looking at the behaviour of some people who have not been through the process of socialisation into human society.

There are a number of famous examples, two of which are given below. They all show how humans who are not socialised into the normal behaviour of society are almost unrecognisable as humans in their behaviour. This shows that our behaviour is not natural but learned.

The case of Anna

In 1978 a girl of about five years of age was discovered on a farm in the United States. Since birth she had been completely isolated, locked up in a room by herself. This was done because she was illegitimate and the grandparents were ashamed. When discovered she could not walk, talk or feed herself and had no control over her bladder or bowels. She had great difficulty in understanding anything that was explained to her or done for her. After being taken from the farm and looked after, she made some progress, learning to feed herself, to speak a few sentences and to dress herself. Unfortunately, she died about three years after being discovered. (Source: Kingsley Davis, *Human Society*.)

The case of Shamdev

In 1978 a boy of about five was discovered playing with wolf cubs in the Musafirkhana forest in India. He hid from people and would only play with dogs. At night he grew restless and it was necessary to tie him up to stop him going out to follow the jackals that prowled around the village at night. If people cut themselves, he would smell the blood and rush across to it. His favourite food was chicken. He caught them, killed them and ate them raw. (Source: *Observer*, 30 August 1978.)

1.4 The process of socialisation

Sociologists distinguish between two aspects of socialisation: **primary socialisation** and **secondary socialisation**.

Primary socialisation

This refers to the process of socialisation that takes place between an individual and a group of people with whom he/she has intimate contact, such as the family and the peer group (which is a group of people close to an individual, against whom he/she measures his or her own behaviour.

The family

This forms the most important agency of socialisation for most people. Children identify with their parents and copy them. Their behaviour is conditioned by the responses of their parents. Because most children want to please their parents, they repeat behaviour that gains approval. Gradually, they learn to **internalise** the correct patterns of behaviour, so that instead of winning the approval of their parents, they *know themselves* when their behaviour is correct or not.

Within the family, the children are generally socialised along gender lines, with girls being encouraged to copy their mothers and boys their fathers.

The peer group

The second important influence a child encounters is the peer group. A child's play patterns with other children influence the way he/she thinks and acts later. Children play together at adult roles, such as cops and robbers, shopkeepers, and mothers and fathers. By playing together in this way they learn the appropriate roles of behaviour for later life.

Piaget, a famous Swiss psychologist, suggested that children pass through various stages in their play as they grow older. In the game of marbles, which he studied, children of two and three at first play with the marbles having no idea of a game. At the age of four or five they begin to understand the idea of rules. The rules are rigidly interpreted. At the age of seven or eight the rules are regarded as flexible and changes can be made. Finally, in adolescence, the rules may be adjusted to give handicaps to even out players' chances.

Conformity among the peer group is strongly maintained and those who in some way fail to meet expectations are picked on, and may be rejected.

Secondary socialisation

Secondary socialisation usually occurs in more formal situations, which are not so personal – the two most powerful are the school and the mass media.

Schools

In complex modern societies, the wide variety of different home backgrounds and values can lead to children being socialised in different ways. One of the roles of the school is to provide a common pattern of socialisation. Thus teachers teach the skills, knowledge and behaviour considered vital for survival in society (the **curriculum**). As well as this, sociologists suggest, children learn the **hidden curriculum** of values and skills that permeate the school. These may include such things as finding out the expectations of males and females in society, through the unintentional comments of teachers, plus the activities of other children in the class (there is a further discussion on this in Unit 4.1.)

The mass media

Apart from the direct experiences we have, which for the majority of us are rather limited, our knowledge about the wider world comes from what we read, hear on the radio or see on film or television. Attitudes towards other countries, ethnic groups and political events are all influenced by what information we receive about them and how this information is presented to us.

1.5 Socialisation in specific settings

Socialisation, however, is not limited to just the family, peer group, education and mass media. Throughout life, people are undergoing new experiences and new processes of socialisation. Two examples illustrated this: socialisation in work and socialisation in total institutions.

Socialisation in work

When people enter the world of work, they must learn the appropriate forms of acceptable behaviour. On the shopfloor in many manual jobs, the newcomer must learn the right pace of work. Someone working too fast or too slow will disrupt the workrate adjudged 'right' by those already there.

For example, employees paid by the amount they produce (piece rate) will limit the quantity turned out to an informally agreed level. The advantage is that the bonus level at which a higher rate of pay is given can be reached without too great a difficulty. A newcomer working fast to earn as much money as possible will mean that the employer will realise the true possible output, and will raise the number of units to be completed to achieve the bonus. Newcomers who break the rules are made the butt of practical jokes; if they continue then they are 'sent to Coventry'.

It is not just output that is involved. Other workers demand conformity in attitudes towards management, in solidarity with workmates, and in most instances doing the job well.

People in the professions have very strong socialisation processes. Doctors, for example, are taught the rules of professional conduct and can be thrown out of the profession for not obeying them. Informally, too, doctors have their own rules - it is extremely rare, for instance, for one doctor to criticise another; this is 'just not done'. Patients, too, help to socialise doctors. They expect them to have a middle-class accent and to dress smartly (and until comparatively recently they expected them to be male).

Total institutions

There exist in society certain institutions in which people have all their choice taken away. Examples of these are monasteries, convents, the armed services, mental hospitals and prisons. In these institutions the individual is often 'stripped' of his or her identity outside the institution and given a new one. Thus the monk is renamed and instead of being Mr Moore becomes Father Stephen; or the prisoner becomes 11657. The person is then encouraged or even forced to accept the rules and values of the new institution. The prisoner must eat and exercise at fixed hours; he/she must learn the appropriate ways of addressing those in authority (to their faces and behind their backs). Total institutions are unusual in that they take people who are already socialised and then completely resocialise them; but they still illustrate the extent of the power of socialisation over individuals.

1.6 Variations in socialisation in modern society

In modern complex societies patterns are different between different groups. The complexity of life is matched by a complexity of patterns of socialisation. People are socialised differently by social class; by ethnic group; by workplace and type of job; by the region of the country; and by age group. However, although there are differences in Britain (unlike some other countries), these differences are not so great as to prevent the society holding together.

Social class

The values of the working class are different from those of the middle class, although the extent of those differences is a matter of debate. Traditional values of the working class included believing in (a) stressing the need for the working class to stick together (particularly at work); (b) that those who are unemployed are simply unlucky; (c) that society is composed of two classes and that most working-class people are stuck where they are.

By contrast the middle class believes (a) in individuality; (b) that the unemployed are generally lazy; (c) that where you get in life depends upon hard work. We could add, too, that the working class tends to have clearer-cut ideas concerning the roles of men and women and a greater stress on traditional ideas of 'masculinity'.

Research

Work by the Newsons (*Seven Years Old in an Urban Community*) has suggested that working-class children are brought up in a more rigid way by their parents: they are not supposed to question their parents' authority and are not given reasons why they ought to do a particular thing – they must obey.

The Newsons suggest there is less stress upon academic success and the working-class children do not receive as much help with reading and writing as the middle-class children. All this has consequences for their future success at school and their future employment.

Ethnic group

Britain is a **multicultural** society. About 7% of the population are immigrants or the children of recent immigrants, from a wide variety of nations. These bring up their children to have specific values that differ from the 'mainstream values' of British society. For example, the children of Indian immigrants to Britain will most likely follow the Hindu or Muslim religions. They have very different views about the role of

Examiner's tip

Remember to emphasise that people are socialised in a wide variety of ways.

the family and the correct behaviour for females. The family is very important and obedience to parents is generally absolute. Females are expected to be extremely modest. Marriages may be arranged by parents.

Age

In particular different youth cultures emerge for each generation and divisions occur within each generation. Thus a variety of competing groups exists at any one time. These reflect in turn class, ethnic and regional differences and the present problems that groups face.

Gender roles

Gender roles (the behaviour expected from members of a particular sex) are socially constructed – they are not biologically based according to sociologists.

Evidence comes from cross-cultural studies where women and men behave in very different ways than in western societies.

1.7 Culture

Culture is the whole of the knowledge, ideas and habits of a society that are transmitted from one generation to the next. Culture is not static, however, and is always changing. The beliefs and values that we hold are not the same as those held in medieval or even Victorian Britain. Sociologists often use the terms **society** and **culture** interchangeably, for a society is generally a group of people **sharing** a culture.

Humans are guided far less by instinct than any other animal. It may be natural to eat and to make love, but *how* these things are done is a reflection of the expectations and values of a particular society.

An example of the importance of culture is the activities of the Japanese *kamikaze* pilots in the Second World War. Near the end of the war, as Japan seemed doomed to lose, volunteers were called for who would fly aircraft packed with explosives into American and allied ships. In the resulting explosion, the pilot was guaranteed to lose his life. Yet there were too many volunteers for the planes available. The pilots considered it a great honour to die for their country and their Emperor. Here the *culture* had completely swamped the *instinct* of self-preservation.

However, clear variations exist in the values that people hold and the patterns of behaviour they engage in. When there is an overall shared culture, but within it there are clearly distinguishable sets of values and behaviour, sociologists use the term **subculture**.

Subcultures are linked to ethnic, social, class, and age divisions in our society.

A typical example would be the youth subculture: in each generation there is a variety of styles of dress, types of music, special language and attitudes that distinguish youth from older people and from children. These values make youth distinct from society, but rarely do they represent complete rejections of the overall culture.

1.8 The components of culture

❶ **Beliefs** These are general, vague opinions held about the world and about the nature of society. They vary by society and sometimes by subcultures. An example of a belief is that Britain is an increasingly dangerous and lawless society. There is no proof that this is actually the case, but the belief is that once, perhaps in the 1950s, there was less crime and a greater sense of community. These beliefs are very important in providing support for changes in the law today and in society's attitudes towards young people.

2 **Values** These are vague beliefs about what is right and correct in the world. They imply that there are certain appropriate forms of action which ought to be taken, e.g. life is precious therefore it is wrong to kill anybody.

3 **Norms** These are socially expected patterns of behaviour. (Actions that are regarded as *normal*.) A norm of our society is to say 'Hello!' on meeting someone, or to stand in a queue without trying to push in front. Norms that are vital to a society and have a certain moral content are sometimes referred to as **mores**.

4 **Roles** Social roles are patterns of behaviour expected of certain people according to the occupation or position they hold in society. The role of a clergyman is to be sympathetic, well-mannered, well-spoken, religious and charitable. A swearing, heavy-drinking, party-going clergyman would be regarded with astonishment by most people.

5 **Role conflict** There are innumerable social roles – father, mother, child, shopkeeper, footballer, old age pensioner, etc. All of us occupy a number of roles, which are generally complementary, but sometimes they may conflict, for instance, the role of being a police officer and of being a friend. If a police officer apprehends a friend who is speeding, does she treat him as a friend or as an offender? This is known as **role conflict**.

6 **Status** This refers to the position of a person or social role in society according to the amount of prestige received from others. In different societies/cultures, status varies. In Britain those with the highest status are the best educated and the rich, although this will obviously vary within subcultures. In traditional Japan, it was the *samurai* warriors who received the greatest prestige, after the Emperor.

1.9 Culture in other societies

It is important to remember that there are and have been a wide variety of different cultures. It is wrong to see British culture as the *normal* culture and to measure all others alongside ours. This is known as **ethnocentrism** and is a common error of those who have no knowledge of sociology.

The Cheyenne Indians

- The Cheyenne existed for thousands of years in the west of what is now the United States.
- Unlike our society, wealth was regarded as a bad thing and there was no status attached to owning goods.
- On the other hand, to give things away was regarded as an action worthy of admiration.
- Therefore, in special ceremonies, those more successful members of the tribe gave away most of their possessions to others.
- The greatest prestige was attached to bravery in battle. This did not necessarily mean killing enemies, but simply showing bravery in whatever respect; for example, an individual brave might ride towards the enemy alone and attack them.
- Power in the Cheyenne nation was held mainly by men and they achieved positions of authority through acts of bravery which impressed other members of the tribe. Powerful positions could not be inherited.
- Children were brought up to be very tough, receiving regular beatings from their parents. This was not done from cruelty but in order to strengthen the children for the extremely tough life they would face.

Summary

1   Socialisation consists of the process of becoming a full member of a society, accepting all of its ideas, values and patterns of behaviour.

2   Socialisation is more important than the biological drives or instincts that we have.

3   Animal behaviour in general is determined by instinct, very rarely by learning. On the other hand, human behaviour is largely determined by learning.

4   This can be seen in the variety of different forms of human behaviour in different cultures.

5   People who are not socialised lack most of the attributes we normally associate with being human.

6   There are two aspects of socialisation: primary and secondary.

7   Primary socialisation is learning that takes place within intimate groups, such as the family and the peer group.

8   Secondary socialisation is the more formal learning patterns that take place in the school and through the peer group.

9   In modern, complex societies it is possible to have differences between the values learned in secondary and primary socialisation.

10 Socialisation takes place throughout life and in specific settings – for example, the workplace. People learn to act according to the way that is normal for those within the work organisation.

11 There are differences in socialisation according to class, gender and ethnic group.

12 Culture is the set of values and ways of acting that mark a particular society.

13 Variations within the culture are known as subcultures.

14 Culture is more powerful than instinct.

15 Culture is learned through the socialisation process.

16 Beliefs are general opinions and understandings about the world.

17 Values underpin how we act by providing the moral framework within which we make decisions.

18 Norms are the accepted patterns of behaviour in a society.

19 Roles are expected patterns of behaviour linked to particular statuses.

20 Role conflict is when two or more roles go against one another.

21 Status is the position of a particular person or social role in society.

Self-test questions

1   What do sociologists mean by the term 'socialisation'?
2   What do sociologists mean when they write about (a) primary socialisation and (b) secondary socialisation?
3   Give three examples of groups that help to socialise us, explaining how they do so.
4   What does the term 'culture' mean?
5   What does the term 'role conflict' mean? Give one example.

Chapter 2
Research methods

In order to discover information about society, sociologists have developed a wide range of research techniques. Unlike journalists or politicians, these allow them to make unbiased, accurate statements about social life, and social life, and allow them to make tentative predictions, based on their research, of how people will act in particular situation.

Within sociology there is some debate between those who believe sociology should aim to follow the lead of the traditional sciences (e.g. chemistry, biology, etc) and those who feel that as sociologists study people's **attitudes** as well as their actions, this makes it different. They advocate placing less stress on much of the scientific method that follows. Usually they argue for participant observation (see Unit 2.9). Those who adhere to the scientific methods are known as **positivists**, while those who stress understanding attitudes are known as **subjective sociologists**.

However, increasingly this division is being bridged with sociologists using a mixture of both types of method.

2.1 The steps in scientific research

When engaging in scientific research, it is customary to follow a number of stages. This is as true for physics as it is for sociology. The stages are: (1) observation (2) hypothesis (3) research planning (4) collecting the information (5) analysing data and drawing conclusions.

Moore and Hendry, in *Sociology*, have analysed a well-known piece of research by Howard Newby (*The Deferential Worker*) under these headings. The research concerned the lives of Suffolk farmworkers.

- **Observation** Whilst studying local community life in Norfolk, Newby noticed the poor pay and conditions of farmworkers; he also noticed little evidence of resentment even though most farmers who employed the labourers were affluent.
- **Hypothesis** Newby tried to find an explanation for this, and finally put forward **the possible explanation** (a hypothesis) that farmworkers hold an attitude called **deference** which resulted, among other things, from working closely with the farmer - this stops them feeling resentful.
- **Research planning** Newby had to find a typical agricultural area without too many commuters who alter the rural community. He therefore moved his research to Suffolk. He next found a **sampling frame** – the *Yellow Pages*.
- **Collecting the information** Newby originally wrote to 312 farmowners, but was only successful in obtaining interviews at 71 farms with 233 farmworkers. He filled out his information using **secondary sources** such as official statistics. He also lodged with a farmworker's family for six months to gain better knowledge of the community.

- **Drawing conclusions** Newby took three years working on his information before he could see if his original hypothesis was correct. He concluded that although much of his hypothesis was confirmed, there were many new areas he had not originally perceived, and so his results were rather different from what he could have foreseen.

2.2 Sampling

Sample

Sociologists frequently make **general** statements about the population, such as 29% of the population think companies make too much profit, while 80% of the population think trade unions have too much power.

Clearly sociologists cannot interview the whole of the British population - the cost and time required make that impossible. Instead sociologists use a **sample** of the population. A sample is a small, representative group selected from the population. The survey that gave the information mentioned above was based on a sample of 1828 people which reflects the general population of Britain.

It is very important that the sample is representative; any error here will be magnified greatly if we use it to make statements about the whole population. Sociologists have therefore developed a considerable number of techniques for ensuring that their information is correct and drawn from a representative sample of the population.

Sample frame

This refers to the source from which the informants have been drawn. To find out people's voting intentions, a useful source (and hence the sample frame) would be the electoral lists. To study workers' opinions about their employers, a useful sampling frame would be the factory personnel records. It is used with random sampling (see below). Oakley (*Housewife*) studied women's attitude to housework, and used the patients' list of two London doctors to find names and addresses of married women aged 20–30 years old with at least one child under five years of age.

Pilot sample

Before undertaking the full sample survey, sociologists usually take a very small 'sample of their sample'. They then test the correctness of their sampling, the usefulness of their questions and, finally, any possible problems. This is a **pilot sample**.

Snowball sample

Sometimes it is not possible to find a sample frame or simply to stop people in the street to ask them questions – particularly if the sociologist is studying a 'deviant' group. In this case the sociologist may find one 'deviant' and then ask him/her to introduce him to a friend. Thus the sample grows rather like a snowball rolled in the snow. (Martin Platt did just this in his study of drug taking.)

Types of sampling methods

There are two types of sampling methods: random sampling and quota sampling.

Random sampling

Individuals are chosen entirely at random from a sampling frame, rather like the idea underlying a lottery – everybody has an equal chance of being selected. Usually sociologists choose at random from a relevant sample frame, by selecting every tenth or twentieth name that appears – depending upon the size of the sample required – or they choose from the sample frame by random number. There are three subtypes of random sampling:

- **Strata sample**: this involves dividing the population according to relevant factors such as age, gender or social class, and once this division (into strata) is complete, taking a random sample within each stratum. This ensures that the sample will be safely representative of the population. It is particularly useful where the sample is very small.
- **Multistage** (sometimes known as **cluster sampling**): if the survey is of widely dispersed population, it is easier to subdivide (by random sampling) the sample into **clusters**. For example political constituencies (MP's districts), upon which electoral lists are based, are subdivided into **wards** which are in turn subdivided into **polling districts**. By choosing certain wards at random, then certain polling districts within those wards, and finally certain people within those few polling districts, the result is a geographically close, random selection of people over 18. The information can then be collected easily.
- **Multiphase**: when the survey is completed the sociologists randomly select a sample of the full sample, to ask further questions. This is useful when further depth is required.

Quota sampling

This is not based on the principle of randomness to ensure a representative sample. If we know a lot of information about the population to be studied (**population** in sociological language means any group which we wish to study), then it can be subdivided proportionately according to important social factors (gender, age, class) and interviewers told to question a specified number (a quota) from each group. This is the type of sampling used by most market research companies.

Random versus quota sampling

Advantages of random sampling:
- statistically very reliable
- there are ways of checking that the sample is representative.

Disadvantages of random sampling:
- expensive
- time consuming
- complex.

Advantages of quota sampling:
- simple
- relatively cheap
- relatively quick.

Disadvantages of quota sampling:
- relies too much on the interviewer's selection of people. If the interviewee chosen does not truly fit the category given to the interviewer, then the sample is ruined
- no possibility of checking accuracy of sample.

2.3 Types of sample survey

❶ **Cross-sectional studies** A study of a representative cross-section of the population at any particular time. This is generally known as 'a survey', e.g. opinion polls. A famous example is Schofield's 1960s study of young people's sexual behaviour, in which 2000 13–18-year-olds were questioned on their attitudes and behaviour. The main disadvantage of these studies is that they represent only a *snapshot* picture of what is happening at one time. There is no attempt to look at changes.

❷ **Case studies** These limit themselves to in-depth study of one particular place or event, e.g. Beynon's study of Ford car workers (*Working for Ford*) in which Beynon talked to Ford production line workers about their attitudes to their work and the management. The main disadvantage of these studies is that as they are restricted to one occurrence it is difficult to generalise from them.

❸ Longitudinal studies These are studies conducted over an extended period of time. The researchers study a selected group of people over time noting the changes and differences between them e.g. The National Children's Bureau Study of 17000 children born in the week ending 9 March 1958. This study has followed their lives, to understand the factors influencing educational attainment. The main problem is the large loss of the sample over time so that it becomes increasingly difficult to make generalisations when so many are missing and there is no information for them.

2.4 Questionnaires

These are sets of written questions which are either mailed to individuals (postal questionnaires) or simply handed out. The respondent completes it alone and then returns it to the researcher. Answers are either **closed** (tick the appropriate box) or **open** (write the answer in own words). The advantages are:

- they can be mailed to a widespread sample;
- they are quick to do. All the researcher has to do is to write the questionnaire, hand the copies out (or mail them) and then collect them afterwards for analysis. Interviews on the other hand can take a long time to complete and so the amount of time must be expanded or the number of interviews cut down;
- people are more likely to answer embarrassing questions (as there is no interview or personal contact).

There are also disadvantages to this method:

- they cannot be used for complex issues;
- the researcher can never be certain who actually completed the questionnaire. Is it the person he or she wants?;
- most people cannot be bothered to return questionnaires (high non–response), which means that the researcher is never certain what the opinion is of those who do not respond.

2.5 Interviews

These are where an interviewer asks a respondent a number of questions and writes down the answers. The interview can fall between the two extremes of the structured interview, which is rather like an oral questionnaire, or the unstructured, where the interviewer converses with the respondent. Within these extremes is a whole range of techniques. As in questionnaires, questions can be **closed** or **open–ended**. The advantages are that the interviewer:

- can examine complex issues;
- can compare the answers with personal observations;
- obtains a lower non–response rate.

The disadvantages are that:

- the interviewer may influence the replies of the respondent by his presence, or inadequate interviewing skill. This is known as **interviewer bias**;
- the technique tends to be relatively expensive.

2.6 Experiments

These are not commonly used in sociology, as sociologists generally argue that individuals in isolation from their normal daily lives do not act in a **natural** manner. Experiments place individuals in closely controlled situations where they can be observed; they then create a particular event to observe the subjects' response. For example, Asch conduced a series of famous experiments which illustrated the power of group pressure. A group of students was asked to estimate the lengths of a series of lines on individual cards. All the students except one were told to give a pre-arranged incorrect answer. The student who did not know would often change his estimate of length to agree with his fellow students. This occurred in 37 out of 100 cases.

2.7 Asking questions

As we have just seen, questions used in interviews and questionnaires tend to be of two types, open-ended or closed. Let us consider them in more detail.

- **Open-ended questions** These are the type of questions which are 'open' in the sense that there is no choice or guidance to the answer – this is left entirely up to the respondent. These sorts of questions are usually asked when an opinion is sought, e.g. 'What do you think about...?'.

    They are very useful in getting people to talk in their own words and they allow people to express quite complicated ideas and feelings. However, they are very difficult to code, and so are complicated to use.

- **Closed questions** These are much simpler and involve giving the respondent a limited choice of answers, e.g. how many hours each week do you spend studying Sociology? One hour or less, more than one hour but less than three, more than three? These are simple to code, but they often simplify issues too much (for instance you might spend 20 hours one week doing Sociology and then nothing for a fortnight).

    They do not allow people to reply in detail. They do not allow people to reply in their own words. They guide the respondent in answering in a certain way, thus possibly biasing the response.

Structured and unstructured interviews

The degree of structure in an interview can have a considerable bearing on its outcome. The structured interview is good for simple issues and provides clear answers which are easy to code.

The unstructured interview can probe an issue in depth and the skilled interviewer can follow up interesting points finding out the true meaning behind the reply of the respondent.

Coding

When the number of questionnaires or interviews have been completed, they need to be put together and analysed. It is much easier if the replies can be grouped in some way. Coding is simply the simplifying and grouping of answers. For example, if questions are being asked about the degree to which people like their jobs, then the type of response can be grouped into three possible boxes, 'like', 'neutral' and 'dislike'. The replies of the respondents are then analysed and placed into the group that is nearest to their reply. Great attention must be paid to ensure that the coding (grouping) by the sociologist reflects the real opinions of the respondent.

2.8 Secondary sources

These are any sources of information that the sociologist has not obtained for him/herself. Secondary sources include:

Official government reports and studies

The **Census** is an example – a national survey of the population conducted every ten years by the government. This, along with regular studies such as the *National Household Survey* keep the government (and sociologists) up to date with changing trends in British society and allow social policy to be planned.

Problems

- The government statistics are collected for official purposes – they are not intended for use by sociologists. The definitions and classifications used by these statistics may not be ideal for the sociologist (see, for example, the discussion on measuring social class in Unit 5.4).
- The figures may be the subject of some controversy, as it may be felt that the government is defining the figures in such a way as to benefit its political image. Criticisms were levelled against the Conservative governments of the 1980s and 1990s for constantly changing the definitions of unemployment and poverty so that the figures seemed to show an improvement when this might not have been the case. Poverty statistics, too, are the subject of heated debate (see Chapter 13).
- The source of the official statistics may be dubious, as is the case with the official statistics on wealth and income. Many people lie to government officials to avoid tax, or figures are presented in such a way for tax purposes that they make the ownership of wealth seem less concentrated than it is.
- Some statistics tell us more about the activities of officials than they do about the actual occurrences they are supposed to represent. Thus crime statistics tell us about the activities of the police more than anything else (see Unit 16.7).

Historical documents

- Official: such as parish records of births and deaths historically kept by clergy in Britain. These were used by Laslett in *The World We Have Lost* to study family changes in Britain between the sixteenth and nineteenth centuries.
- Unofficial: such as diaries and novels; these give a picture of how people felt and lived at a particular time. Here, however, the researcher has to be very careful as the contents will reflect the bias of the writer.

Newspaper reports

These are useful to fill in information for a researcher and to give the background to an event; they may also be useful as a piece of research in themselves. This form of studying events through newspapers is sometimes called **content analysis**. Often it is the only way to find out information about the activities in the past of certain groups without an official history, such as gangs of delinquents or criminals.

Problems

The problems of bias are particularly strong in content analysis.

- Newspapers need to sensationalise events in order to sell copies and so facts are often distorted.
- Newspapers are generally politically biased, in the majority of cases towards the Conservative Party. Political reporting may not therefore be 'balanced'.

2.9 Subjective sociology – observation

This is sometimes called **observational sociology**.

Earlier we saw that some sociologists believe it necessary to observe, or even join in, social activities in order fully to understand them. This does not mean they are opposed to the stricter scientific methods, it is just that they place less emphasis on statistics and more on their own observation. Sociological knowledge has traditionally come from blending the two approaches.

Observational methods are particularly useful:

- in digging below people's answers to questions, in order to see how they actually behave;
- for certain **deviant** groups, delinquents etc, who may not reply to questionnaires or interviews;
- where it may be inappropriate to use interviews or questionnaires, at a football match for instance, when the sociologist may be trying to understand football crowd violence.

There are two types of observational method: nonparticipant and participant. In practice the two methods are often intermixed.

Non-participant

The observer watches the behaviour of a group, perhaps following them around and asking questions. He/she does not join in group activities. It often happens, however, that the observer gets drawn into the group through his or her close contact. In certain circumstances the observer may use mechanical methods of recording information such as a tape recorder or a video camera.

Advantages:

- the researcher is able to observe a group who could not be studied in any other manner;
- the researcher exerts minimal influence on the group's actions;
- the researcher is able to study the group as they behave normally.

Disadvantages:

- observations are only superficial if the observer does not join in the group activities;
- lack of statistical evidence – all based on observation.

The most famous example of observational research is the Hawthorne Studies of 1924 conducted by Elton Mayo. He examined the effects of changing the working environment on the productivity levels of a group of workers. He found that virtually any change in working conditions improved productivity. Apparently the influence of Mayo's presence actually encouraged the workers to greater efforts. This illustrates the influence of the researcher.

Today researchers overcome this by using various forms of recording. Stanworth (*Gender and Schooling*) tape recorded lessons in a number of Cambridge schools to illustrate the point that boys receive more attention in class than girls. The tape recorder was far less obtrusive than her presence would have been.

Participant observation

Here the observer joins the group as a full member and is accepted by them. The researcher also participates in all group activities.

Advantages:

- deep contact with the group who confide in the observer as group member;
- full understanding of the reasons behind group's actions, as the observer is participating.

Disadvantages:

- the observer may lose his or her objectivity and become biased through too much contact with the group under study. This makes any observations very suspect;
- lack of statistical information to confirm the observer's conclusions;
- the group may be influenced by his or her presence, for instance an older middle-class sociologist joining and observing a group of working-class delinquents may end up advising them, so altering the **natural** pattern of events.

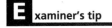
Examiner's tip

Point out that whatever method of research is chosen, the sociologist tries to keep his/her values from influencing the outcome of the research.

For example, James Patrick (*A Glasgow Gang Observed*) joined a violent Glasgow gang without telling them his true identity as a sociological researcher. He stayed with the gang over a period of months, joining in their criminal activities and behaving similarly to them.

The result is an in-depth description of gang life and beliefs. It is clear that Patrick disliked the gang, and this dislike may perhaps have biased his conclusions and observations.

Participant versus non–participant observation

When choosing the particular from of observation, the sociologist must be aware that participant observation:

- gives a greater depth of information;
- is more likely to be coloured by his or her identification with the group;
- is more likely to influence the group under study.

Nonparticipant observation:

- gives more superficial observable information only;
- there is less chance of influencing the group or
- being influenced by it.

Summary

1 There is a wide range of techniques used by sociologists to understand society. Sociologists select whatever methods seem most appropriate.

2 There is a division between those sociologists who stress more the method of using social surveys and those who stress more the use of observational methods.

3 There are specific steps to be followed in conducting a survey. These are observational hypothesis, research planning, collecting of information, the drawing of conclusions.

4 When studying society, sociologists use sample surveys, which are representative selections of the population.

5 A sampling frame is the list from which the sample is drawn.

6 Pilot samples are small samples taken before the main sample to check for problems that may be encountered.

7 There are two main types of sampling technique – random and quota.

8 There are various ways within these two methods of varying the data collection – snowball sampling, cluster sampling, multiphase, etc.

9 There are different types of studies which vary in depth and width. Types of study include cross-sectional, case, longitudinal.

10 Sociologists collect sociological information using questionnaires (written questions), interviews (oral questions) and experiments, and secondary sources (material collected by other people).

11 Questionnaires and interviews are dependent on the quality of the questions asked. The sociologist must beware of making them confusing, or biased.

12 Experiments are not commonly used in sociology because they do not reflect the situation of real life.

13 Secondary sources provide many problems for the sociologist – in particular the sociologist has to be aware of the reasons why the information was originally collected and the biases built into that information.

14 Some sociologists prefer to use the observational approach because they argue that it gives them greater understanding of what people actually do, rather than what they say they do.

15 There are problems with observational studies in that the sociologist often becomes too involved in the group and therefore becomes biased.

16 Sociologists choose the best research method available for them under the circumstances – there is no one correct or best method.

17 Sociologists must always try to keep their own biases and values out of the studies they do, otherwise the study will be of little value.

Self-test questions

1 Explain what is meant by the following types of study:
(a) cross-sectional study (b) case studies (c) longitudinal studies.

2 What are secondary sources? In what ways are they useful to sociologists?

3 In what circumstances would a sociologist choose to use (a) a mail questionnaire and (b) participant observation?

4 What are the advantages of using observational methods? Are there any drawbacks?

5 What is meant by the following terms:
(a) open-ended questions (b) interviewer bias (c) experiment?

Chapter 3
The family

3.1 Family forms

A family group is a group of people living with or near each other, who are closely related by marriage or blood. **Kin** means a wider circle of people who are related to one another and who generally give each other help.

There are **four** main types of family form:
- the extended family;
- the nuclear family;
- the lone-parent family;
- the reconstituted family.

The extended family

This generally consists of three generations of people – grandparents, parents and children who maintain close contact.

The extended family is usually found in societies where a large group of people living together is economically useful. For example, in an agricultural society where people live off the produce of the land, a larger group of people can do all the farming tasks. In industrial societies (as opposed to post-industrial, such as most of western Europe today), where there is poverty, the mutual aid provided by a large group of workers is useful.

There is clear evidence for the extended family in nineteenth-century Britain right up to the early 1950s and it continues to exist today amongst Asians in Britain.

The nuclear family

This is smaller than the extended family and usually consists of parents and their children. Contact with the wider kin is weaker and less frequent than amongst members of the extended family.

The nuclear family is usually found where a large group would be less useful than a few people living together. In some technologically simple societies based on hunting, known as hunter-gatherers, where food is in short supply, a small, fast moving group is more likely to survive.

Nuclear families are also found in post-industrial societies, such as Britain, where there is less need to rely upon the family for help. This appears to be the most common form of family in Britain today.

The lone-parent family

This consists of a single parent plus his or her dependent children (it is more commonly the mother). In Britain, the growth of lone-parent families reflects:
- the rise in the divorce rate;
- pregnancy outside marriage;
- death of a partner.

Reconstituted families

This form of family reflects:

- the increase in the number of divorces and remarriages;
- the increase in the number of people who change from cohabiting with one partner to another;
- (which leads to) an increase in the number of families which are headed by step-mothers and step-fathers, each of whom may bring their own children to live together.

Being the head of a lone-parent family is normally only a temporary condition as 75% of men who divorce, and approximately 70% of women, remarry within five years. It is estimated that about six million people live in reconstituted families of one type or another; 10% of children are currently living with step-parents.

Marriage

All forms of the family as we describe it here are based on a sexual relationship between at least one member of either sex, producing children. The relationship is based on some form of religious or cultural ceremony which marks them as married – this can take two different forms: monogamy and polygamy.

Monogamy is the marriage of one man and one woman only (as in Britain).

In Britain people who divorce are often likely to marry again. Sometimes this can occur several times to the same person. Sociologists have suggested the term 'serial monogamy' for the situation when a person divorces and then remarries, that is they have only one partner at a time, but a number of partners over a lifetime.

Polygamy is the general term for the situation where one of the partners has more than one partner from the opposite sex. In particular polygyny and polyandry.

Polygyny

This is the marriage of one man and a number of wives. The Koran (the sacred book of Islam) permits Muslims to have up to four wives at the same time. Polygyny is common in the Muslim Arab states of the Middle East, such as Saudi Arabia, and in Africa, such as Senegal.

Reasons for polygyny:

- In many societies the balance of males and female may not be more or less equal. Usually there is a shortage of males because male infants are weaker than females and more likely to die. As adults, it is generally men who engage in warlike or dangerous behaviour. As a response to this polygyny absorbs the surplus of females.
- In pre-industrial societies, the mortality rates are very high. In order for the society to continue, the maximum possible number of children must be born. Women who are able to bear children, but who are 'surplus', must therefore have a sexual partner.
- Religion and culture are extremely important influences. Many societies, for example ones based on the Muslim religion, allow more than one wife.
- Polygyny is useful for a family in an agricultural society where it produces more children to help in planting and harvesting crops.
- Although polygyny is stressed as ideal in certain societies, in fact it is often only the better-off males who can afford to have more than one wife.

Polyandry

This is a marriage of one woman with a number of husbands at the same time. Polyandry is much more unusual than polygyny. It occurs in Tibet, where there is little land suitable for agriculture. In order to keep the population down to realistic survival levels, one woman will marry a number of brothers. This means that all the brothers are restricted to the number of children that one woman is able (or willing) to bear, rather than each one having a wife to bear children.

3.2 Changes in the family over time

Fig. 3.1 Shows how industrialisation altered the family.

Fig 3.1   The family and industrialisation
(Source: Stephen Moore, *Sociology Alive!*, Stanley Thornes, 2nd edition, 1996)

	The pre-industrial family	Industrialisation and the family	The family today
Structure	Mainly nuclear families, but the better-off had larger households, as people came to stay with them; late marriage; small families because of the high death rate of children	Working-class families – became extended as numbers of children increased because of higher child survival rates (results of medical improvements) and people crowded into limited housing available in towns Middle-class families – became extended, as younger generation remained at home until they were economically free to leave and set up own house	Nuclear families, with connections by telephone/car to wider kin (although Asian families are extended)
Relation-ships	Not very close or warm; marriage and child-rearing mainly for economic reasons; idea of 'love' is unusual	Working class – children close to mother; father and mother not close at all; women oppressed by men Middle class – children not close to parents; father-mother, cold relationship; women oppressed by men	Close family relationships, the 'privatised' family; husband and wife fairly equal, 'symmetrical'; but women still expected to be responsible for domestic matters; children are seen as extremely important
Functions	Family very important as all worked together in the home or on the farm; family looked after its members if they survived to old age	Working class – family very important for survival; pooling of economic resources; helped each other where possible in all matters; older generation looked after by younger generation	Mainly emotional, but still practical and financial help (loans, etc) when needed; state and voluntary services assist or replace the family in many of its functions
Wider setting	Agricultural society; people living in the countryside in small villages	Industrialised society; people living in large towns	A mobile family moving for promotion and to take job opportunities; people living in suburbs; light industry and offices are places of work

---

3.3 Households and families in Britain today

Most people hold an image of the typical British family as consisting of a wife and husband plus two or three young children. The wife stays at home and the husband goes out to work – yet only about 23% of households in Britain are composed of a married couple and their young children.

As Fig. 3.2 shows 29% of households are composed of married couples with no children, 30% of households (the total of all the groups under the headings 'one person' and 'two or more unrelated adults') do not live in a family at all, 6% are married couples with their grown–up children, and the remaining 10% are one-parent families.

It is most important to remember that a family is a dynamic institution, which is changing all the time. Each family will typically go through a family life cycle, passing from one stage to the other. These stages may typically include:

❶   young marrieds, both working, no children;
❷   young marrieds with children;
❸   middle aged with older children leaving home;

④ old with all children living independently;

⑤ one remaining original partner (usually wife), with other original partner dead.

Fig. 3.2   Households in Britain: by type of household and family
(Source: *Social Trends 27*, 1997)

			Percentages
	1981	1991	1995–6
One person			
Under pensionable age	8	11	13
Over pensionable age	14	16	15
Two or more unrelated adults	5	3	2
One family			
Married couple [1]			
No children	26	28	29
1–2 dependent children [2]	25	20	19
3 or more dependent children [2]	6	5	4
Non-dependent children only	8	8	6
Lone parent [1]			
Dependent children [2]	5	6	7
Non-dependent children only	4	4	3
Two or more families	1	1	1
All households			
(=100%) (millions)	20.2	22.4	23.5

[1] Other individuals who were not family members may also be included.
[2] Households may also include non-dependent children.

An analysis of family life would have to take into account all these stages. So although there are only 23% of households with young children, many of the 29% of married couples without children may be in stages 1 and 4 of the family life cycle. Furthermore, the majority of the 15% of one-person households over retirement age may be the widow/widower in stage 5.

Lone-parent families

Today over 10% of British households are headed by a lone parent. This is the result of:

- increasing divorce rates – this is the single most important explanation, with over 52% of women heading a lone-parent family as a result of divorce or separation;
- the decision of women who become pregnant not to marry/cohabit – reflecting a change in the attitudes of women to marriage and their role in society. Approximately 34% of lone parents are women who have never married, though they may have cohabited;
- widowhood – approximately 6% of lone-parent families are the result of the death of a partner.

Conflicting views on lone-parent families

The rise in single-parent families has been seen by some as a threat to marriage and the conventional family. Writers such as Dennis argue that children need two parents ideally, as one parent is unable to look after the children adequately if he/she (usually the mother) works. This means that the children may be looked after by child-minders. According to this approach, this may lead to inadequate socialisation.

On the other hand, if the single parent does not work, he/she may be forced to claim benefits and may be unable to provide an adequate standard of living for his or her child.

Against this is argued that:

- only a relatively small proportion of families are headed by one parent;
- unhappily married partners give their children an unstable home background, which is often linked to later social problems with the children;
- it is not that being a lone parent creates poverty for the children, but that the levels of state benefits are too low.

3.4 Ethnic minority family life

Research

❶ Ballard in *South Asian Families* has described Asian families (such as Indians and Pakistanis) as extended in form. They consist of the father, sons and grandsons with their wives and unmarried daughters. The man (father) is the head of the household, controlling family finances and making most of the important decisions. The style of family life has been transferred from the country of origin to Britain. Women have very distinct roles from men, mainly working on household duties and having to accept that men are regarded as superior. Girls and women are expected to behave modestly in western terms, and are more likely to be discouraged from having boyfriends or any form of social life outside the kin network. This is known as *purdah*.

Marriages are still commonly arranged, which means that the parents find a partner for their children, although in practice today the majority of parents accept that their children will have some say in which partner is acceptable or not. In the past the view of the son or daughter has not been very important.

Once married the bride is regarded as having joined the husband's family. The family is much closer than the typical British family, and is often not just a 'unit of consumption', for they may work together in a business in a way that is rare in Britain.

In the last twenty years, there has been some difficulty with the notion of 'identity' for Asians, with some younger Asian people influenced by the western values, They have begun to reject some of the values of obedience to parent, of extreme modesty and arranged marriages that are expected of them by the older generation. However, the majority of those studied simply adapted their behaviour, behaving as expected at school and then switching to the values of their ethnic community in their private lives.

❷ Oakley studied Cypriot families in London (*Cypriot Families*). She concluded that here the male dominates the female and the women are trapped in the house with a purely domestic role to play. The husband has all the dealings with the wider world and effectively makes all the decisions. The honour of the family is very important and neither male nor female should do anything that could be regarded as staining this honour – such as sexual promiscuity on the part of the females. The family is of the extended type.

❸ Driver studied families of West Indian origin (*West Indian Families*). He suggested that there are two types of black family structure in Britain. The first is the nuclear family in which both parents share all the domestic tasks. However, there is another form – the mother-centred family. This is the result of lack of stable employment for the men, and a culture norm borrowed from the West Indies. The mother is left on her own to bring up the children and provide an income. The husband is a person who appears only occasionally and provides little regular support for the family. The mother is the dominant figure in the household and it is around her that the family forms. This form of family accounts for about one-third of families in the West Indies.

3.5 The role of the family

The family, in whatever form, performs a number of important **functions** for its members. The extent of these functions depends primarily on the economic nature of society. On the whole, it appears that more functions are performed by extended families in simple tribal societies than by nuclear families in modern industrial societies like our own.

A positive view: the functions of the modern family

Families perform the following functions in society:
- regulate sexual behaviour;
- reproduction;
- socialisation;
- economic;
- emotional support.

Regulate sexual behaviour

Firstly, uncontrolled sexual activity is a possible source of conflict in any society as disputes can easily break out between rivals for the same lover. Therefore, by restricting sexual activity to one's married partner the degree of conflict is lowered. Secondly, if blood relatives are clearly marked by family membership, so that everybody knows his or her relationship to others, there is less risk of incest.

Reproduction

Every society needs to reproduce itself in order to continue. The family is the culturally approved unit in which we have children. If the family is stable then the infants are guaranteed a safe and secure early life. The family, therefore, ensures that enough healthy children survive to continue the society.

Socialisation

Fundamental to any society is the need to teach each new generation the socially correct ways of behaving and acting. Without these common standards of values and behaviour societies could not continue. Shared forms of behaviour ensure that we are able to live together with a minimum of conflict.

The family is the first, and perhaps the most significant, agency of socialisation that most people encounter. Parents teach their children:
- who they are, e.g. their social class, their gender, the colour of their skin;
- the behaviour expected of them by society according to who they are;
- the values of the society in general, which they must know and copy.

Economic

The family is an economic unit of **consumption**, by which we mean that family members dispose of much of their earnings on buying items for the family, as opposed to individuals. From house purchase through to daily groceries, the family members may well pool most of their earnings together. This is different from agricultural societies where the whole family worked together as a unit of **production**.

Emotional support

Modern western societies are highly competitive and, many think, unfriendly. Our contact with others is generally superficial. In this sort of world, it is claimed that the family ideally provides the warmth and emotional support that is missing in the wider society. Often, the closest social bonds are between family members.

A critical view: the negative side of family life

The **functionalists** in the previous section make a crucial assumption that the family is beneficial (good) for its members. many sociologists criticise this assumption. Although there is certainly good in the family, they balance this out with comments on the harm the family can do its members.
- **Emotionally intense** The narrowness of the nuclear family and the intense bonds between the few family members can lead to great strain and conflict. The rise in divorce rates is seen as evidence of this.
- **The repression of women** Feminists state that the family as we know it operates to the benefit of men. Women are expected to do most of the housework and cooking and to disrupt their working lives in order to raise the children.
- **Violence in the family** This is linked to the two previous points. Wives and children are physically abused in the family and in the last 25 years there has been a growth in the women's refuges where they can go to escape from violent husbands. Research in North London suggests that 10% of women have been victims of

serious violence by their partners. It has also been estimated that approximately 12% of children have had significant violence used against them by parents.

- **Psychological disorders** The psychiatrists Laing and Cooper, among others, have suggested that certain psychological disorders such as schizophrenia are closely linked to family life. When intense pressure is put upon children to conform to the parents' wishes, it can lead to psychological disturbance.

Fig 3.3   The family life cycle
(Source: Stephen Moore, *Sociology Alive!*, Stanley Thornes, 2nd edition, 1996)

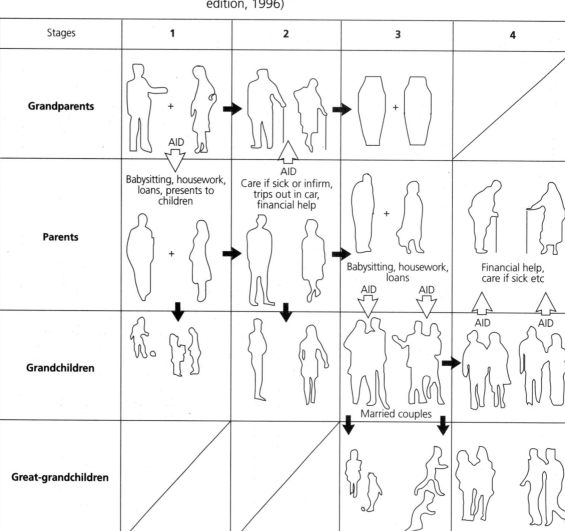

3.6 Changing relationships between partners

Traditional relationships

From the late nineteenth century until 1950 the relationship between husband and wife could be described as **male dominated** (patriarchy). The father/husband was the undoubted head of the household, his needs, his values, his viewpoint were always considered first.

Women were regarded as inferior and spent their lives as mothers, looking after their children; as wives, looking after the husband; and as housewives, looking after the home.

The wife's role, that is the typical pattern of behaviour expected of a wife, reflected the attitudes held about women at that time. These attitudes were basically that women were naturally inferior to men and should accept their authority. However, in the 1950s a change began to take place, with a greater emphasis on a more shared home life.

Equality within the family: the symmetrical family

By the 1970s sociologists such as Willmott and Young argued that a significantly new form of family relationship had emerged. What they termed 'the symmetrical family'. This was characterised by:
- equality between husband and wife;
- a sharing of domestic tasks;
- leisure time spent together as a family;
- a greater pride in the home.

These changes started in the middle class and spread rapidly to most of the working class.

The following factors have led to this form of relationship between partners:
- The increasing importance of the home to couples, with partners more likely to spend time there together.
- The increased geographical mobility of families in the search for employment or better housing have isolated the nuclear family, pushing its members closer together.
- The general rise in the status of women is reflected in legal and social changes.
- The increase in the number of women working led to a degree of financial independence, so that economic decisions had to be joint ones between partners.
- Decrease in family size has led to higher standards of living and greater freedom for the women from child care.

The feminist criticism of equality within marriage

The idea that the relationship between husband and wife can best be described as symmetrical has been severely criticised by feminists, who point out that women benefit far less from marriage than men.

Childcare
Women are expected to shoulder the larger proportion of the housework, and take the responsibility for the children.
- In a study of North London, Oakley found only 14% of husbands helping in the house.
- Edgell studied middle-class families (*Middle Class Couples*) and could find no evidence to support the existence of the symmetrical family.
- Boulton (*On Being a Mother*) found less than 20% of male partners taking an equal share in child rearing.
- Government statistics show that mothers spend an average of 62 hours per week on household tasks, compared to 23 hours spent by fathers (*Social Trends 27*, 1997).

Violence
Feminists also point out that violence against women is still common in family life and that this is generally ignored by the police unless it is extremely violent.
1. In a study of over 1000 married women by Painter in the early 1990s, over 14% of wives claimed that their husband had raped them, and that in 50% of these cases, violence had been used. The chances of being raped by a husband were seven times higher than by a stranger.
2. In a study of domestic violence in North London in 1994, Mooney discovered that over their lifetime up to 25% of women had experienced some form of domestic violence, which included assaults by other members of the family including parents, siblings, step-brothers and even children. In all, 10% of women had suffered serious violence against them by their partners.

Decision making
Pahl's study (*Money and Marriage*) of 102 couples with at least one child under 16 found that in over 60% of the couples, the husband dominated decision making concerned with spending money.

3.7 Cohabitation, marriage and divorce

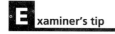
Cohabitation

Today almost 25% of 18–49-year–olds are cohabiting, compared to less than half that figure in 1981. The figure of the 28–35-year-olds is even higher, with over 30% of these cohabiting. It has been suggested that this is an alternative to marriage. However, only a relatively small percentage of women are cohabiting on a permanent basis, and the majority of cohabitees are in a stage which precedes marriage or as the result of a breakup of a marriage. For example, more than half of cohabitations last for less than two years, and the main reason is not a break up of the partners, but their decision to marry. This is linked to the decision to have children, or the fact that the woman is already pregnant.

However, the statistics do not fully bear out the claim by some writers that cohabitation is merely a stage which takes place before or after marriage. Today about 30% of births are outside marriage, and about 13% are registered by both parents living at the same address. This would imply a long-term commitment, which is similar to marriage in its degree of permanence. These figures fit in with what has already happened in Scandinavia, where almost 40% of couples cohabit rather than marry.

Marriage

Decline in the proportion of people marrying

Marriage rates have declined steeply across Europe since the 1970s. In 1961 there were 340 000 first marriages, yet in 1995, this had fallen to 208 000. As a partial compensation for this, the numbers of people marrying for a second time has increased over the same period from 5000 to 137 000 marriages, so that remarriages form over 40% of all marriages in the UK compared to 14% in 1961. In 1971 only 4% of women remained unmarried by the age of 50, today the figure is 17%. Furthermore, the fewer people who are marrying are choosing to do so at a later age, typically following cohabitation. Britain still has the third highest marriage rate in Europe after Portugal, but also has the third highest divorce rate after Portugal.

Marital breakdown

There are three types of marital breakdown:
- **divorce**, which is a legal dissolution of marriage;
- **separation** where partners live apart;
- **empty-shell marriages** where the partners remain married, but have separate emotional or social lives.

Since 1971, marriages have fallen by one-fifth and divorces have doubled. On the face of it, this suggests a collapse in the institution of the family, but, it could be argued that all that has happened is that today unhappy marriages are more likely to end in divorce, and the number of 'empty-shell' marriages has declined.

Explanation for marital breakdown

Legal changes

The divorce rate partially reflects legal changes. When the law is liberalised, to make divorce easier to obtain, there is an increase in the numbers applying for divorce. This is not a cause of divorce, but a reflection of unhappy marriages.

Goode has argued that this process of 'liberalisation' is part of a wider process of secularisation in western societies, by which he means that it reflects the decline in the institution of religion.

Examples of the sudden increases in divorce include the **Divorce Reform Act** which came into force in 1971, and in 1984 the shortening of the period that a couple had to be married before they could petition for divorce.

The divorce rate is an almost exact reflection of the gradual liberalisation of divorce in the twentieth century. There appears to be a **dam effect**, with a build-up of people wanting divorce leading to a change in the law, and as a result a sudden rise in divorce.

- In 1857 divorce became available for the first time in the courts, although the law for men was different from that for women, allowing men to obtain divorces more easily.
- In 1937 divorce was made easier, with one partner having to **prove** that the other partner had committed some offence against the marriage vows, such as adultery or cruelty.
- In 1950 there was an extension of legal aid to divorce. This meant that many people, particularly women, who previously could not afford to start divorce proceedings were able to proceed.
- In 1969 the law was changed so that the **irretrievable breakdown of marriage** became the only reason for divorce. This meant separation for two years if both partners wanted the divorce, or separation for five years if only one partner wanted the divorce.
- It has to be remembered that changes in the law reflect changes in public opinion, so we cannot say that the changes in divorce laws caused a rise in divorce, rather they allowed a rise in divorce.

Expectations of marriage

Goode has suggested that historically marriage in most societies was not based upon love, but was supposed to be an economic relationship with limited expectations regarding companionship. Partners did not expect marriage to provide partnership and sexual fulfilment as we do today.

This links to the work of another sociologist Parsons, who claims that the family has lost its wider functions and instead today is relegated to providing the emotional needs that are not available in the broader society.

Furthermore, the decline in the extended family and the move to the nuclear family places greater emotional pressures on the fewer family members. The result of all this emotional loading is that the family becomes an emotional 'pressure cooker', with the heat of the emotions leading to chances of an 'explosion'. If the family fails to provide all the emotional and social needs then the marriage breaks down.

Changing attitudes of women

Three-quarters of divorces are started by wives. This suggests that:
- the increasing economic independence of women,
- the increasing belief in their own rights, and
- the availability of legal aid for divorce have allowed them the opportunity and desire to divorce if they feel restricted in their marriages. Traditionally, the dominant economic role and the values of patriarchy (male dominance) meant that it was difficult for wives to initiate divorce proceedings.

Community and peer group pressure

The informal social control and community pressure which helped marriages to remain in place have weakened as a result of increasing urbanisation and the related decline in community.

Social status and divorce

Marital breakdown occurs with greater frequency amongst certain social groups than others.
- There are higher divorce rates amongst the working- and lower-middle classes.
- The younger the partners at marriage, the higher the chances of divorce. This reflects possible emotional immaturity, the fact that the woman is more likely to be pregnant at marriage, their personal development may take place at different speeds and in different directions.

  However, the increase in cohabitation and the availability of terminations and contraceptives have decreased the numbers of people marrying young, and/or when the partner is pregnant with an unplanned pregnancy.
- Partners who come from very different backgrounds have increased chances of divorce. Thomas and Collard *(Who Divorces?)* argue that often divorce occurs because the couple are unable to communicate their feelings to each other, so they are unable to work through their differences and problems.

Conclusion: the stability of the family

More than 90% of people still marry today. Although divorce rates are high, remarriage rates are high too, suggesting that people may reject their partners but they are not rejecting the institution of marriage.

However, cohabitation is increasing rapidly and it is now normal to cohabit before marriage. In Sweden, cohabitation has moved further and begun to replace marriage for certain groups, although in neighbouring Denmark, marriage has 'returned to fashion'.

Summary

1   There are two extreme family types, extended and nuclear; most societies have a mixture of both.

2   There are a number of different forms of marriage, including polygamy, polyandry and monogamy.

3   The type of marriage varies with the culture and economic situation of the society.

4   The typical family in Britain before industrialisation was the nuclear type. However, better-off households were larger because orphans, related kin and child servants all lived in.

5   Early industrialisation brought an increase in the number of extended families living in industrial towns and giving mutual assistance. These lasted right up to the 1950s in some cases.

6   The family performs some functions for society and its members, including the regulation of sexual activity, socialisation, production of children, economic activity and emotional support.

7   However, it is also agreed that the family can be harmful to its members, because of the intense emotional ties within it.

8   Relationships have changed considerably among family members.

9   In particular children are treated with greater consideration and there is an acceptance of their right to have a viewpoint and a say in the affairs of the family.

10   There are significant differences between the way that male and females are raised. They are socialised into different gender roles.

11   Women have gained a greater measure of equality in the home (and in society generally). Some sociologists have gone so far as to argue that there is now equality in the household and that men do as many household chores as women. This form of relationship has been called the symmetrical family.

12   Feminist sociologists have argued that this is an exaggeration and that women have to do the bulk of the housework and child rearing. The family remains a place where women are unequal.

13   The idea that the elderly are isolated from the wider family seems to be untrue. Most of the elderly who have family are in regular contact with them.

14   There is a wide variety of family forms in Britain today, including lone-parent families, families formed through divorce and remarriage, couples without children, etc, and the families of ethnic minorities.

15   Families as we know them are not the only form of group life – there have been communes and there are *kibbutzim*, for example.

16 Industrialisation has also affected family life in other societies, for example in Japan, where the authority of the male head of the household has been undermined, and the extended or 'stem/branch' family has given way to the nuclear family.

17 People are marrying later and are more likely to live together before marriage. Cohabitation is now a normal stage which precedes marriage.

18 Couples are having fewer children, and having them later.

19 Divorce has increased rapidly since the 1960s, and first marriages have declined. The continuing popularity of marriage is reflected in the fact that those who divorce are still likely to remarry.

21 The increase in divorce reflects changing attitudes and expectations from marriage and the fact that divorce is now easier to obtain.

22 Marriage still remains very popular, with 90% of the population marrying.

Self-test questions

1 What is meant by the terms 'nuclear family' and 'extended family'?
2 According to sociologists how have the functions performed by the family changed in recent times?
3 Why is the assumption that the family is beneficial for its members criticised by some sociologists?
4 How have the roles of men and women changed within the family since the beginning of the century?
5 How has the position of children changed within the family during the twentieth century?
6 What useful part do old people play in the modern family?
7 Why is the image of the typical British family consisting of a wife and husband plus two or three children not a wholly accurate one?
8 In what ways does marriage mark a crucial change in a person's status in society?
9 Why might divorce statistics not accurately reflect the true extent of marital breakdown?
10 Why might it be argued that 'in recent years we are witnessing the end of marriage as we know it'?

Chapter 4
Education

4.1 Socialisation and education

Learning about society does not start or finish at school, but happens throughout our lives. Schools contribute to this learning process in two ways. through **formal learning** and through **informal learning**.

Formal learning

- This is the academic or practical knowledge taught to us at school or college.
- It consists of clearly defined skills or bodies of knowledge taught in an organised manner (the lesson), which can be graded and tested (examinations) after a set period (the length of the course). Each subject we are taught at school, such as mathematics or history, is an example of formal learning.
- Formal learning is the official reason for the existence of schools.

Informal learning

- This form of learning is part of the socialisation process, in which we learn social skills and values that are necessary in order to function as a normal person in society.
- Informal learning is not organised or examined (except that if we are badly socialised we may be regarded as deviant by others).
- It is learning in our daily lives through interaction with other people and through the mass media. The most important people who influence our informal learning are family, the peer group (people of our own age), and especially our friends and teachers.

All complex industrial societies have education systems for formal education in order to train people how to carry out the tasks necessary to maintain the economic system of rapidly changing society. The education system trains scientists, clerks and tradespeople.

In simpler societies without industrialisation and rapid social change, there was no need for a formal education system. All learning took place informally through the family, religion and the peer group. Knowledge of farming or hunting useful to one generation was also of use to the next.

Informal learning in the school: the hidden curriculum

The distinction between the two forms of learning is not totally clear, however. Formal learning may occur in the home, e.g. where a mother teaches her child to bake a cake or repair a car; while in school informal learning takes place alongside formal learning. An English lesson may be about a comprehension exercise, but the teacher may choose an extract on old age. Through the lesson the pupil may be socialised informally to expect certain patterns of behaviour from the elderly.

In fact informal learning as a part of the process of socialisation occurs as much in the school as does formal learning. All the things that the pupils learn at school which are not officially part of the lessons are known as the **hidden curriculum**. The term is used because all the lessons that form the typical school timetable are collectively known as the curriculum.

Examples of the hidden curriculum
- **Gender roles** Through the action of teachers in responding to girls and boys differently and expecting different forms of behaviour from them (see Chapter 6) children learn the behaviour expected of the sexes.
- **Racial differences** Just like gender roles, children also become aware of the differences in ethnic groups. This is partly through the attitudes and expectations of teachers, and partly through the content of books and lessons they study. For example, very few books, if any, studied at school have a black heroine or hero (see Unit 4.6).
- **Class differences** Research by Sharpe and Green indicates that teachers are more sympathetic towards middle-class children and find it easier to relate to them, possibly because the teachers come from middle-class backgrounds themselves.
- **Streaming and examinations** These prepare children for the inequality of later life when some groups take the better jobs with higher prestige and better rates of pay. Children come to regard it as natural that people are graded.

FORMAL ·LEARNING * INFORMAL LEARNING

- **Language** Working-class children and those from ethnic minorities discover that the forms of English they use are inferior to the middle-class language of the school books they study.
- **Social control** Children learn that they must do what they are told, even if this is not what they want to do. They are therefore prepared for work later when they must obey their bosses even if the work seems pointless and boring.
- **The peer group** Pupils of the same age are known as the **peer group** and they are extremely important in influencing the attitudes and behaviour of their colleagues. In lower streams, for instances, it is not regarded as 'the done thing' to be helpful and polite to teachers. This can lead to anti-school groups who will develop values that will lead to school failure.

The research of Paul Willis *(Learning to Labour)* is important here. He shows how lower-stream pupils learn to see school as completely unimportant. They develop values that enable them to cope with the boredom and irrelevance of school – for instance, they muck around, playing tricks on teacher, and the result is they fail. However, these very values that led to their certain failure, also allow them to cope with the boring work they might later obtain.

4.2 Educational change

1988 Education Reform Act

This Act introduced a number of significant changes.

- **Local management of schools** This gave much greater control over budgets to schools, and very significantly reduced the roles of local education authorities.
- **Grant maintained schools** A further development was that schools could opt out completely of local education control, choosing to take money directly from the government.

    What this did in effect was allow **selection**, which had diminished greatly as a result of the growth of comprehensives, to reappear. Schools which decided to take grant maintained status (after a parental ballot) were able to adjust their intake policies – that is, to choose which pupils they wanted.

- **The National Curriculum** Traditionally in Britain, schools had decided what they would teach, and how they would teach it. The National Curriculum stated exactly what schools had to teach, the pace of teaching and the targets that had to be achieved at the ages of 7, 11 and 14 and 16.

    In order to measure whether the achievements had been attained, assessments (SATs) are carried out nationally and the results published.

Criticisms of the National Curriculum, publication of results and testing

- The **content** of the National Curriculum has been criticised for being too nationalistic and even racist, in that it teaches a single view of history which ignores the experiences of many of the ethnic minorities.

    For example: the teaching about the British Empire in History can demean those who came from the ex-colonies, as it is not seen from their viewpoint; English teaching can stress that only one form of English writing and speech is correct and deny the background of many others.

- **Testing** has been criticised because it puts great pressure on young children, who are being assessed as early as 7. Pupils become aware of this and judge themselves according to their level of attainment. Therefore pupils are feeling failures at an early age. This may affect their attitude to school. The tests fail to recognise that pupils may develop at different paces, and to impose one overall level of development may be wrong. The tests also use a significant amount of time which could be better put to use in teaching and learning.

- **Publication of results** Schools have their results published and parents are encouraged to compare the results. It is unfair, however, to compare schools in poorer neighbourhoods with those from affluent ones, with different intakes of pupils.

Vocational education

State education provision has always been closely related to the perceived needs of the economy. State education was originally introduced partly as a response to the need for numerate and literate workers for industry. From the 1980s onwards, the importance of the job, or 'vocational' relevance of education has returned to the top of the agenda. Employers and employer organisations have been requested to suggest what they think should be taught in schools.

Local employers as opposed to elected representatives from local authorities have been put on the managing bodies of schools and colleges. Schools, colleges and universities have been encouraged to take on the business ethos of efficiency and competition. Rather than the question 'how does this develop the mind of the student?' the question is rather 'how can this help the student to get a job?'.

Vocational qualifications

Britain has always had a two-tier system of educational qualifications. Traditionally these were apprenticeships for skilled manual and craft work, and academic credentials such as A-levels and degrees for the 'more academic'. The academic credentials were always held in higher esteem.

However, during the 1980s, the government began to replace apprenticeships with various forms of vocational qualifications, which eventually developed in the early 1990s into the NVQ and GNVQ system.

NVQs are specific recognised skills for a particular job.

GNVQs are a rather more general range of transferable skills, within broad vocational categories (for example there is a GNVQ for Health and Social Care).

Critics of vocational qualifications argue that education becomes job training rather than a true preparation for life.

Supporters point out that the UK has fallen behind other countries as it has failed to teach adequate job skills and therefore is in danger of companies investing in other countries with higher levels of skilled labour.

Training councils

In order to implement job training, a series of agencies have had the task of running this form of education. These have replaced local education authorities on the one hand, and apprenticeships on the other. Currently, Training Enterprise Councils (TECs) have the job of running much of local training. These are organisations which are dominated by local businesses and funded by central government to buy job-related education. Young people who leave school without employment are required to attend a training scheme if they wish to receive any government benefit.

Criticisms of the employment schemes run by TECs include:

- that the things taught are less educational and more about learning the right attitudes of attendance, punctuality and acceptance of the power of employers;
- those on training courses have few employment rights;
- that the claims that they lead to higher levels of employment at their completion are wrong, and that the figures are manipulated;
- that the unemployment statistics are kept down by sending large numbers of people on to various employment training schemes.

(At the time of writing the Labour government is committed to addressing these problems, but it is too early to tell how effective its new measures will be.)

Research

Cohen (*Against the New Vocationalism*) has argued that there is little real knowledge learned in employment schemes and that it simply draws attention away from the real 'structural' cause of unemployment, which is a lack of investment.

Buswell (*Training for Low Pay*) found that training schemes were highly sexist. She argues that the sorts of training which females are given reflects traditional assumptions about the sorts of jobs that women do – in industries such as retailing – and that the females were being socialised into taking low-paid work.

4.3 The functions of education for society

The functionalist school of sociology analyses each social institution (e.g. the family, the political system, religion, education) in terms of the **functions** it performs for the existence of society, in much the same way that to understand the purpose of the heart, we look at the function it performs for the existence of the body.

Functionalists conclude that there are four functions of the education system:

1. the transmission of culture;
2. social control;
3. economic training;
4. social selection.

1 The transmission of culture (or socialisation)

To exist every society needs a basic set of shared beliefs and values. In order for society to continue, it is necessary to pass on these values from one generation to the next. It is a particularly important function in our complex form of society, where many different cultural groups must exist together. The school transmits a core set of values around which society adheres.

This cultural transmission function may be reinforced by other agencies such as the family or the mass media. However, in certain cases, such as among the children of immigrants, the school alone teaches them the values of our society (see Unit 4.1).

2 Social control

Closely allied to the transmission of culture is the need for each society to regulate the specific behaviour of its members. We cannot be allowed to do just what we want. Schools teach us the specific behaviour expected of us. We learn about acceptable and unacceptable, perhaps even illegal, behaviour. Part of this social control function is to pass on an acceptance of the political system of our society.

3 Economic training

Each society needs to produce its economic necessities in order to survive. Our economic system, based upon industry, needs a wide variety of skills varying across the range from scientist to plumber to chef. The education system produces an adequate supply of trainee manpower for every skill required.

4 Social selection

Society needs the more able children to perform the more complex jobs. Ideally, the education system should grade children according to their ability, so that they may learn the level of skill best suited to their ability. In such a way society best uses its available talents.

The functions of education: a criticism

The functionalist viewpoint we have just read implies that the education system benefits everybody in society equally. Many sociologists – particularly those influenced by the Marxist approach – disagree with this viewpoint. They argue instead that powerful groups in our society use education to *impose* beliefs and values that benefit them on the rest of society. So children are taught at school to do what they are told, to accept society as it is without questioning why it is organised so that a few are extremely rich and the rest work for a wage in order to keep the few rich.

In reality education does not reflect the needs of society, but the needs of the owners of industry and commerce for a docile workforce with enough skills to do the jobs needed.

Bowles and Gints *(Schooling in a Capitalist Society)* studied 237 final year US secondary school pupils. They found that pupils who received the highest grades were more likely to be the hardworking, quiet, reliable ones who did what they were told without question. On the other hand, low grades were associated with students who were creative, aggressive and independent. There was no evidence to suggest that the aggressive, low-grade students were less intelligent than the high-grade obedient ones. Schools are not then rewarding intelligence, but conformity.

4.4 Social class and educational success

Examiner's tip

Do not fall into the trap of writing that all working-class children 'fail' at school – it is much more complex.

Statistics indicate that social class is directly related to educational success or failure. The higher a person is in the social class structure, the more likely his or her child is to succeed in the education system. Explanations which have been put forward include:

- poverty and deprivation in the home;
- family socialisation;
- cultural explanations;
- the school as an institution.

Poverty and deprivation in the home

The National Child Development Study found that at age seven children from overcrowded homes with low incomes are over nine months behind other children in their educational levels. The study went on to point out that one in sixteen children suffered from 'multiple deprivation', which included such things as low income, poor housing, poor diet – all of which impact on the educational chances of children.

In a study of education and its relationship to job success later in life, Halsey, Heath and Ridge found that material circumstances significantly affected the type of secondary school attended and the decision whether to take A-levels.

However, other sociologists have pointed to the fact that many poor children do succeed in the education system. What they point to is the importance of parental interest and cultural background – family socialisation.

Family socialisation

Intelligence

Psychologists such as H Eysenck argue that differences in educational attainment reflect the fact that individuals inherit their intelligence from their parents in much the same way that a person inherits his or her facial features. (The term used to describe this view of intelligence is **innate intelligence**.) Furtermore, intelligence can be measured by IQ tests such as those used in the 11+. A person's IQ can be measured by dividing his or her mental age by his or her chronological age, and multiplying by one hundred. So a person with a mental age of twelve but a real age of ten has an IQ of 120 (12/10 × 100). Most sociologists argue that although we inherit a degree of mental capacity from our parents, most of our intelligence is determined by our culture and our upbringing. In particular they make the following points:

- What is considered to be intelligence varies from society to society. An intelligent person in a tribal society may be considered stupid in ours.
- IQ scores vary over time and a person can improve them with practice.
- IQ tests measure only the ability of the person tested to conform to the tester's idea of intelligence. This varies with class and background culture.

Parent's interest

Douglas' longitudinal study of a national sample of British schoolchildren stressed that the single most important influence on educational success was parental interest. This was supported by a study of childrearing patterns in Nottingham, by the Newsons who claimed that middle-class parents provide more stimulating home environments.

Deferred gratification

Sugarman stressed how middle-class children were brought up with the concept of 'deferred gratification', that is being prepared to give up short-term benefits for long-term ones.

Language development

Bernstein stressed the differences in language use and development. Middle-class families were more likely to bring up their children to use language forms which developed 'conceptual' thought and the ability to express oneself.

Bernstein distinguishes between two codes of speech:

- **Elaborated**, where a wide vocabulary is used with the child and he/she is encouraged fully to explore his or her language potential. This code is most often found in middle-class homes.
- **Restricted**, where the child is spoken to with a narrow range of vocabulary. This is more often found in working-class homes.

The result is that middle-class children are more likely to be adept at language when they attend school and this gives them a great advantage when speaking or writing

Cultural explanations

Cultural deprivation

Closely linked to the idea of family socialisation is the argument that certain groups in society may be 'cut off' from the mainstream values of the society. This lack of culture can influence children's ability to benefit from school, as the work there does not reinforce knowledge learned in the home. This is part of the argument used to support the idea of the underclass in British society.

Cultural capital

This approach suggests that rather than certain groups being **deprived** of culture, children from middle- and upper-class homes are seen as having very significant advantages at school. The values of school are those of the middle class, and therefore the child 'fits in'.

Indeed one of the functions of schools, it is claimed by writers such as Bourdieu, is that they should ensure that these values are passed on from one generation to the next. Those who come from the appropriate backgrounds have a very great advantage in that their home and the educational values mutually support one another. The working-class pupils have much further to go to achieve these values. Bourdieu calls this advantage of the middle and upper classes **cultural capital**. However, Bourdieu is unclear exactly what the *content* of cultural capital is.

Structural explanations

These are explanations which look to the much wider economic and social structure of society for explanations for school failure.

Functionalist writers point out that schools act as sieves, grading out higher ability children. The least able therefore do less well. However, this approach can be criticised for failing to explain why so many intelligent working-class and black children do not succeed in the education system.

Marxist writers claim that the education system:

- imposes the dominant values of the ruling class on the population,
- ensures that failure is inevitable for the majority of the population. That is the point of the system – to make sure that the majority of people accept that the upper class are cleverer and deserve to be in their positions.

Willis (*Learning to Labour*) argues that working-class boys, aware of their inevitable failure, cope with the boredom of school and its irrelevance to their lives, by 'mucking about'. This behaviour actually guarantees their future failure.

Griffin and Lees have found a very similar process happening to working-class girls, who prepare themselves for a perceived career as a housewife/mother and part-time employee.

However, the Marxist approach has been strongly criticised as working-class children do succeed – about 60% of those in social class 1 come from origins outside that class.

The school

This approach stresses the importance of the school itself, as an **organisation** to influence success or failure. There are two main explanations of why the school fails many young people:

- poor organisation;
- the role of teachers.

Organisation approaches

Rutter (*15 000 hours*) studied 12 London comprehensives and measured four factors: attendance, achievement, behaviour and level of delinquency outside the school. What he found was that schools varied very greatly in their levels of success with their pupils. He suggested that, even after allowing for social class differences, the following factors were crucial:

- the ethos of the school (a general commitment to good practice shared by all staff members);
- good teaching (teachers are punctual, well organised, patient, encourage pupils, inspire by example);
- an established and consistent set of rewards and punishments.

Teachers

The labelling of certain students as good or bad can have a very important impact on their levels of success. If teachers expect children to do well and encourage them it can actually bring this about. On the other hand, low expectations can lead to an 'anti-school' culture amongst the students.

Research

- **Ball** (*Beachside Comprehensive*) showed that teachers' attitudes to lower-band pupils helped to produce an anti-school culture amongst the middle band by the third year. But, even when banding was abolished and mixed ability groupings brought in, teachers continued to distinguish (informally) between 'bright' and 'dull' pupils and treated them accordingly – with the expected consequences.
- **Halsey, Heath and Ridge** (*Origins and Destinations*) studied 800 males and concluded that:
  - family cultural background and attitudes of parents were crucial up to the age of eleven;
  - at this point their influence declined and then the organisation of the school was overwhelmingly important;
  - however, material circumstances were crucial in determining whether boys stayed on to take A-levels and therefore attained better academic results.

4.5 Gender and educational attainment

Attainment differences by gender

Girls are more likely to be successful throughout the education system up to degree level, when both achieve equally.

However, although females are more successful in the education system, feminists have pointed to the fact that females are more likely to study social science, language and caring subjects than males, who are in turn more likely to study science and engineering subjects. The significance of subject choice is that it strongly influences the choice of further/higher education and the type of employment.

However, the impact of the National Curriculum has not yet fully worked through the education system. It may be that in the future there will be greater similarity. Kelly argues that it will make little difference as long as science has a 'masculine' image.

Explanations for differences in education

Explanations for the different choices and routes in education include:

- socialisation;
- peer groups;
- the impact of teachers and the hidden curriculum.

Socialisation

Girls are treated differently to boys by parents and relatives. As early as six months of age, Goldberg and Lewis found parents expected daughters to be quieter, cleaner and more restrained than six-month-old boys.

According to Sharpe, young children are given sex differentiated toys, with construction toys regarded as more appropriate for boys.

Loban, in her research, had pointed to the way that schoolbooks and children's books generally continue to reinforce gender stereotypes.

The peer group

Feminists point to the way in which girls actually police themselves by helping to impose gender stereotyping and trapping themselves in certain poorer paid, dead-end jobs.

Griffin studied a group of low achieving secondary schoolgirls in the Midlands and found that although there was no clear anti-school culture amongst the girls, they did think that academic success was 'unfeminine'. Their aim was to get what was perceived as glamorous white-collar jobs, with relatively little power or income.

The result of the socialisation both in the family and the wider society is such that girls actively choose jobs in the caring professions or courses in the humanities. They regard these as appropriate and 'natural' courses of action.

Sharpe and Lees in two separate studies point out the acceptance by teenage girls of the inevitability in the longer term of motherhood.

The impact of teachers and the hidden curriculum

In school teachers respond differently to boys and girls and expect different patterns of behaviour from them. This reaffirms socialisation in the home and wider society. It also helps to direct girls (and boys) into different subject choices and hence different future areas of employment.

In primary schools, French found that boys were more active and demanding, so teachers responded more to their wishes and views. When organised for discussion around the teacher, French found the teachers organised the seating so that the girls were on the periphery.

In secondary schools Stanworth claimed that teachers spent disproportionately large amounts of time dealing with boys to the exclusion of females. Girls also suffered from very low self-esteem, underrating their ability when compared with the views of teachers.

Teachers also advise girls on subject choice based partially on the girl's choice of future career, and partially on a realistic awareness of where girls are most likely to be successful which, according to Thomas and Stuart, is in 'female' areas, such as the health and caring professions.

Teachers are influenced by the values of the wider society and import these values into the classroom. Deem noted in her study how interaction in the classroom is built around these values. For example, boys were asked to help lift things.

Textbooks and readers in primary schools are still often gender biased, with males being the more dominant characters.

It is not just teachers who seek to marginalise females, notes Kelly (*Science for Girls*) who studied science lessons in secondary schools. She claims that the boys in science classes dominate the classes by insisting they do the experiments, by shouting out answers to teachers and generally taking control. Kelly sees this as a microcosm of the wider patriarchal (male-dominated) society. She also points out that the majority of books are illustrated by male figures.

Finally, feminist sociologists have pointed out the way that the school curriculum consistently ignores the contribution of women to the advance of knowledge, such as in the area of scientific research where the overwhelming majority of great scientists are men and the role of women has been ignored or covered up.

4.6 Ethnicity and education

Under achievement and race

The Swann Report (*Education for All*) in 1985 found very significant differences between the results of pupils of Afro-Caribbean origin and those of whites.

Only 5% of children of Afro-Caribbean origin obtained an A-level, and less than 1% went to university. Those of Asian origin had similar success levels to whites, though those of Bangladeshi origins had the worst performance of all groups in the education system.

Race, gender and stereotyping

The problem with any discussion of race and gender issues is of stereotyping the debate. Although children of Afro-Caribbean origin do relatively less well overall than whites and Asians, it is not true that all children of Afro-Caribbean origin do worse educationally than whites – merely that they are less likely to be successful. Indeed, females of Afro-Caribbean backgrounds achieve well above average. Driver studied pupils in five inner city comprehensives. His conclusion was that black girls were more successful than either white girls or boys, whereas black male pupils performed worse.

Ethnicity and educational achievement

Explanations for the differences in achievement include:
- innate differences;
- language and cultural differences;
- social class;
- family and socialisation;
- racism both inside and outside the school.

Innate differences

A number of writers have suggested that there are innate differences in intelligence between blacks and whites. Jenson in the USA and Eysenck in the UK have both argued this on the basis of IQ tests. However, the Swann Committee found that when environmental differences were taken into account, the differences were so slight as to be irrelevant to the debate.

Language and cultural differences

Where the home background is not English or is a variation of English, it is claimed that this may hold back the pupil. However, the Swann Report found this was only a significant factor in a small number of cases – primarily for Bangladeshi children.

Family and socialisation

Driver and Ballard (*Contemporary Performance in Multi-Race Schools*) found that the Asian children in their study did particularly well because of the strong emphasis of the family on educational success. They discovered that the Asian families were prepared to make sacrifices for the success of their children in the system. The Swann Report argued that the Asian family structure was more tight knit than those of either whites or Afro-Caribbeans, and that this may be responsible for higher achievement.

Tizzard (*Young Children at School in the Inner City*) studied 343 primary school children (171 black, 106 white). The study took place over three years in thirty schools. She concluded that:
- white and black parents of primary school children were equally likely to support their children and to read to them at home, so the argument of the less supportive Afro-Caribbean was a myth;
- that race was of much less importance than gender in predicting overall success at primary school.

Social class

The differences in performance by pupils from different ethnic backgrounds may be heavily influenced by social class. We know, for example that the income, employment, and housing standards of those of Afro-Caribbean origin are significantly lower than the majority of the population. Therefore much of the poor performance could be related to the same factors that make the white members of the working class perform relatively poorly. The Swann Report suggests that this probably explains about 50% of Afro-Caribbean under achievement.

Race inside the school

Examiner's tip

The relationship between 'race' and educational success can only be understood if linked to issues of social class and gender.

According to Green's research in junior and middle schools, some teachers favoured white pupils when teaching. Teachers appeared to have lower expectations of Afro-Caribbean pupils and failed to encourage them as much. The result was a lowering of the pupils' self-image.

Tomlinson points out the way that teachers expect less from Afro-Caribbean origin pupils. The teachers in the study claimed that they were slower learners, lacking concentration, and less well behaved.

Brah and Ninhas claim that teachers expect Asians to be industrious and courteous, but Asian girls are often overlooked by teachers as they are regarded as 'passive'. Often this can result in them being underestimated.

Fuller studied black girls in a London comprehensive, and although they were often academically successful, and not overtly anti-school, they were not interested in attaining a good reputation with the teachers. Fuller suggests that more important to them was their identity as female and black, rather than as successful and attentive pupils.

Stone (*The Education of the Black Child in Britain*) in a study of 264 pupils of Afro-Caribbean origin found that they were often hostile to the teachers and felt that they discriminated against them on the grounds of race.

Coard (*How the West Indian Child is Made Educationally Subnormal in the British School System*) argues that children of Afro-Caribbean origin are made to feel inferior by the way that the curriculum ignores black perspectives (on history/music etc) and by the way blacks appear in subservient roles, or are totally absent, in books. Coard claims that this leads to Afro-Caribbeans having low opinions of themselves and this contributes to their failure. However, the Swann Report found no evidence of low esteem amongst those of Afro-Caribbean origin. Nor did Stone find evidence of low esteem amongst her sample.

Reasons for the relatively better performance of Asian compared to children of Afro-Caribbean origin

- **Family background** There is generally a very great stress in the Asian family on obtaining good qualifications. The Asian family is very closely knit and provides an exceptionally stable background for study.
- **Rejection of racism** Although Asians face racism just as much as people of Afro-Caribbean origin, they seem better able to reject it. It has been suggested that this is because they have a greater sense of cultural identity than those of Afro-Caribbean origin. They have managed to retain a sense of community and independence of culture which makes them sure of their own worth.
- **Children of African Asian backgrounds** These generally have middle-class educated parents who had professional jobs in Africa before coming to Britain. They therefore receive all the same advantages as middle-class white children.

Summary

1   Socialisation is the process whereby a person learns the expectations and rules of society. Primary socialisation takes place in the home and family. Secondary socialisation takes place in the school.

2   The curriculum consists of all the subjects taught at school that prepare the pupil for adulthood.

3   The hidden curriculum consists of all the values and expectations that are taught to the pupil in the informal relationships between teachers and pupils and amongst pupils themselves. These may actually conflict with the official curriculum. Pupils learn expectations regarding social class, gender and race in particular.

4   The education system in Britain has developed mainly as a result of the need for more and better skilled manpower. Recent developments today such as NVQs and YTS all show that education is closely related to skill training.

5   However, it is not just demands for skilled workers that caused the changes in the education system. Political demands by the working class for better schools for their children were also important.

6   There is some dispute about the wisdom of abolishing grammar schools and replacing them with comprehensives. However, comprehensive schools appear to have had some (limited) success in helping the children of the working class to do better in the educational system.

7   There is a division between **functionalists** and **Marxists** over the functions of the education system. Functionalists argue that the education system has four functions: the transmission of culture, social control, economic training, and social selection. These all benefit society. Marxists disagree; they argue that the education system operates to the benefit of the rich and simply trains an obedient, skilled workforce.

8   Working-class children are less successful in the education system. Sociologists have explained this by the facts that (a) the home background is often not as helpful for educational success as that of the middle class; (b) the neighbourhood may also weaken the chances of the working-class child; and (c) what happens inside the school, particularly the actions of the teachers and the peer group, can help the middle-class child and harm the working-class child.

9   Girls perform differently in the educational system from boys. It has been suggested that this is mainly due to the way society crates **gender roles** which stress how males and females ought to behave. The result is that girls are directed towards caring and routine white-collar types of courses.

10   The ethnic minorities differ in their educational performances from whites. Although some Asians in particular perform exceptionally well, others, such as those of Afro-Caribbean origin and Bangladeshis, perform poorly. Explanations vary, but it is generally agreed that as the majority of people in the ethnic minorities belong to the working class, the same explanations are useful for their failure. On top of this, intentional and unintentional racism are important.

11   Britain cannot be said to be a **meritocracy** as so many of the children of the working class, the ethnic minorities and many girls fail to achieve their full potential from the education system.

Self-test questions

---

1   Clearly explain the difference between formal learning and informal learning.
2   (a) Explain the meaning of the term the 'hidden curriculum'.
    (b) Give two examples of the things that the hidden curriculum teaches us.
3   Explain the meaning of the following: (a) labelling, (b) social control.
4   In what ways do the functions of the education system relate to the needs of society?
5   What changes did the 1988 Education Act introduce?
6   What is meant by vocational education? How has this influenced education?
7   Suggest benefits and give any criticisms of vocational education.
8   Describe any two social effects of streaming.
9   Give two examples of the differences in educational patterns between males and females.
10 (a) Do all children of the ethnic minorities do badly at school?
    (b) Give two reasons why some children of migrant original do better than others.

Chapter 5
Social stratification

5.1 The meaning of stratification

Social stratification means the division of people into various social groups who have different levels of prestige, economic rewards and power according to their membership of these groups. Most societies have some ways of dividing people into social groups. The main ones are:

Caste
Estates (Feudalism)
Slavery
Social class

However, running alongside these forms of social divisions are those of:

Age
Gender
Ethnic group

In this unit we will concentrate mainly on **social class**, as it is generally accepted to be the most significant influence on our lives. In the following units we will concentrate on **gender, age** and then **ethnic divisions**.

5.2 Comparative forms of stratification

1 Caste

Caste stratification is based on the principle that people are born into a group and nothing they can do in their lifetime alters their group membership – different groups receive greater or lesser rewards and prestige as their birthright. This idea that you are born into a particular group is called **ascription**.

The caste system exists in India, although it is being increasingly weakened by industrialisation. It is based on the **Hindu** religion which preaches that people are reborn (**reincarnation**), i.e. have more than one life. The form of life and the caste you are born into depends upon your conduct in your previous life; the worse your conduct the lower your caste.

The various castes are rigidly separated; contact with a lower caste member **pollutes** a higher caste person. Thus social intercourse and marriage are strictly forbidden.

Each caste is traditionally association with a form of work. The castes are in descending order of status:

- Brahmin Priests
- Kshatryas Soldiers
- Vaishyas Merchants
- Shudras Servants and manual workers
- Untouchables Regarded with disgust by the rest of the population

The Indian system of caste is the classic example, but it has also been applied in other countries where strict unbreakable divisions are enforced.

Until the end of apartheid in South Africa, the colour of a person's skin would determine his or her economic and social position. In Peru and Columbia today the indigenous people (the so-called Indians) are treated very differently from the majority of the population. In Brazil there have been accusations that there is a systematic attempt to kill the native inhabitants of the river region who are seen as preventing the exploitation of the forests for oil and gold prospecting.

2 Feudalism

This system of stratification is traditionally associated with medieval Europe – but it also existed in Japan, Russia and Eritrea until this century.

The basic principles are very simple. Ownership of the land was in the hands of a small group of **nobles**. Each noble divided his land and allowed a lesser noble to have that land as long as he swore personal loyalty to the senior noble, swearing to provide him with fighting men in the event of war. The lesser noble then subdivided his land in return for personal oaths of allegiance. The resulting system was rather like a pyramid with the king at the top and working through all the nobility right down to the serf who swore personal allegiance to his local lord in order to have the right to work on the land. In an agricultural society to have land meant to have wealth.

Each layer of the society was known as an **estate**, and like the caste system each estate was based on ascription (or the assigning of land/wealth/loyalty to other groups in society).

3 Slavery

One of the earliest and most widespread forms of stratification was slavery. In societies such as Ancient Greece or Rome it was customary for the society to be divided into freemen (amongst whom great differences in wealth existed) and slaves – who were owned by freemen. This ownership of one man by another existed until the nineteenth century.

4 Social class

In modern industrialised societies the dominant form of social stratification is social class. People are grouped according to **hierarchy** (a series of steps) based on economic and status differences.

The main differences between social class and other forms of stratification are that:

(a) Social class is **open** in the sense that one can move up or down the hierarchy, as opposed to the **closed** stratification systems of slavery and caste etc. This is known as **social mobility**.
(b) The basis of class is primarily economic.
(c) The separate strata are not clearly marked off from each other.
(d) Social class, unlike caste, is not formally legalised.
(e) Intermarriage between social classes is possible in a social class system.

5.3 Explanations of social class

Although it is clear that social class exists and that it influences our lives, sociologists have disagreed about how it developed and exactly what the basis of class is. There are three different explanations:

1 The ideas of Karl Marx (often know as **conflict theorists** or **Marxists**);
2 The ideas of Max Weber;
3 The **functionalist** approach.

Karl Marx

The basis of Marx's explanation of social class is economic. Marx, who lived and wrote in the nineteenth century, argued that although the class structure appeared very complex, in reality a clear distinction could be made between two groups who formed the only two classes in society:

- Those who own wealth and property – the **bourgeoisie**;
- Those who sell their labour to the wealthy – the **proletariat**.

The bourgeoisie

Marx argued that those who own wealth and property (he used the term **the means of production**) are in a fundamentally different position from those who have to work for a wage. They have power and influence to shape the political and social nature of society. He sees society as a reflection of their interests. They pass on their wealth and power to their children.

The proletariat

Everybody who works for a wage or salary falls into this social class. Marx argued that the distinctions between groups as far apart as doctors and unskilled labourers are really unimportant. Both groups have to work for their living, and have little power compared to the wealthy bourgeoisie.

The origin of classes according to Marx

Marx's division between bourgeoisie and proletariat is only part of his explanation of the political and social history of man. According to Marx in every society two classes exist – one that owns the wealth and the other that is exploited by the wealthy.

- In Ancient Greece and Rome – there were freemen and slaves;
- In feudal societies – nobility and serfs;
- In industrial societies – bourgeoisie and proletariat.
- The struggle between the wealthy and the workers has caused most social change.

False consciousness

Many people criticise the Marxists' view of the class structure by arguing that if the people really were so exploited they would rise up in revolution. However, Marxists believe that the bourgeoisie control the television and newspapers, as well as the educational system. These all promote ideas which benefit the bourgeoisie, creating the belief that what is good for the rich, is good for everybody. Because they are constantly told this, people believe it. There is therefore no revolution. Marxists call this acceptance of the views of the bourgeoisie **false consciousness**. If people are aware of their exploitation this is **class consciousness**.

Criticisms of Marx

Amongst the many criticisms (and replies to the criticisms) of Marx's work are the following:

- Marx argued that there are only ever two social classes, but in practice the class structure is much more complicated, with a wide variety of groups existing in society. It seems a mistake to group doctors with production line workers.
- He claimed that a revolution must occur in industrial societies when the tension between proletariat and bourgeoisie becomes too intense. Yet no signs of such potential revolutionary activity exist, instead the Labour Party and trade unions have developed to look after the interests of the working class.

Marxism today

Modern Marxists accept the criticism that Marx's stress on only two social classes in society needs to be modified. They suggest that although the basic division between owners (bourgeoisie) and non-owners (proletariat) is correct, there are a number of splits within them, which they call **social class fractions**. For example, they see white-collar employees, such as junior managers working in offices, as having different views and life styles from many factory workers, even though they both work for the same employer. Marxists suggest that these are still members of the proletariat (because they do not own), but are different fractions of it.

Max Weber

Weber lived shortly after Marx and his work on class was influenced by him. Although he agreed that a small group of people had excessive power and wealth, he disagreed that the most important division was into two groups based on ownership and wealth.

Weber suggested three elements that divide people in our society:

- **Economic factors** How much wealth or income a person has or inherits from his or her parents;
- **Status** The amount of prestige we give to a person based on such characteristics as occupation, accent, education, etc;
- **Power** The amount of power and influence a person has.

When all three are added together they indicate a person's **life chances**, that is a person's chances of success in life. Weber argued that the divisions between people in society are very complex and the class structure resembles a ladder with a long series of small steps.

Weber points out that although the three elements (economic factors, status and power) usually go together (for example, a rich person is often powerful and has high status in society) this is not always the case. There are many rich people who do not have high status, and some people who are powerful without being very well off, for instance Labour politicians. So people are ranked on each element separately. The important point here is that Marx only stressed one (economic factors) of the three elements that form class according to Weber, and saw the other two as deriving from it, which Weber saw as wrong.

The functionalist approach

In the 1940s Davis and Moore put forward what has now become the classic **functionalist** explanation of social class. Functionalists see society as similar to a human body. Each part of society performs a function to keep the society 'alive', just as each part of the body has its role to play.

Clearly there are some parts of the body that are more important than others. For example, the heart is much more important than the little finger. In society there are certain jobs that are more important for society than others. Functionalists would claim that doctors are more important, for example, than car salesmen. In order to persuade the very best people to take these difficult but very important jobs, such as doctors, they need to be paid more and receive higher social status. The result is the differences in status, power and prestige to be found in our society. According to this explanation of stratification, the differences in income reflect differences in the importance of those jobs to society.

Functionalists see little conflict among classes.

Criticisms of functionalism

The explanation of the origins and basis of social class has been criticised because it seems a justification by the better paid for their higher incomes. Although some jobs are clearly more important than others, it is extremely difficult to grade most jobs.

The levels of income reflect less the social importance of the jobs than the success of trade unions, professions, or simply individuals by their wits, to negotiate high wages. A simple comparison of some obvious jobs shows the weakness in the argument.

Doctors, for example, earn much less than advertising executives on average, but most people would see the doctor as more important to society.

5.4 Measuring social class

The importance of occupation

In investigating society, sociologists need to use a simple measurement of social class – as a result most surveys have been based upon occupational differences. We know that occupation is related to:

- Differences in income;
- Differences in prestige – for example, people rank doctors as more prestigious than factory workers;
- Differences in education – usually the higher educated a person is the higher his or her occupation;
- Life style – different incomes earned in different levels of occupation are generally reflected in different spending patterns, and therefore different life styles. Differences in education are important here, too;
- Differences in speech and dress – differences in occupation reflect educational differences and this shows itself in different types of speech patterns. It also influences taste in and ability to pay for different types of clothing.

Problems with using occupation as the only measure of social class

In using occupation to measure class as the following classifications do, there are some problems:

- Classifications based on occupation omit the very rich who own the factories, and commercial institutions.
- They ignore the fact some people in similar occupations may have very different backgrounds and resources. For example, a teacher from a rich family, who is given regular financial help by his or her family, is in a very different situation from a teacher from a working-class background.
- These classifications ignore the unemployed.
- Classifications based on occupation ignore or gloss over the fact that the same job title can mean very different things in different circumstances. For instance, a doctor can mean a very successful general practitioner with a 'practice' in a pleasant part of a city, with some private patients; or it can mean a junior hospital doctor in an inner city hospital earning low wages.

Classifications used

Based on the assumption that occupation is the most useful indicator of class, the following classifications are used.

The Registrar-General's classification

Class	Type of occupations
1	Professional and higher administrative, e.g. lawyers, architects, doctors, managers, university teachers
2	Intermediate professionals and administrative, e.g. shopkeepers, farmers, actors, musicians, teachers
3	Skilled
	(a) Non-manual, e.g. draughtsmen, shop assistants, clerks
	(b) Manual, e.g. electricians, coalminers
4	Semi-skilled, e.g. milk roundsmen, bus conductors, telephone operators, fishermen, farm workers
5	Unskilled, e.g. night watchmen, porters, refuse collectors, cleaners, labourers

The Registrar-General's classification divides the workforce into five groups, with a further division in class three between manual and non-manual workers. This division reflects the fact that sociologists are aware that manual workers (those who work with their hands) and non-manual workers (those who work in clerical or professional occupations) have a very wide gap between them in values held and life styles, even though their incomes may not differ greatly. The Registrar-General's classification is the one used in official government studies.

The Hope-Goldthorpe classification

Eight occupations		%	Classes
1	Higher-grade professionals, administrators, managers and proprietors	7.7	
2	Lower-grade professionals, administrators and managers Supervisors and higher-grade technicians	6.0	Service
3	Clerical, sales and rank-and-file service workers	7.4	
4	Small proprietors and self-employed artisans	12.6	Intermediate
5	Lower-grade technicians and foremen	11.3	
6	Skilled manual workers in industry	27.2	
7	Semi- and unskilled workers in industry	22.6	Working
8	Agricultural workers and smallholders	5.2	
All		100	

Hope and Goldthorpe have developed a refined version of the Registrar-General's classification of occupations. It divides the eight groups into three classes, service, intermediate and working, reflecting the changing occupational structure of Britain. In particular, it divides the white-collar workers with some degree of power and control over their working situation, such as accountants or managers (the service class) from those white-collar jobs that are routine and have relatively lower wages (the intermediate class). Included in this class are manual workers who have authority, such as foremen. Finally, there is the working class composed of the rest of the manual workers.

Measuring the social class of women

With the large increase in women working, it has become increasingly important to construct a measurement of social class which will be accurate for women. One drawback of using measurements such as the classifications of the Registrar General and Goldthorpe are that they were based upon the different sorts of jobs that men do, and we know that women are generally employed in very different sorts of jobs.

Feminist sociologists have, therefore, suggested that classifications need to be developed which incorporate the sorts of job women do. One such measure is that provided by Arber, Dale and Gilchrist:

1. Higher professionals
2. Employers and managers
3. Lower professionals
4. Secretarial and clerical staff
5. Supervisors and self-employed workers
6. Sales and personal services
7. Skilled manual occupations
8. Unskilled occupations

5.5 The changing working class

The decomposition of the working class

Sociologists have argued that the changes in employment patterns, leisure pursuits and the spread of affluence amongst large sections of the community have 'decomposed' the working class. The divisions which have been proposed are:

- the new working class;
- the underclass.

The debate on the 'new' working class

During the 1980s and 1990s a division, it has been claimed, has opened up between:

- those in secure employment and those in insecure occupations;
- the unemployed and the employed;
- those living in private housing and those in rented local authority or housing association dwellings;
- those in suburbs and those in large out-of-town local authority estates, and inner city areas;
- those who are affluent and those who are on low incomes.

The **new working class** are said to be characterised by:

- home ownership;
- well paid, relatively secure employment;
- materialistic life style;
- declining allegiance to socialist or traditional working-class values.

The idea of an emerging new working class was not new in the 1990s; in the 1960s the idea first emerged under the term the new 'affluent workers'. In the 1960s a series of studies took place of male manual workers in Luton car and chemical industries, (no women were included in the study) and these suggested that a new type of affluent worker had emerged who was different from the traditional male manual workers (Fig. 5.1).

Fig. 5.1   Changes in the working-class male

	Traditional working-class male	The new working-class male
Income and employment	Relatively low wages; employment in manual work.	Relatively high wages; employment in newer industries – using greater skills beyond just manual work.
Housing	Inner cities or large-scale, working class, local authority housing estates.	Buying own homes, living in suburbs or newer developments.
Leisure patterns	Working-class patterns of solidarity, with clear distinctions between the sexes.	Great emphasis on home life, patterns of leisure traditionally associated with the middle class.

Arguments for the new working class

Changes in employment patterns

A move has occurred away from unskilled manual work in traditional industries, towards office and leisure-related employment.

Today, there are less than 7.5 million manual workers, compared to 15 million in 1951. They comprise less than half the workforce. The manual work most people engage in now is more likely to be skilled. Most importantly, it is increasingly likely to be performed by women.

Affluence

- Wages are higher than ever before in real terms for those skilled workers in secure employment.
- The development of credit has hastened the expansion of consumer goods for those in employment.
- As a higher proportion of married women have entered the workforce, there has been a growth of two-earner households, which has significantly increased the income of these households.

Home ownership

Seventy per cent of homes are now owned or being purchased through mortgages. There has been a long-term decline in rented properties, and the selling off of local authority housing in the 1980s had led to only 18% of housing being rented from local authorities. There has also been a significant move away from inner city areas to suburbs and newer developments by those who are buying homes.

Family life

There has been a move towards a more integrated and shared family life, particularly with the growth of women working. Women still retain the prime responsibility for household chores however, and relationships are not equal.

Leisure

There has been an increase in home-based purchase into traditional middle-class activities and holiday patterns.

Politics

A process of de-alignment from class-political party loyalties has occurred. Voters of all classes look for immediate benefits for themselves and their families. This resulted in Conservative voting in the 1980s and New Labour voting in the late 1990s.

Arguments against the new working class

Marshall et al (*Social Class in Modern Britain*) studied over 2000 people in the UK, and drew from comparative studies elsewhere, to argue that social class is still very important in people's lives, and still remains one of the clearest guides to understanding people's attitudes, behaviour and life chances. They also argued that there have always been divisions within the working class, and these have been commented on as far back as the nineteenth century.

The underclass

Apart from the possible emergence of a new working class which is more affluent than the traditional working class, there is also the claim that at the other extreme an underclass is emerging which is composed of the long-term unemployed or unemployable living in large local authority housing developments or in the inner cities.

Income levels

There is a dispute over the exact meaning and implications of the term, however. Field and Giddens define the class in terms of income levels, so underclass is a group below the working class who are the very poorest, primarily composed of the sick, the elderly, single parents and the long-term unemployed. The state benefit system is seen as the main culprit in maintaining the underclass, because it pays such low benefits it is impossible to have a decent standard of living, or to escape from poverty.

Culture

A more negative view of the poor is associated with Charles Murray, who argues that there exists a group of poor who have little or no interest in contributing to society. They have a distinctive set of values which justify crime, living off state benefits and are uninterested in finding employment.

Evidence for the existence of an underclass?

Heath used material from British Attitude Surveys, and found that there were few differences in values between what would be defined as the members of the underclass and the 'traditional' working class.

However, there is clear evidence of a growth in the number of people living in poverty. These are often people, like never-married lone parents, who are unable to obtain employment because of child-rearing responsibilities and costs, who are trapped by the state benefit system. These people are often excluded from the general rise in standard of living.

5.6 The middle class

The traditional middle class

Traditionally, the middle class was composed of white-collar workers, such as clerks at the lower end and managers/traditional professionals, such as solicitors and doctors, at the other end. They tended to live in different areas of the towns and cities from the working class, had greater job security and higher wages (although the wages of highly skilled manual workers and clerks overlapped) and better working conditions. The values of the middle class stressed individual hard work and the desire for a career. Although the income levels varied within the middle class, those engaged in office jobs saw themselves as having higher status in society and felt that they did form a clear class.

Changes in the middle class

The middle class, like the working class, has been fragmenting and is nowhere near as cohesive as in the past.

According to Goldthorpe, the middle class can broadly be divided into two:
- the service class, composed of professionals and managers;
- and the intermediate class, composed of routine white-collar workers.

The best way to understand the differences is by comparing their:
- market situation (what their work is worth);
- work situation (what their working conditions are like);
- status situation (how much prestige other people give them);
- gender.

The service class

This is composed of members of the higher professions such as law and medicine, as well as managers. Generally they come from middle-class backgrounds themselves.
- **Market situation** These are the top managers who have skills that are very well rewarded in commerce and industry. They have very high earnings.
- **Work situation** They usually work in a pleasant and varied atmosphere with real control over their working lives. Often they are in charge of others and are the ones making the crucial decisions.
- **Status situation** Managers and professionals have managed to define what is regarded as high status work. They are the model for most people as to what constitutes success.
- **Gender** Most of the members of the service middle class are male.

The growth of the professions

An important part of the service class are the professions. Between 1971 and 1981 numbers of people working in manufacturing industries (actually making things) fell by a quarter. At the same time the numbers of people engaged in the service industries (providing services such as insurance, banking etc) rose by a quarter.

The occupational group that benefited most from this growth in services were the professions, who increased their numbers by over a quarter in this period. Since the beginning of the twentieth century the proportion of the workforce in the professions has increased from only 4% to over 12%.

The rise of the professions is related not just to the expansion of service industries owned by private companies, but also to the growth of the state. The biggest expansions have taken place in the areas of education, health and welfare. Within the professions, however, there is a clear division between the 'traditional' professions of solicitor and doctor, who are generally well paid and enjoy great status, and the 'newer' professions of teacher and social worker, who are less well paid and have lower status in society.

The intermediate class

This is composed primarily of routine white-collar workers. Typical jobs include clerks, shop workers, and employees in the leisure industries.

Market situation These jobs are the replacement of the semi-skilled jobs which existed in industry before technological changes had their impact and the numbers of people employed declined dramatically. There is competition for the employment and salaries are relatively low. A moderate degree of education is required.

Work situation Generally workers in these jobs are doing routine jobs with very limited freedom of action. They are responsible to superiors and have clear hours of employment and responsibilities.

Status These jobs carry with them the prestige of white-collar work, even though the wage levels and degree of responsibility are low.

Gender This group reflects the 'feminisation' of this sector of employment. Males have moved away from this type of work into management (or unemployment). What is most important to realise is that middle-class jobs are therefore divided by **gender**, with higher paid and higher status jobs more likely to be occupied by men.

Proletarianisation

This division of the middle class has led some writers to argue that a process of 'proletarianisation' has taken place (Fig. 5.2). That is, people in the lower section of the middle class have now got wages and working conditions which are effectively the same as the working class. All that distinguishes them is that they work in offices instead of factories and no longer wear overalls.

Fig. 5.2   Arguments for and against the process of proletarianisation of the middle class

Market situation	Status situation	Work situation
For proletarianisation	**For proletarianisation**	**For proletarianisation**
Traditional clerical skills not needed, technology pushing it aside, decreasing levels of pay – overtaken by many in manual work.	No longer high status work. Style of life indistinguishable from clerical and manual workers. Fastest growth in unions has taken place amongst white-collar workers.	Style of offices (open plan) is similar to the factory floor. The introduction of computers has deskilled workers.
Against proletarianisation	**Against proletarianisation**	**Against proletarianisation**
Nothing has changed, there has always been an overlap between clerical and manual pay. Although declining, some differences still exist in the better quality of the work situation and the provision of a range of benefits, including job security, pensions, holidays etc.	The growth of trade unions reflects an attempt to maintain the differences between white collar and manual work, not to join the working class. The similarity in lifestyles does not reflect changes in the middle class, but the increasing affluence of the remaining working class.	Promotion prospects still exist. Stewart et al studied the career prospects of *male* clerical workers and found a majority were promoted out of it, while 30% left for manual work. So *males* move into and out of white-collar work. It is therefore suggested that the work of clerical workers has been proletarianised, but not clerical workers themselves.

Proletarianisation and gender

The debate is in some ways misleading, in that the clerical workers of the past cannot be compared to white-collar workers of today, in that white-collar work is increasingly dominated by women workers, whereas in the past, clerical work was dominated by men. A process of proletarianisation of white-collar work may have taken place, but the males who would once have occupied these jobs in the past are likely today to be in professions or management.

Feminisation of the intermediate class

As routine white-collar work has expanded, it has been women who have filled these roles, such that 75% of routine white-collar posts are now taken by women. The lower position of clerical workers can be seen as simply reflecting the lower position of women in our society generally. Furthermore, this tells us that we need to study class as only one element of stratification.

5.7 The upper class

A unified upper class

Some radical sociologists argue that Britain is controlled by a ruling class, who own the main industries and commercial institutions and use the power deriving from economic control to gain and continue to enjoy political power.

Westergaard and Resler (*Class in a Capitalist Society*), for example, argue that there is a ruling class comprising 5–10% of the population, who are the very rich and either directly or indirectly very powerful. They claim that they are linked through a network of intermarriage and mutual benefit.

A fragmented upper class

Scott (*The Upper Classes, Property and Privilege in Britain*) argues that there is no single ruling or upper class in Britain, but like the middle and working class it is fragmented. According to Scott, in the nineteenth century there were three overlapping strata of the upper class:

- landowners;
- financiers;
- manufacturers.

In the nineteenth century, firms became so large that they gradually moved away from being under the direct control of the founding family. By the end of the Second World War, the top three strata had become almost indistinguishable through intermarriage and financial overlap. But, in the last part of the twentieth century, the proportion of shares owned by individuals has declined as pension funds, and unit trusts have become ever more significant in the City of London in terms of ownership. In this contemporary period, a **business class** has emerged which dominates the upper class.

The business class

The business class comprises the directors, top executives and main shareholders of the 1000 largest British companies, which Scott estimates as about 0.2% of the population. A further less important group consists of senior people in the armed forces, the church and the universities.

This business class can further be subdivided into:

- **Entrepreneurial capitalists**, holding large shareholdings in their own firms – these are the remains of the traditional family firms. Those still existing include Tesco, Sainsbury's, Rothschilds (bankers), Baring Brothers (bankers).
- **Internal capitalists**, senior executives working for companies and who are in employment, though very often today they have some shareholdings in the company that employs them.
- **Finance capitalists** These are involved in the financing and ownership of more than one company. They are particularly important in linking ownership and control of different firms through a network of overlapping directorships. This ensures a continuity and a coherence of response to perceived trends and problems. Very often the finance capitalists own, or part own merchant banks.

The continuation of the ruling class

The ruling class manages to reproduce itself from one generation to the next by:

- passing on wealth from one generation to the next;
- passing on 'social and cultural capital', that is shared culture through public schools;
- appointments in senior positions in business, arts and finance of family and members of the network.

5.8 Changes in the distribution of wealth

Income and wealth: definitions

- **Income** Earnings from employment, investment or from state benefits.
- **Wealth** Ownership of property, shares or other assets.

Wealth distribution

The ownership of wealth has remained very unequal, although there had been a decline in the extent of inequality amongst the various groups throughout the twentieth century until the late 1970s, when the decline stopped. This was the result of government policies to maintain inequalities in wealth distribution.

The main trends are:

● That the wealth has shifted from the richest 1% to the richest 25% – this reflects the ability of the very rich to distribute their wealth within their family, and thus to avoid duties payable on death.

● Three has been little significant spread of wealth across the population as a whole. Today, the wealthiest 10% of the adult population own just under 50% of all marketable wealth.

Share ownership

Share ownership increased significantly in the 1980s and early 1990s as a result of government privatisation schemes. In 1981 approximately 7% of the population held shares, and this had increased to 25% by 1996. But although more people own shares, they only own a very limited proportion of all the shares, so that the great majority of shareholdings remain in the hands of the top 5% of personal shareholders.

There has been a large increase in shares held by such organisations as pension companies, banks and insurance companies in the last thirty years.

Income distribution

This is much less unequal in its distribution than wealth. Nevertheless significant inequalities exist, so for instance, whereas the bottom fifth of the population receive only 10% of the income, the top fifth earn approximately 35%. The gap between the two extremes grew between 1979 and 1997.

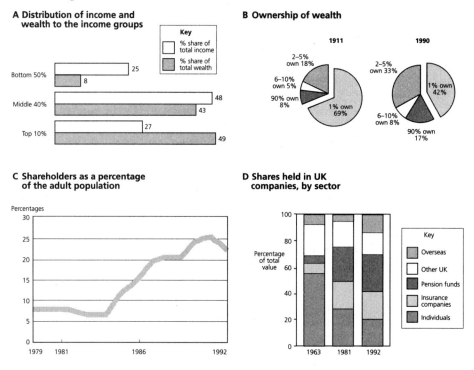

Fig. 5.3 Winners and losers: how wealth is distributed in Britain

Not only is income distribution noticeably unequal (Fig. 5.3), but the proportion of people in the lowest income categories has been growing.

Redistribution

Although there is some redistribution as a result of income tax and state benefits, in total the highest income groups lose only a small proportion of their income as a result of the redistribution by the welfare state, once welfare benefits are taken into account, according to government statistics.

	Broad social class groupings	Groups within social classes	Divisions other than social class		
			Gender	Ethnic group	Region
The upper class	The rich	The 'establishment' or 'ruling class'	Women concentrated in the lowest-paid jobs in each class	Blacks concentrated in lowest-paid groups / unemployed	The worse-off found in the North and the inner cities
The middle class	● Managers and professionals (mainly men); high pay	The 'service class'			
	● Routine white-collar workers in offices, banks, shops and caring services (mainly women); low pay	The 'intermediate groups'			
The working class	● Better-paid manual workers in secure employment in newer light industries	The 'new working class'			
	● The self-employed				
	● Less-skilled, less well-paid manual workers; job increasingly under threat as industry contracts	The 'traditional working class'			
	● The poor; the unemployed	The 'underclass'			

Fig. 5.4   Divisions in Britain today
(Source: Stephen Moore, *Sociology Alive!* Stanley Thornes, 2nd Edition 1996)

5.9 Social mobility

The meaning and measurement of social mobility

The main distinction between caste and class societies is that in a class-based society, such as Britain, there is social mobility. Social mobility means the movement of people up and down the social scale.

❶ There are two types of social mobility (sometimes called *vertical mobility*);
  - **Intragenerational** movement within the occupational structure by one person over a period of time. In other words a person's career;
  - **Intergenerational mobility** – occupation of a person compared to his or her father.

❷ The **measurement** of social mobility is usually based on either the Registrar-General's scale, or the Hope-Goldthorpe classification (see p. 48), and so is based upon **occupation**.

❸ The **extent** of social mobility is usually described in terms of:
  - **Long-range mobility**, which is movement of two or more occupational groups up or down the social scale;
  - **Short-range mobility**, which is movement up or down by only one occupational group;
  - **Self-recruitment**, the situation when children are in the same occupational group as their parents.

For example, a man is working as a doctor, and his father was a labourer on a building site. This type is **intergenerational mobility** (parent/child being compared), and the extent is long range (he moved more than two occupational groups up, compared to his father); if the man was a labourer, this would be an example of **self-recruitment**.

Problems in measuring social class

In measuring social mobility in research, certain problems arise:
  - Most studies use occupation, and so encounter the same problems as are discussed on p. 47 in creating categories of class, as they ignore the differences within occupations, and they assume that all non-manual work is 'higher' than manual work (whereas many manual workers earn more than routine white-collar workers);
  - Over time the status and significance of certain jobs change. For example, a clerical worker in 1900 had a job considered to be of far higher status than today. Any comparison over time needs to take this into account;

● At what point in a person's career do you measure his or her social mobility? For example, if the son/daughter of a rich London stockbroker has his or her first employment as a manual worker on a building site for a year, while he/she waits for a suitable opening in the City of London as a stockbroker, do we measure the mobility from the first job or from the second job in the City?

Social mobility in Britain

In 1972 a group of sociologists at Nuffield College, Oxford, started to study the extent of intergenerational mobility in Britain. The *Oxford Mobility Study*, as it is known, was based upon interviews with 10000 men, from all social classes. They compared the social mobility patterns of men born between 1908 and 1917 with those born between 1938 and 1947 in order to obtain a view of the changes in social mobility during the twentieth century.

In order to simplify the results of the survey, the seven occupational groups were put into three classes;

The service class, composed of those in professional and managerial positions – that is the most successful;

The intermediate class, which includes those in routine white-collar jobs, the self-employed, technicians and supervisors;

The working class, which includes most manual workers. The results are illustrated in Fig. 5.5.

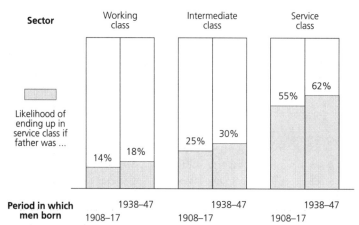

Fig.5.5 Likelihood of ending up in service class

Fig. 5.5 shows that for all groups the chance of going into the service class has increased.
● 18% of the 1938–47 generation who were born into the working class achieved the service class, compared to 14% of the 1908–17 generation.
● 30% of the 1938–47 generation who were born into the intermediate class achieved the service class, compared to 25% of the 1908–17 generation.
● 62% of the 1938–47 generation who were born into the service class succeeded in staying in this class, compared to 55% of the 1908–17 generation.
This means that upward mobility has certainly increased.

At first sight it would seem that by 1972, the class structure was more **open** (there was greater movement, so that talented people from working-class backgrounds could be successful) than previously. Indeed, 25% of all higher professionals (the highest occupational group in the survey) came from working-class backgrounds.

However, the **relative** chances of children of each group entering the service class did not alter over time. The sons of the service class have four times the chance of following their fathers into the service class themselves compared to the sons of the working class, and twice the chances of the sons of the intermediate class. This has been dubbed the '1:2:4 rule'.

The explanation for the movement of so many people, according to Halsey and Goldthorpe who led the survey, is that the changing **occupational structure** means that there are a lot more jobs available in the service class than ever before. So, there is a lot more room at the top. There are also fewer working-class jobs. This is illustrated in Figure 5.6. It shows that of all jobs:

Men born 1908-17			Men born 1938-47
13%	SERVICE	25%	
33%	INTERMEDIATE	30%	
54%	WORKING	45%	

Fig.5.6   The changing occupational structure

- the proportion of service class occupations has increased from 13% to 25%;
- the proportion of intermediate class occupations has increased from 33% to 30%;
- the proportion of working-class jobs has decreased from 54% to 45%.

Women and social mobility

There have been few studies of the patterns of social mobility of women. This is mainly because of the fact that sociologists have traditionally taken the social class of wives from the class of the husbands – even though it is known that women often marry 'outside' their class.

Research

Heath in *Social Mobility* found that single women tend to be more upwardly socially mobile than single men, although in a more restricted range of professions. He suggests that in order to be successful in their jobs women have to make a choice between marriage and children (and the consequent disruption of their careers during child raising) and concentrating all their attention on work. For men, on the other hand, it is accepted that they ought to concentrate on their jobs. So for men, careers and marriage fit together. For women, they are opposed.

What are the causes of social mobility?

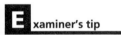

xaminer's tip

Occupational change is the most important reason for social mobility.

- **Occupational change** As the occupational structure alters in response to economic and technological change, different types of employment arise. These may be of higher or lower status. Since the end of the Second World War, there has been a considerable expansion in middle and high status jobs and a decline in labouring work. (For a full discussion of occupational change in Britain, see pp. 83–5). This has meant that there is more 'room at the top' and less at the bottom. Individuals who may have entered manual work twenty years ago will enter clerical positions. This appears to be intergenerational mobility, although some sociologists have suggested that there has been a decline in the status of clerical work, so that no 'real mobility' is taking place. It is just low paid, low status work adapted to changed technological circumstances.
- **Differential fertility** If the top groups fail to produce enough children to fill all the top positions, then there is space for the children of lower groups. (This argument is based on the fact that there is a high rate of self-recruitment in the class structure.) Since the turn of the century the expansion of the non-manual job sector has been greater than the birth rate of the middle class.
- **Educational change** Since the 1944 Education Act there has been greater opportunity for intelligent working-class children to succeed. The introduction of comprehensives and the expansion of university provision have been further attempts to expand the chances of working-class children. Today 25% of the professions are from working-class backgrounds. However, the education system in Britain has never fully succeeded in eliminating the differences in the success rate between the middle and working classes. (For a full discussion of this, see pp. 35–7.)
- **Individual motivation and aspiration** Although sociologists stress that social mobility is mainly outside a person's control, it is true that certain people may be more motivated to succeed. The different ways in which middle-class children are socialised from working-class children is an example of this. Middle-class children may have been brought up with higher aspirations and have received greater encouragement to be successful.

- **Gender** As a woman's social class position is usually measured by her husband's occupation, it is therefore possible, and common, for women to switch social class through marriage. Many women have their careers interrupted, however, in order to have children.

The significance of social mobility

There are two very different views on social mobility: the **functionalist** and the **Marxist**.

- **The functionalist view** This is that the greater amount of social mobility in society, the greater the degree of reward exists for ability. Those who are able and hard working can move upwards and the less able sink down. This is known as a **meritocracy** or **open society**, as opposed to a **closed society** where the higher classes ensure that their children will follow them into those occupations.
- **The Marxist view** is that social mobility is really a smokescreen that obscures the fact that only a tiny proportion of the population own significant wealth in Britain. People compete against each other in order to reach managerial or professional jobs, yet hardly anyone progresses beyond this to join the ranks of the owners. The owners get the very best people into the managerial jobs to look after their interests for them.

Summary

1. **Social stratification** means the division of people into various social groups having different status and prestige.

2. The main types of divisions are **caste** (as in India); **estates** (as in feudal times); **slavery** and **social class**. Other divisions are based on age, gender or ethnic group.

3. **Social class** is the main form of social stratification in modern industrialised society. It is based on economic and status differences.

4. **Social mobility** occurs between different classes, i.e. movement between classes in a social class system; but not in a caste system.

5. Objectively, **life chances** are affected by social class. Unskilled working-class people will have poorer health and larger families. People in social class 1 will have better education and more material possessions.

6. Subjectively, **views and ideas** on politics, leisure and social issues will be very different, although there is an overlap in attitudes between classes.

7. There are three different explanations of social class:
   - **The Marxist theory** based on economics where society is divided between those who own wealth the bourgeoisie) and those who sell their labour to the wealthy (the proletariat); such theories have been developed from the work of Karl Marx.
   - Followers of **Max Weber** say that three elements divide people: economic factors, status and power; and these together influence a person's life chances.
   - **The functionalist explanation** compares society to the human body with some parts more important than others.

   There are criticisms of all three explanations.

8. In measuring social class **occupation** is very often used as the most important factor. This leads to the **Registrar-General's classification** and the **Hope-Goldthorpe classification**.

9 It has been suggested that a separate classification is necessary for women.

10 Certain factors have caused changes in the class structure in British society. Such factors include the growth of affluence; unemployment; far more people owning their own homes; changes in the educational system giving increased social mobility.

11 Some maintain that there is a 'new' working class as well as the 'traditional' working class which still exists. **Fragmentation** of the working class has taken place.

12 The middle class has also been fragmented or decomposed, e.g. clerical workers have undergone a process of **proletarianisation** (have sunk into the working class). Their importance has decreased.

13 The growth of the professions – but here again there is a distinction between the traditional professions, such as doctors or solicitors, with their income and status higher than that of the new professions, such as social workers or teachers.

14 Britain is a **capitalist** society. The top 10% in Britain own 50% of wealth. Wealth means assets that are worth money if sold, made up of property or stocks and shares.

15 Attempts to redistribute wealth have been largely ineffective.

16 **Social mobility** is movement up or down the class structure. There are a number of political difficulties in trying to measure social mobility.

17 In Britain social mobility has involved more people entering the 'service class', i.e. the professional and managerial occupations.

18 Heath in *Social Mobility* suggests that for women to become upwardly mobile they have to make a choice between marriage/children and concentrating on their careers.

19 Other factors affecting social mobility are individuals' motivations and aspirations – the 'will to succeed'.

20 The **functionalist** view of social mobility is based on a **meritocracy**, where those who are able can succeed and move upwards.

21 The Marxist view says that really only a tiny proportion of the population own significant wealth and nothing changes this. Nobody joins the owners, but the owners simply benefit from this limited social mobility by getting the best managers to run things for them.

Self-test questions

1 Class is one example of social stratification. Give three other examples.
2 What are a person's 'life chances'?
3 Explain how divisions between people in society are very complex according to Max Weber.
4 Why are simple measurements of social class often based on occupational differences and why are there problems in using such an approach?
5 List the changes that have taken place in British society over the last 30 years which help us to understand the changes in the nature of social class in Britain.

6   What evidence is there for the existence of an underclass?
7   Some sociologists have argued that social class is less important than it once was. What arguments do they use?
8   Define the term 'wealth' and explain briefly why wealth is said to be divided unequally in Britain.
9   Define 'social mobility' and explain why it is difficult to measure accurately.
10 To what extent may it be said that upward social mobility has increased in Britain?

Chapter 6
Gender

6.1 Gender roles

Definitions

Sociologists use the term **sex** to refer to the biological differences between males and females. The term **gender** is used to refer to the social expectations (or roles) which are related to the physical differences.

In British society, there are certain forms of behaviour that are regarded as appropriate for one gender and inappropriate for the other. For example, it is seen as normal for women to be gentle and emotional by nature; to wear dresses, skirts and make-up; to be better at cooking and dressmaking. On the other hand, men are supposed to be less emotional than women; to be tough and physical; to have a strong sex drive; to regard clothes and their appearance as less important than they are for women; to have mechanical and decorating abilities, etc. These differences of behaviour which we expect from men and women are known as **gender roles**. It is also commonly felt by men that women are inferior in some ways to men as a result of these differences.

Gender roles are learned. Gender roles are so obvious and common that often we fail even to think about them, simply accepting them as somehow 'natural' ('boys will be boys'). The reasons normally given for these differences are that they reflect biological differences between men and women and that it is quite impossible for them to be changed. For example, men are supposed to be naturally stronger than women, and women are said to have a natural 'mothering' instinct for their infants.

Sociologists disagree. They argue instead that the difference in the way men and women behave is the result of socialisation into a culture that artificially stresses whatever differences there are between men and women. They point out, for instance, that there is no reason why men should do all the manual work in society – in Britain in the past, and in the countries of the former Soviet Union and much of Africa today, women perform just the same sort of hard, physical labour as men. As for the 'mothering instinct', if it were natural, then all women in all societies would show a natural 'mothering' instinct to their young. Yet no clear pattern emerges; in some societies mothers are gentle and caring with their children as in Britain today, in others they are hard and apparently uncaring as was the case with the Ik tribe of Northern Uganda (studied by Colin Turnbull in the mid-1960s).

The social construction of sexuality

Not only are gender roles socially constructed, but sociologists argue that expectations regarding 'normal' sexuality are too. An example of how discourses in sexuality are socially constructed can be found in the perceptions of homosexuality.

Homosexuality

Traditional accounts of homosexuality treat it as deviant and abnormal, even if studies, such as that by Wellings in 1994 suggested that as many as 6% of males and almost 4% of females have had at least one homosexual/lesbian experience in their lives. Therefore, sociologists have suggested that sexual identities are not as clear cut as generally believed, and that there is a case for arguing the normality of bisexuality.

Weeks (*Sexuality*) argues that it was not until the nineteenth century that the only accepted form of 'normal' sexuality was heterosexual sex, with other forms of sex coming to be regarded as deviant. In fact, the term 'homosexuality' was only coined in 1860, both reflecting and helping to construct the emergence of a clear-cut sexual identity.

Foucault (*The History of Sexuality*) points out that in the eighteenth and early nineteenth centuries new ways of thinking and discussing sexuality developed regarding different groups in the population and their sexuality. The discourses divided sexuality into four types:

- **Women's sexuality** – women were not supposed to have the same sexual drive and needs as men.
- **Children's sexuality** - children were removed from sexuality altogether.
- **Married sex** – married sex was normal (though not necessarily pleasurable).
- **Homosexuality** – homosexuality was a form of deviant sexual activity engaged in by 'perverts'.

Foucault argues that the ability to impose a particular way of viewing sex reflects differences in power between social groups, so that the views on sexuality reflect the power of heterosexual males.

Gender socialisation

This is performed by (a) the family, (b) the school, (c) the media and (d) is reinforced by the general culture of society.

The family

The most important institution to teach us the values and expectations of society is the family. Gender roles are taught here, too. In the hospital as the birth is about to begin the midwives might ask conversationally whether the couple would prefer to have a girl or a boy?

Gender roles are constructed in a range of ways: (a) in the sort of toys given – a ball for a boy, doll for a girl; (b) in the language used – 'Stop crying, you're behaving just like a little girl!'; (c) in the activities they are encouraged to engage in – boys to help their fathers and girls to help their mothers; (d) in the clothes they wear – boys in active clothes such as jeans and tracksuits, girls more carefully dressed in dresses with their long hair combed; (e) as they grow older the boy will be allowed greater freedom; (f) in some families the education of the boy will be regarded as more important than that of the girl, as it is argued that the girl will most likely marry and have children rather than a career.

Statham (*Daughters and Sons; Experiences of Non-Sexist Childraising*) studied thirty middle-class adults heading eighteen families. The families were committed to raising their children in a manner which broke down gender roles. However, they found it very difficult to combat the influence of the wider society and even the expectations of their relatives.

The school

At school the differences between boys and girls are strengthened. In some places they even send children to boy or girl only schools. In side the school girls are often encouraged to follow subjects seen as appropriate to them. So far more girls than boys study languages, human biology, word processing and commercial arts (and sociology!). Boys are more likely to take science and maths subjects. This reflects both the attitudes of the pupils themselves, and also the advice given by teachers.

Apart from the official choices of subjects given by the school (the **curriculum**), there is also a **hidden curriculum**, which refers to the way certain ideas and values of the teachers about the way the girls and boys ought to act are imposed upon pupils in the school. These values influence the way teachers talk and behave towards girls and boys, encouraging them in certain forms of behaviour and discouraging them in others. Girls learn to see their future in terms of low-level white-collar or caring jobs. They see that teachers pay more attention to males which may discourage them from trying.

Research by Walker and Barton (*Gender, Class and Education*) suggested that girls are rewarded for silence, neatness and conformity, but the more rebellious attitudes of boys are tolerated by teachers, both male and female.

Race, gender and school
Bryan et al (*Learning to Resist: Black Women and Education*) found in their research of black female pupils that they tended to be enthusiastic about school initially and it was only gradually that they became disillusioned, because of the activities of teachers in labelling them as troublemakers. However, this was not the view in Fuller's study (*Black Girls in a London Comprehensive School*) of black female pupils, where the importance of the future career was emphasised by the girls. The importance of teachers and other pupils was not regarded as particularly important. Indeed, the female pupils of Afro-Caribbean origin were likely to be more successful than the white girls in Fuller's study.

The media
The images presented of women in newspapers, radio and television still stress either their sexuality or caring qualities.

- Newspapers such as the *Sun* print pin-up pictures. Women are described as 'attractive blond' or 'beautiful brunette', even in quite serious papers, yet it is rare to have a man described in such a way. There are women's magazines that are devoted to explaining how women can (and should) make themselves more attractive to men. In such ways as these women come to see themselves as desirable or not, depending upon their attractiveness to men.

- The other major role of a woman is to be a good mother and wife. Certain women's magazines are filled with knitting patterns, recipes, child care and domestic hints. Often, too, romance stories are published which strengthen the ideal of true love and the importance of finding a good husband.

Both these images are strengthened by the millions of pounds spent on advertising. The advertisers stress how alluring certain perfumes, clothes and make-up can make a woman. On the other hand, the advertisers present women in the home feeling proud and fulfilled because their children's clothes are really white.

Ferguson (*Forever Feminine*) studied women's magazines over more than twenty years. She found a 'cult of femininity' in which the dominant values regarding women were enshrined. Today the message of the magazines is that the ideal woman combines a successful career with motherhood.

The wider culture
Gender roles are strengthened in the wider culture of British society. For example, the Christian religion stresses the role of the woman as mother and wife. In daily life girls are complimented on their good looks and encouraged to seek this approval from men. Certain attitudes towards sex are expected from females, which are not expected from men.

Social control

The family
Parents exercise stricter control over daughters compared to sons, regulate where they go and what time they return.

Husbands have expectations of wives concerning their behaviour – in the most extreme cases this can lead to 'marital violence'.

The peer group
Girls' behaviour is constrained as much by other girls as by males or parents. Research by Lees has pointed to their fear of gaining a 'reputation' (e.g. for being sexually available). This influences how they behave. In a study of Midland schoolboys, Willis found that boys sought out girls defined as available, but did not want a long-term relationship with a girl like that.

Public sphere
Women are controlled in public through fear of harassment or even violence, if they go out in the streets at night or into pubs, etc alone.

Hammer and Saunders found that women's behaviour was inhibited by fear of sexual assault and violence. The only way to overcome their fear was to request the 'company' of a male, but this creates a situation of dependency on men, who are the cause of the trouble in the first place.

Employment

Women are usually employed in least responsible positions, with male managers. They are also paid less than men. This means that they are more likely to be controlled and supervised by men in employment, and in the wider spheres of their lives.

The significance of gender

- In childhood girls are expected to help their mothers in housework and parents keep much stricter control over them.
- In books and magazines girls are rarely shown as the central characters. Usually they are seen in the role of helper to the male. Magazines written for girls are usually based on romance stories about 'getting their man'.
- Education. Girls are generally more successful than boys at school, but they study different subjects from boys – less often maths and science, more often languages and commercial subjects such as word processing. After school they are less likely to go into further training or higher education.
- Employment. Females are concentrated in a few areas of work, such as 'caring' jobs (e.g. nursing) and clerical work. They earn less than men – on average about two-thirds the male wage – and are less likely to be promoted into positions of responsibility.
- Family. Care of the children and running of the household are seen as more the responsibility of the wife than the husband. Women are much more likely to give up jobs and careers to look after the home and bring up the children.

6.2 Women and employment

Women, work and the family circle

There is a close relationship between family life and female employment. As women are expected to stay at home to look after their children, they generally leave work for a few years while bearing and raising them, then return once more to paid employment. This is illustrated by the fact that according to the Labour Force Survey (1996), 28% of women gave child care as their main reason for not working, compared to 1% of males. Today, on average, women return to work $3\frac{1}{2}$ years after the birth of their last child.

However, the length of child-bearing period has reduced, as has women's willingness to remain at home as full-time mothers and houseworkers, so the time out of employment for child rearing is becoming increasingly shorter.

Reasons for the increase in the numbers of women working

- The changing economic structure since the 1950s has seen a shift in Britain from heavy industry (e.g. steel, engineering) towards light industry (e.g. electronics) and service industries (e.g. shops, catering). Employers were more likely to accept women in the growing industries.
- Women are a cheap source of labour; on average women earn only 72% of the wage of men. This has made them economically attractive to employers.
- Women are a far more **flexible** form of labour than men, and can be employed part time.
- An increase in educational opportunities for women has meant that they are better able to compete for work and less content to remain at home.
- A general rise in the status of women has meant that they are more likely to want, and to be given, work.
- Smaller families in a shorter period means greater freedom for women who are less tied to the home.

Type of employment

Over 70% of full-time female workers are employed in clerical or service work. They are concentrated in a narrow range of employment sectors, particularly in caring and service occupations. Sixty-three per cent of women workers are employed in jobs done exclusively by women, and 81% of men are in jobs done exclusively by men. This division into different sectors of the economy is known as **horizontal segregation**.

Wages

The pay of women is significantly lower than men's. Women earn approximately 75% of male net earnings. Part-time female workers earn only about half the male average wage. Reasons for low pay include:

- women are concentrated in occupations which are traditionally low paying;
- women are less able to work overtime because of (a) the nature of jobs, for example, clerical work offers little overtime and (b) because of domestic responsibilities;
- women are concentrated in lower grades of employment;
- women are more likely to be working part time.

The level of employment

Women are more likely to be found in the lower levels of any occupation. Although 24% of male workers are employed in managerial or professional occupations, only 9% of females are. Furthermore, those employed in these positions are likely to be the 'lower' professions such as teaching/social work, and in the lower management positions. On the other hand, 61% of women are in routine non-manual occupations compared to only 17% of males.

Within occupations men are still more likely to be in senior positions compared to women. The situation where men are more likely to have the more senior positions is known as **vertical segregation**.

Attitudes of men

Coe (*The Key to the Men's Club*) found that:

- it is difficult for women managers to combine child rearing and senior management, and therefore they often felt that they had to make a choice;
- when women are managers they face prejudice from men who work for them, with 20% of men saying that they did not like working for women.

Workplace facilities

Workplaces are not organised to provide facilities for women, for example providing free workplace creches.

Hours of work

Women are more likely to be employed in part-time jobs: 44% of women in employment are part time, and they form 90% of all part-time employees.

Employment markets

Sociologists have explained the position of women in the labour market in two ways.

Dual labour market theory

Barron and Norris *(Sexual Divisions and the Dual Labour Market)* argue that there are two very distinct types of jobs:

1. secure, with the possibility of promotion;
2. insecure, with no definite future and no benefits such as pension, paid holidays etc.

Women are much more likely than men to be trapped in the second 'marginal' labour market. This is because they are more likely to have to work part time because of child care responsibilities. They also find it difficult to have careers because of the problems caused by a break in their working lives having children. The growth of lone-parent families headed by women has made it difficult for them to have careers, particularly with the cost of paying for child care. Women are more likely than men to be offered this sort of insecure work.

Reserve army of labour

A second explanation for the position of women in employment is that they are treated as a cheap pool of labour which employers can draw on when they are short of workers. When they no longer need them they are laid off.

Women workers and unemployment

The overall figures for unemployment are lower than those for men. This can partially be explained by the fact that as women are generally more lowly paid than men, employers are more likely to dispose of the more expensive male workers first. However, it should be remembered that (a) women are more likely to accept part-time work than men; (b) married women are less likely to sign on the official unemployment register as they do not receive any social security benefits, so they do not appear in the unemployment figures.

Homework and caring

It is commonly believed that when we talk about women working, it means paid employment in offices, factories and shops. But the job of being a **housewife** involves just as much work as any form of labour outside the home. In *The Sociology of Housework*, Ann Oakley has suggested a number of characteristics of housework:

- it is unpaid – women rarely receive any form of regular salary they can call their own in exchange for all the cooking, cleaning and ironing, etc they do;
- it is low-status work – most men do not even regard housework as work, as they have an untrue image of its consisting of playing with the children, cooking a meal and watching television. In reality the tasks of cleaning, shopping, cooking and caring for the children can be exhausting labour;
- it is monotonous. Oakley's study of housewives in North London found that they found their work to be more boring and repetitive than assembly line workers in factories;
- housewives are isolated, tending to be cut off from people other than their young children. They are often trapped in the home most of the day apart from visits to the shops;
- long hours of work. Oakley estimated that housewives worked an average week of 77 hours – more than any group of workers employed in factories or offices. She points out that the activities of clearing up, of cooking and ironing continue well into the evening, long after the hours of outside employment have finished.
- housework is female work. The role of housewife, as the word suggests, is almost exclusively female. It is women who give up their jobs to stay at home to care for children and this is expected of them. The occasional husband who does this is regarded as highly unusual. (This exclusivity to women is closely linked to the whole idea of male and female roles as discussed in Unit 6.1.)

Women and education: please turn to Chapter 4.
Women and the family: please turn to Chapter 3.
Women and social class: please turn to Chapter 5.
Women and crime: please turn to Chapter 16.

Summary

1 Gender roles are how sociologists describe the idea that there are certain different activities, attitudes and ways of dressing which society regards as appropriate for males and females.

2 Sociologists argue that these differences are not natural, but are learned in childhood and constantly strengthened in everyday life.

3 Social identity is learned, and is not as clear cut as generally believed.

4 The most important influences in forming gender roles are the family, the school and the media.

5 Today women are legally equal to men, but they still suffer many disadvantages, particularly in the world of work.

6 Women work in more low-paid, lower-grade occupations than men.

7 Women, unlike men, have to combine the responsibility of running a household, looking after their children and working – this means that they are more likely to do part-time work and more likely to give up all paid employment for a few years while they have their children and bring them up.

8 The job of housewife is performed almost exclusively by women and, although it is hard work, it is often not seen as work at all.

Self-test questions

1 What do we mean by the term 'gender role'? Give one example of a male role and a female role.

2 Explain how sexuality is created, using the example of homosexuality.

3 Give two examples of how women are socially controlled.

4 Why is it possible to say that although women have achieved legal equality with men, this does not mean that they have full equality today?

5 Explain what is meant by the term 'employment market' with reference to women.

6 Why do so many women work part time?

7 Why are women likely to be employed in low-status, low-paid work?

8 What are the main characteristics of housework? Is housework really work?

Chapter 7
Age

7.1 Childhood

Variations in childhood

Childhood is as much a social construction as a biological stage in ageing. The meaning of childhood has varied over time, and both within and across societies. For example, even in Britain today, the childhood of a white working-class boy may be extremely different from that of an Asian-origin, middle-class girl.

Malinowski, in his study of the Trobriand Islands in the early part of the twentieth century, showed how distinctively different the lives of Trobriand Island young people were from those in the west, even today. They were much freer, were openly engaged in sexual activity and were not regarded as having to be subservient to parents.

Turnbull (*The Mountain People*) showed how groups of children, abandoned by their parents, and aged only three to five, were able to survive.

In contemporary Brazil and Peru, gangs of street children survive by street trading, theft and other marginal activities. As a result of their perceived threat to adults in the larger cities, groups of vigilantes, reputed to be off-duty police officers, have murdered significant numbers of them.

The development of childhood

The modern idea of childhood has emerged over time. Aries (*Centuries of Childhood*) has argued that in medieval society, the concept of childhood did not exist. As soon as the child was no longer an infant then he/she was regarded as an adult. This meant that children were included in all types of social activity including sex, war and heavy work.

Gradually from the fifteenth century religious theorists began to claim that there was something 'special' about young people and that they should be treated differently from adults. However, it took three hundred years for the idea that childhood was a special period of life to take hold.

Musgrove (*Youth and the Social Order*) has stressed that the nature of childhood alters with the economic usefulness of children. Where they are of great economic use, as in peasant societies where they are of use working on the land, and in societies in the early periods of industrialisation, the concept of childhood, as we know it, was not present.

On the other hand, when the children become of little economic use, such as in the UK when compulsory schooling was introduced, and laws were passed forbidding child labour, then the nature of childhood changed. The lengthened period of childhood has developed as a result of the prolonged education of modern society.

Childhood in contemporary Britain is viewed as a period of great innocence. The 'realities' of life, such as sex and violence, are generally hidden from children. The general view is that they are human beings who are to be 'moulded' into values of society through socialisation. It is not considered correct for them to undertake certain activities that are regarded as only for adults, which vary from voting through to drinking alcohol. All this is based on the notion that children are not able to make sensible choices for themselves, but as they grow they become more 'mature' and better able to exercise choice.

7.2 Youth culture

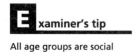

Youth as a distinct phase in life

Traditionally, individuals moved directly from childhood to adulthood – there was no intermediate stage of **youth** as there is now.

This transition from childhood to adulthood, with its assumption of rights and responsibilities, was clearly marked in a ceremony known as a **rite of passage**.

A well-known example of a rite of passage is the traditional initiation ceremony for males in the Murring aboriginal tribe in Australia. The adolescents were initiated by having a tooth wrenched out, during a ceremony which involved special dancers and the wearing of masks. The missing tooth was a symbol of manhood and an indication of the ability to withstand pain.

For women, the initiation was usually one related to onset of puberty and the first period. Among the Wanomani Indians in South America, for example, girls were expected to retire to a specially constructed hut for their first period and to be attended by older women.

In contemporary western society there are no rites of passage linked to the movement from childhood to adulthood – instead there is the period of youth. In this period, the individual is not expected to behave like a child, but is denied the status and rights of an adult. There is also no clear age at which childhood and youth end or adulthood begins. The only accepted age of adulthood is 18, which marks the right to legal powers, voting, borrowing money, and purchasing alcohol.

Although the boundaries of youth are unclear, it is accepted that it now forms a distinctive phase in people's lives, and those boundaries are expanding in both directions, so that youth begins earlier and ends later.

Subculture

Since the early 1950s, young people have adopted certain patterns of behaviour that are noticeably distinct from those of the older generation, particularly in dress and music. This has led some sociologists to argue that a separate **youth culture** exists.

When sociologists use the term **culture** they mean the whole way of life and set of beliefs of a particular society. The anthropologist, Ralph Linton, describes culture as 'the way of life of its (a society's) members: the collection of ideas and habits which they learn, share and transmit from generation to generation'. Youth culture therefore refers to the distinctive values and activities of young people. It should more correctly be referred to as either of the following:

- **Subculture** This means a distinctive way of life *within* a wider social circle. After all, youth may have a **distinctive** way of life but it takes place *within* the wider culture of our society;
- **Contra-culture** This is where a set of values arises in *opposition* to the wider culture, for example, New Age Travellers.

7.3 The nature of youth culture

As the focus of sociological research has come to bear on youth culture two viewpoints have emerged:

1. that youth culture is one culture shared by all youth of every social class and has led to a clear-cut **generation gap** between the younger and older generations;

❷ that youth culture is really an **umbrella** term that covers a wide range of divisions *within* youth. The divisions are based on social class, gender and race.

The single youth culture view

Early sociologists studying youth culture, such as Talcott Parsons, argued that the period of adolescence is one in which young people are passing through a transitional stage between childhood and adulthood. This transitional stage gives the chance to rebel against parental and adult authority; it also allows society in general to change its values slightly to cope with changing social conditions. The variations within youth are not regarded as being very significant: they are viewed merely as different reflections of the same youthful rebelliousness and the search for pleasure.

Youth culture and the activities of the peer group serve a very important psychological function for young people. As they are unsure of themselves and their developing identity, they look to others in the same situation with the same fashions and values for guidance, reassurance and support.

Youth culture as an umbrella term

The idea that there is *one* all embracing youth culture has come in for considerable criticism in recent years. In particular it is argued that there are a number of *different* youth cultures which reflect the particular problems (and advantages) of youth of the different social classes. Middle class, working class and black youth have their own distinctive subcultures.

Examiner's tip

Youth culture is one area where students often know more than examiners, but try not to get carried away with too much detail.

Middle-class youth culture

Middle-class youth are more likely (i) to stay on in education and (ii) to have good chances of future success in life. The result is that their versions of youth culture focus on student life and political protest. Very often they develop clear-cut alternatives to the present system, e.g. the New Age Travellers.

Working-class youth culture

Working-class youth have a wider variety of subcultures than the middle class. Sociologists such as Mike Brake argued that their versions of youth culture 'attempt to infuse into this (working class) bleak world, excitement and colours, during the respite between school and settling down into marriage and adulthood'. For working-class youth, school is largely irrelevant as most will leave at the minimum age with low academic qualifications to undertake manual work or be unemployed. Their cultures are far more of a **response** to their **experiences** of life, which are very different from the middle–class student.

Youth culture is seen as a way of solving problems. Brake claims that each generation of working-class young people begins to realise that their parents have bleak lives with limited income and opportunities. They therefore construct a subculture which 'helps them to cope' with their lives and which they believe will provide them with a different life from their parents.

Black youth culture

Surveys of job opportunities and living conditions, often find black youth of Afro-Caribbean descent with the worst conditions. Black youth also faces racism as an integral part of British society, it is claimed.

Sociologists have suggested that, rebuffed from British society, a distinctive black youth culture has emerged which has borrowed elements from the inner city 'ghettos' of America and from the Caribbean.

Asian youth culture

After a long period of remaining relatively isolated from the wider society, varieties of Asian youth cultures have emerged. Like working-class and black youth culture, traditional or distinctive elements of music and culture have been adopted and modified to provide a separate youth culture which gives them a distinctive identity.

Female youth culture

The 'male' model is inappropriate for females because they are socialised differently into a subordinate role. They experience the world in a different way because of this and have developed very different means of 'solving' their problems through a different form of youth culture from boys.

Griffin (*Typical Girls*) studied a group of white working-class girls at school and then at work, over a three-year period. This was backed up with 180 interviews with a wide variety of schoolgirls. She found no real evidence of a gang; instead the girls tended to have 'best friends'. Rebelliousness was expressed through sexual activity. There was no development of a clear anti-school group, but nor was there any real enthusiasm for school.

Lees (*Losing Out*) studied 15–16-year-olds in three schools over a two-year period. For Lees, the experience of youth for girls was totally dominated by the concept of 'sexuality'.

- Behaviour at school was strongly influenced by the concept of the 'slag' – a girl who has slept with a number of boys. Girls did not want to be known as this, but nor did they want the label of being a 'tight bitch' (a virgin, not interested in sex). The result was a control of their own behaviour to conform to the expected role of a girl.
- He found that girls saw their lives in terms of the inevitability of marriage and child raising, but did not look forward to the prospect with joy. They saw as an important aim of their lives, according to Lees, to delay marriage for a number of years.

McRobbie and Garber (*Girls and Subcultures*) studied girls in one school who lived on a single council estate. They argue that parental control and gender attitudes that effectively prohibit females from 'hanging around' street corners, create a 'bedroom culture'. Girls go around to each other's houses to stay in listening to music, dancing and chatting. But the 'culture' exists in private – at home. This is regarded as the appropriate place for females in our society.

7.4 The importance of the peer group

A **peer group** is a group of people of similar characteristics who identify with each other. This term is generally used to refer to youth – although, as it can be seen from the definition, this is not necessarily the case.

A peer group usually plays an important part in the **socialisation process**:
- It teaches people how to behave in groups outside the family;
- It is often in youth peer groups also that individuals learn how to treat others of the opposite sex;
- Peer groups develop their own norms and values and those in the group who break the informal rules may well be punished;
- Status differences appear within peer groups. These can be based on a wide variety of factors, but in adolescence it is typically such things as attractiveness, wit, toughness and ability at sport;
- At its most powerful, in adolescence, the peer group may actually develop its own subculture (as discussed earlier) and so in a wider sense, people use the term **peer group** to refer to **youth subcultures**.

Research
Paul Willis in *Learning to Labour* studied the influence of the peer group in education. His study was a group of secondary school, lower stream boys. These rejected the school system and instead committed themselves to an anti-school culture of avoiding work, being tough, having a laugh, and making fun of the teachers and those pupils who worked hard. Each member of the peer group measured his behaviour against his fellow anti-school group and no one else was of real importance to him. The 'lads', as they were called, egged each other on to be the most awkward or the toughest at school.

7.5 Old age

The rite of passage of retirement marks the end of a person's economically useful life to the community. Old age has become the phenomenon of modern society, as before the twentieth century, the numbers surviving to old age were very small. Today there are over 10 million people of retirement age in this country. In contemporary Britain, the elderly have low status and are regarded as having little to contribute to society.

As a person's employment often gives him or her an identity, the movement out of paid employment often creates problems of self-identity. Modern Britain has not yet developed an adequate status for the elderly (see Unit 11.5 for further discussion of the elderly in Britain).

In a comparative study of 14 different societies, ranging from the simple tribal (the Aborigines of Australia), through the underdeveloped (Mexico) to the modern industrialised (Britain), Cowgill and Holmes found that:

- Being elderly is seen in most societies not just as having lived for so many years, but as achieving the status of a tribal elder or of becoming a grandfather. Actual age, which is important to us, is not generally seen as so important.

- There are many more elderly people in modern industrialised societies than in tribal or underdeveloped ones. This can be explained by better standards of living and to a lesser extent improved medical services.

- The status of the aged is at its lowest in modern societies.

- In simpler societies older people hold most positions of power. This is generally not true in modern societies.

- The faster the rate of social change, the lower the status of the aged in society. This is because the skills and knowledge they have are not relevant to the younger generation – so they are not regarded as having worthwhile knowledge. In agricultural societies where the knowledge of one generation is generally useful to the next, the old, therefore, have high status.

- Retirement is a modern invention. Traditionally, the elderly gradually withdrew from manual tasks as their ability declined – but there was no abrupt stopping of work. This is important, as in modern societies an individual's status and self-perception are related to his or her job. On retirement, the person has lost his or her identity.

- In modern societies, there is a process called **disengagement** which is the gradual withdrawal of old people from other people's company. This does not occur in other societies.

Summary

1   The idea of appropriate behaviour being attached to certain ages is a social creation and is not the result of biology.

2   Childhood as we know it now developed over a long period – starting in the eighteenth century.

3   Before that time, children were seen as 'little adults'.

4   There have always been class differences in the way that children have been treated. Possibly the greatest gap was in the early part of the nineteenth century, when the children of the working class were forced to work longer hours and in much worse conditions than even adults today.

5   The proof of social creation of childhood comes from comparing childhood in different cultures and over time. In one culture (of the Ik) children are expected to look after themselves from the age of three.

6   Rites of passage are the ceremonies that most societies have to mark the transition from one age grade to another – for example from childhood to adulthood.

7   British society has lost most of its rites of passage relating to age – although the eighteenth birthday is still commonly marked by a party.

8   The idea of youth is a new invention that occurred in the 1950s.

9   The main factors influencing the growth of youth culture were: (a) pace of change, (b) length of education, (c) affluence, (d) growth by the media.

10   Subculture means to has a distinctive set of values within the wider culture, but not, however opposed to it.

11   One group of sociologists has argued that youth culture is a way for young people to cope with the change from childhood to adulthood by giving them confidence.

12   A different approach is taken by most other sociologists who argue that there is no one youth culture at all, and that youth culture is really closely related to differences in class, gender and ethnic group.

13   The peer group is a group of people of the same age or situation against whose behaviour we measure our own. The peer group is particularly important to youth.

14   The idea that there is a clear generation gap is not proved by research. It seems that most youth are conventional in their attitudes.

15   The number of the elderly is increasing in society, so there are now more of them than ever before.

16   The number of the elderly has never been so low in advanced industrial societies.

17   This low status is related to the fact that the skills and knowledge of older people is of restrictive value in a rapidly changing world.

18   However, the degree of status of the elderly is not equal in all advanced societies; in Japan the elderly have considerable higher status than in Britain.

Self-test questions

1   Why is age a topic of interest to sociologists?
2   Give a brief account of how 'childhood' is viewed in Britain today.
3   How does the experience of childhood in Britain today differ from the experience of childhood over 300 years ago in this country?
4   What is youth culture? Is there only one youth culture?
5   How are the old commonly regarded in modern British society?

Chapter 8
Race, ethnicity and migration

8.1 Race and ethnic group: definition

Race is a term that has been used to indicate a group who are assumed to share some common biological and social traits. It is an extremely difficult concept to define, as it has been used in a number of ways. Perhaps the most infamous attempt to define race was by the Nazis in the 1930s in Germany, who claimed that one could distinguish pure races. However, they were unable to substantiate this claim in practice.

A commonly accepted division of people into races is into Negroid, Mongoloid and Caucasoid. Interestingly for those who argue that Indians are of a different race from the British, they are both, in fact, Caucasoid. Over the millions of years of man's existence and various migrations over the earth, these three groups have become intermixed.

Ethnic groups (ethnic minorities) are groups of people who share a common culture which is different from that of the majority of society. Sometimes this is the result of migration from one country to another. The new society to which they move is known as the **host society**. Ethnic minorities usually only remain noticeable if their culture, form of dress or skin colour make them stand out, and if they form a distinctive community slightly separate from the main host society.

8.2 Enriching the culture: patterns of migration and settlement

Fig. 8.1 on the next page shows the population of Britain by ethnic group.

Fig. 8.1   Population of Britain by ethnic group, Spring 1996
(Source: *Social Trends 27*, 1997)

	Population (thousands)
White	52,942
Black Caribbean	477
Black African	281
Other Black	117
Indian	877
Pakistani	579
Bangladeshi	183
Chinese	126
Other Asian	161
Other ethnic minorities	506
All ethnic groups	56,267

People of Afro-Caribbean origins

The majority came to Britain during the 1950s and early 1960s, when they were recruited by British companies to fill job vacancies, when there was a severe shortage of labour.

Although the majority of the original migrants came from Jamaica, almost half came from a range of islands such as Trinidad and Tobago and Barbados, and also from Guyana on the South American mainland.

The cultural background of the migrants who came here was English and local 'Creole' dialects of it, and they were educated in English language, in schools based on the British system. The religion of the Caribbean islands and Guyana is Christianity. The British colonialists had maintained the fiction that Britain was the home or motherland, and it was with considerable shock and hurt that the original migrants to Britain encountered the racist, hostile reactions to their arrivals. The first generation tried hard to integrate, but successive sociology surveys have demonstrated that those of Afro-Caribbean origin are one of the groups in Britain with the lowest 'life chances' in education, employment, housing and law enforcement.

People of Asian origins

East African Asians

A fifth of Asians are of East African origin. Most had originally gone to East Africa, with British encouragement, from north India and Pakistan, where they formed the commercial and administrative middle class, usually highly educated and fluent in English. They are generally Muslims and Hindus.

After independence a policy of Africanisation took place in Kenya, Uganda and Malawi, so many were forced to give up their positions and businesses and settle in the UK. Because of their high levels of education and business acumen, they have been outstandingly successful. The highest achievers in the state education system come from this type of background.

Pakistan

Migrants came from Kashmir and Punjab from the 1960s onward. There is a major division between urban Pakistanis, who are generally well educated, and rural Pakistanis who may have more traditional customs and be less literate.

Most Pakistanis live in Yorkshire, Manchester, Lancashire, West Midlands, Glasgow and Cardiff. The pattern of migration was usually through kinship networks, such that entire families gradually migrated here, and therefore a fairly close set of communities has developed.

Many Pakistani communities are encapsulated from much of the wider society by religious difference, racism and the fact that they are concentrated in low paid jobs, living in inner city areas.

India

People of Indian origin originally came to Britain in the 1950s and 1960s. There are two distinct groups:

- Sikhs from the Punjab, who settled in Leeds, West London, the West Midlands and Glasgow.
- People from Gujarat. These are mainly Hindus, speaking Gujarati, who live in North and South London, Leicester, Coventry and Manchester.

Bangladesh

Bangladesh is the poorest of the Indian sub-continent nations. Originally, the males came to Britain from the 1950s to the 1970s for low skilled, low paid jobs. Most came from the rural Sylhet district. They tend to have settled in East London.

Other migrant groups

Britain has always had a history of immigrant groups arriving here including Chinese from Hong Kong, Poles who came after the Second World War, Jews who have settled here over one hundred years, Italians who came in the 1950s to Bedfordshire and Glasgow. However, the single biggest 'immigrant' group in Britain are the Irish.

8.3 Reasons for migration

We can divide the reasons that people migrate to another country under the headings push and pull.

Push reasons

- **Poverty and unemployment at home** If there is widespread poverty and unemployment in the home country, with little prospect of the situation improving, then people search elsewhere for a better life. In the ex-colonies of India, Pakistan and the West Indies, Britain had left little industry and poorly developed agriculture. These, combined with high birth rates, led to widespread poverty.
- **Persecution** If certain groups are undergoing persecution then they will attempt to flee. It was for this reason that Jews came to Britain at the end of the nineteenth century, and in smaller numbers in the 1930s. Most of the Asians who came here in 1972 and 1976 were escaping from policies of Africanisation followed by the Ugandan government, which wanted to replace Asian British passport holders with locals to limit unemployment.

Pull reasons

- **Recruitment** Britain was undergoing an acute labour shortage in the early 1950s. This was the result of the take-off of the economy after the end of the Second World War. The limits of the British workforce had been reached and so Britain turned to the West Indies (and later India and Pakistan). Immigrants were encouraged to come; and some institutions such as London Transport and the National Health Service actually set up recruitment offices in the Wesr Indies. The immigrants who came generally took the jobs that nobody else wanted. In recent years, only the long hours of work and low pay of Pakistani workers has kept the British textiles industry in existence. As nobody else wanted to do this work, the employers continued to recruit from Pakistan right through the 1970s.
- **To join relatives** If part of the family is living in one country and part in another, then there is an understandable desire to reunite; 70% of immigrants from the New Commonwealth and Pakistan are wives and children of immigrants already settled here.
    The amount of immigration has been dependent on:
    - the economic situation and need of Britain compared to the immigrants' country of origin;

- the legislation limiting immigration, which is heavily influenced by the economic situation.
- the number of dependants of those immigrants settled here.

8.4 Racism and discrimination

- **Racism** is the belief that there are distinct races, and that some races are superior to others.
- **Racial prejudice** is when people are disliked, not for any personal characteristics, but because they belong to a certain group.
- **Racialism or racial discrimination** is when a group of people are unfairly treated simply because they belong to a particular ethnic group.

Explanations for racism

About 35% of the British population admits to having some degree of racist feeling.

There are three basic types of explanation for racial prejudice:

- those which stress individual reasons;
- those which stress cultural reasons;
- those which stress competition for scarce resources.

Individual explanations

This approach argues that certain personality types are more prone to have racial feelings. Psychologists argue that people who are brought up to have rigid or **'authoritarian' personalities** are most likely to have racist tendencies.

Culture

The second set of explanations is based upon the idea that the British culture has racism woven into it. People are brought up with **stereotypes** about race and the differences between the various groups in society. This is most vividly shown by racist jokes which are still common.

Sociologists have suggested this might be a result of the colonial past. In order to justify having colonies and imposing slavery, the myth of inferior beings was created.

Scarce resources

Sociologists have noted that racism often turns into racialism when the employment situation worsens or there is a shortage of housing. They argue that 'outsiders' of any kind are made **scapegoats** to substitute the real reasons for the economic downturn or the lack of housing. This was the basis upon which Nazi Germany persecuted Jews.

8.5 Race and life chances

People from the ethnic minorities are, on the whole, likely to have worse 'life chances' than the majority of the population.

Housing

Those of Asian origins are most likely to live in overcrowded conditions, and 35% of them do, compared to only 3% of the rest of the population. They are also more likely to be living in older properties than the majority of the population.

Those of Afro-Caribbean origins are more likely to live in local authority accommodation and to receive the least desirable housing in local authority stock.

Criminal justice system

A survey commissioned by the Metropolitan Police in the mid-1980s showed that the police routinely used racist language and attitudes. According to the Prison Reform Trust, the proportion of the male black population in prison is almost eight times higher than that of the population as a whole. Less than 1% of police officers nationally are drawn from the ethnic minorities.

Employment

There are clear differences in the levels of employment and type of employment by ethnic group. Members of the ethnic minorities are, on average:
- limited to lower level jobs;
- working in sectors of the economy in decline;
- employed in shift work;
- earning lower wages.

However, it is important to stress that this is a series of general statements. People of Indian origin, for example, are more likely than the majority of the population to be in managerial and professional positions.

Wage levels are significantly lower on average for ethnic minorities than for whites. However, it is also true that East African origin Asians are particularly successful.

Unemployment

Levels of unemployment for members of the ethnic minorities are higher than of the majority of the population. Overall, they have unemployment rates which are in some cases twice the average British unemployment rate. Amongst Pakistanis/Bangladeshis it is three times the national average. Fig. 8.2 shows male unemployment by ethnic group.

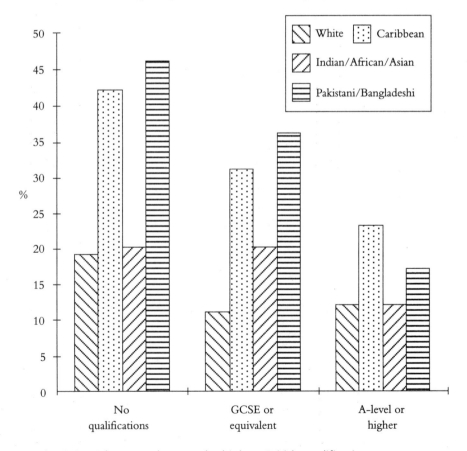

Fig. 8.2 Male unemployment by highest British qualification
(Source: Based on T. Modood, R. Berthoud et al, *Ethnic Minorities in Britain,* Policy Studies Institute, 1997)

Education

Indians and African Asians are the most successful in the British educational system, while Pakistani and Bangladeshi men fare the worst. Afro-Caribbean women are particularly successful up to A-level, but few go on to university.

Health

The poorer living conditions of the ethnic minorities mean that their health levels are worse than the majority of the population. However, this is masked because the patterns of migration when young, fit people came to Britain in the 1960s means that there is not yet a very large elderly population from the ethnic minorities. It is the older people who tend to exhibit the worst health levels. However, infant mortality levels are higher amongst those from Pakistan and Bangladesh origins. There are significantly higher levels of mental illness amongst those of Afro-Caribbean origins.

8.6 Preventing discrimination

In order to limit racial discrimination, a number of Acts have been passed. The **1965 Race Relations Act** made it illegal to discriminate in the provision of goods or services to the public, or in the areas of employment and housing. It became illegal to incite racial hatred.

The Community Relations Commission (CRC) was established to promote inter-racial harmony. The Race Relations Board (RRB) was established to investigate complaints of racial discrimination. The CRC and RRB were criticised for ineffectiveness. This resulted in the **1976 Commission for Racial Equality** (CRE) which was established with greater powers than the RRB. The CRE can bring cases to court, whereas the RRB acted only in cases of **direct** discrimination (for example, when a person was denied employment because he/she was black); the CRE can bring institutions to court for **indirect** discrimination, which is really discriminating in intent, but attempting to hide this in some way (for instance, if it is prohibited to wear any form of headgear apart from the official cap, this discriminates against Sikhs who must wear turbans).

Other ways to eliminate prejudice and discrimination include the teaching of Third World studies or African history. These show that non-whites were not uncivilised people without any culture until the white colonialists came, but had complex cultures already which were often deliberately destroyed. This helps to break down stereotypes held by young people.

How effective has the legislation been? A study in 1994 still found 35% of people with racist views. Discrimination still exists and strongly affects the quality of black and Asian people's lives. They have been affected more by the growth of unemployment since 1985; they pay more for housing and are more likely to have lower incomes than white people.

Passing laws can outlaw obvious discrimination but it cannot really alter people's racist attitudes if these are embedded in our culture. As long as our culture continues to reaffirm stereotyped views of people who are not white, then prejudice will continue.

Summary

1 Although the term **race** is commonly used to describe people of different skin colour, there is no biological evidence to show there are any important differences that can distinguish one so-called 'race' from another.

2 The term ethnic group is usually employed by sociologists to distinguish one form of cultural group from another.

3 In the late 1940s and early 1950s, Commonwealth immigrants were welcomed into Britain because they were needed to fill job vacancies.

4 People came to Britain for one of two reasons: the amount of work available or because of relatives already here.

5 Afro-Caribbeans and Asians face problems of prejudice (which means to be disliked simply on the grounds of the colour of their skin) and of discrimination (to be treated differently because of the colour of their skin).

6 Explanations of prejudice include: (a) the authoritarian personality; (b) stereotyping, and (c) scapegoating.

7 Discrimination has been shown to exist in areas such as employment and housing.

8 There have been various government attempts to eliminate discrimination. However, it is difficult to change attitudes held deep within the culture.

Self-test questions

1 What is the difference between 'race' and 'ethnic' group?
2 In which areas of Britain did migrants settle? What reasons can you suggest for this pattern?
3 Give three reasons why migrants came to Britain after 1950.
4 What are the main causes of racial prejudice?
5 Give brief accounts of the discrimination which people of Afro-Caribbean origin and Asians face in: (a) employment, and (b) housing.
6 What steps have been taken in recent years to reduce the amount of racial discrimination in Britain?
7 How effective has government legislation been in reducing racial discrimination?

Chapter 9
Work

9.1 The meaning of work

Although it may seem easy to define work when asked, in fact it is very difficult, for no particular action can be described exclusively as **work**. What is considered as work varies, depending upon such things as time, place, society and individual preferences.

Examples
- The **task of planting seeds** If this is done by a farmer growing crops for sale, or for professional use in an agricultural society, then it is work. If it is done (even by the same people) as the leisure activity of growing flowers for pleasure in a garden, then it is not work.
- **Playing a sport** If a professional plays football, then it is work; if a sociology student plays it is likely to be for pleasure.

The **most common elements of work** are that (a) it is paid, (b) it is not done primarily for pleasure, (c) most commonly, there is an employer who imposes his or her authority on the worker in exchange for wages, (d) usually work takes place in a special place put aside for that purpose – the office or factory, (e) usually there is some productive or useful outcome of the work – the building of a part of a car, the assessment of someone's insurance claim, etc, (f) the amount of time spent at work is clearly marked off from the hours of non-work.

Not all the above elements of work need to be present, however, for an action to be considered work.

The **division of a person's time** between non-work and work is a relatively modern happening. Throughout history, the activities people engaged in to make a living and to survive have simply been a central part of their lives. There was no division into completely separate spheres. In agricultural or hunting societies, people simply lived their lives without any awareness that work could be divided from **leisure**. The two elements of life were closely integrated.

The division, as we know it now between work and leisure, developed during the Industrial Revolution, as the machinery in factories needed to be started and stopped at precise times. Furthermore, the precise integration of all the jobs in a factory required a strict work discipline.

Before the Industrial Revolution most production had been carried out at home, and the family or kin was the economic unit.

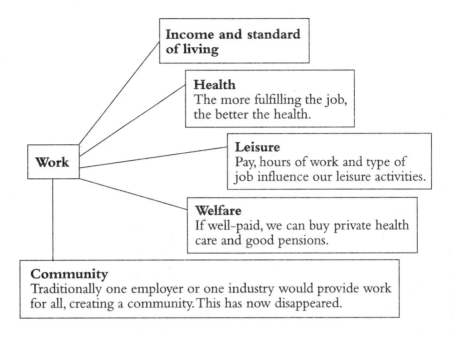

Fig.9.1 The impact of work on our lives

9.2 The occupational structure

The occupational structure refers to the type of jobs performed by the working population. Very broadly defined, there are two forms of labour:

1 **Manual labour,** work that involves physical labour of some kind such as a miner, bricklayer or a mechanic performs;

2 **Non-manual (or white collar) labour,** work that involves little physical labour but relies more on mental effort or force of personality. For example, shop assistant, clerk or teacher.

There are three types of industry:

1 **Primary,** such as mining or agriculture, which involve our nature resources;

2 **Secondary,** or manufacturing, such as industry, where objects are created to be sold;

3 **Tertiary** or services, involving providing a service of some kind, such as banking or transport.

The changing occupational structure

Historically, industrialisation brought a move away from agriculture towards manufacturing. The 150 years from the beginning of the nineteenth century to the middle of the twentieth saw the vast majority of the population employed in the secondary or industrial sector, as Britain was one of the countries dominating world manufacturing.

Since 1950, and at an increasingly fast pace, there has been a move towards the tertiary sector. Today, more people are now employed in this than in manufacturing. Agriculture has shrunk to a tiny proportion of the workforce, accounting for only 2% of employment.

Britain has therefore been described as a **post-industrial society** – meaning that it no longer earns its living by manufacturing, but by service industries including banking, leisure and tourism.

In 1966 there were approximately 8 million people employed in manufacturing, and today the figure is less than 5 million. This has been described as a process of de-industrialisation. Today, Britain actually imports more manufactured goods than it sells.

Causes of change in the sectors of the economy

Explanations for the changes in the British economy include:

- The growth of a **world economy**, in which Britain has had to compete increasingly against newer industrialised nations. In itself, this may not have caused great change in manufacturing, however it can be linked with

- The growth of the **multi-nationals**. The multi-national companies now dominate the world economy. These companies (such as Ford, Mitsubishi, etc) search out the cheapest places where production can take place, and therefore have a tremendous advantage over companies which are located in higher wage economies. In the past this has often led to the multi-nationals producing in Third World countries (even though the profits flow back to the owners in the First World). However, as Britain is now a low wage economy and presents a cheap production site for companies (such as Nissan cars) who wish to produce in the European Union, this flow out of Britain of manufacturing jobs may be slowed down.

- **Changing technology.** The introduction of computer aided machines and robotics has generally replaced workers rather than enhanced their jobs. So, the numbers in employment in manufacturing have declined.

- **State intervention.** Approximately 25% of all employment is state related, as there has been massive growth in health and social welfare provisions since the 1960s. The growth of the professions in the post-war years has been primarily as a result of the expansion of the state.

The consequences of the changes in economic sectors

The changes in the economic sectors have had consequences on **employment patterns**.

Occupations

- Manual work has declined, in line with the decline in manufacturing. Overall, manual workers now form less than 50% of those in employment, although there are differences between the sexes. Today, approximately 56% of employed men, compared to 36% of women are engaged in manual work.

- White-collar work has, in comparison, expanded rapidly. Since 1950, the number of white-collar workers has increased by 400%.

- There has been a similar expansion in the numbers of people defined as managers and administrators.

- The most rapidly expanding occupational group since 1950 has been that defined as 'professional', with a 500% increase.

- The self-employed number approximately 8% of the working population.

Full-time and part-time employment

The changes in the sectors of the economy have been closely related to the changes in the hours and conditions of employment.

Part-time employment has increased dramatically. Today, 23% of all employment is part-time, with more than 5 million people in part-time employment, 90% of whom are female. Most of this increase in part-time employment has been in the service sector, in catering, tourism and leisure. However, increasing use of what is known as '**post-Fordist**' production (where much more flexible work patterns are adopted by industry) techniques have increased the numbers of part-time women workers in industry too.

Full-time employment has decreased since the 1960s, and this process has speeded up since 1980. Since 1960, more than 4 million full-time jobs have disappeared in Britain. The full-time jobs that have been lost are those traditionally regarded as 'male', and generally concentrated in the older 'heavy' manufacturing industries.

Unemployment

Long-term unemployment developed in Britain in the 1970s and intensified greatly in the 1980s.

This was partly the result of government policy, and partly of the changes in the sectors of the economy described earlier. Decline in the industrial sphere and in the amount of manual workers needed has been the main force behind the increase in unemployment, but government policies in the 1980s were to make British industry operate with the smallest and cheapest workforce possible. Employers were encouraged to lay off workers, and the traditional defenders of employees – the unions – were weakened by legislation.

Unemployment does not hit all groups equally. The unskilled manual workers, particularly in the traditional heavy industries, have the highest rates of unemployment. Also, the ethnic minorities have significantly higher levels of unemployment than those experienced by whites. Official statistics show that male unemployment rates are higher than for females, but this is probably the result of obstacles to married women 'signing on' as officially unemployed, for example.

According to Therborn, long-term unemployment will create a two-thirds/one-third society in which the unemployed third will be permanently excluded.

Perceptions of social class

One of the consequences of the changes in the nature and types of people's jobs, has been the effect on social class and people's perception of their class. The enormous growth in the non-manual occupations, and in particular the growth in the 'professions', has meant that the middle class has now grown at the expense of the working class. The reality of employment in routine clerical work may be similar to traditional working-class jobs in that they are lacking in autonomy, they are poorly paid and they have limited career structure, but the circumstances of the employment give the perception of middle-class work. This has affected traditional patterns of class consciousness.

One of the causes of the dominance of politics in the 1980s by the Conservative Party, was its ability to capture the vote of the new 'middle class', whilst appealing to the affluent sections of the working class. The weakness of the Labour Party had been that its traditional base of male, manual workers in heavy industry had largely disappeared, at least as an electoral force.

The formal and informal economies

Sociologists claim that there are two types of economy which co-exist. These are:
- the formal economy and
- the informal economy.

The **formal economy** consists of paid employment which is usually covered by legal boundaries and constraints. We have already analysed the changes taking place in this part of the economy in the previous section. However, these changes do not give a full account of working life in Britain without an understanding of the informal economy.

The **informal economy** consists of work which is either not paid – the payment is in 'kind', or is outside the tax system. There are three types of work within the informal economy:
- **Household economy** Production by members of households for other members of those households of goods and services, for which substitutes may have to be paid for (e.g. the work of a 'housewife').
- **The hidden economy** Work which is remunerated, but which is not declared for tax purposes (e.g. work for 'cash-in-hand').
- **Communal economy** Production of goods or services for which the group would normally have to pay, but which is not for the consumption of the producers themselves (e.g. voluntary work).

The relationship of informal and formal economies

Traditionally all discussions of work have centred on the formal economy. Statistics on economic activity, on levels of pay and on attitudes to employment have all been based on formal occupations.

In reality, work performed outside the formal sector is important to understanding all the 'facts' mentioned above. For example, understanding the roles men and women play in the home and the amount of unpaid work done there, helps us to understand the different situation of men and women in the 'formal workplace' of the factory and the office.

Examples of the significance of the formal economy include:

Examiner's tip

Make sure you understand the terms used in this chapter, e.g. formal and informal economies, post-Fordism, etc.

- The overwhelming majority of the elderly and disabled are cared for by women at home, without pay. If the government had to pay for these then taxes would need to rise. Studying the informal economy helps us to understand the 'real' costs of social care for society.
- Pahl studied people who did work in their spare time to earn extra cash. This is cash-in-hand and never shows up in official statistics. Pahl shows that those who are already doing well out of the formal economy are also more likely to be successful in the informal one (for example skilled electricians who receive relatively high wages and are able to supplement their income with 'private' work).

Feminisation of labour

(More on women and work can be found in Chapter 6 Gender)

The work force is changing significantly in its composition. In 1961, for example there were 16 million men working and only 8 million women. By the 1990s there were 15 million men and 11 million women. Women now represent over 40% of the labour force, and by the end of the 1990s the numbers of women at work should be almost equal to (or possibly greater than) the number of men. This has been called, the '**feminisation** of the labour force'.

However, women tend to be concentrated
- in lower paid work;
- in a narrow range of occupations (particularly in the clerical and service industries);
- with less responsibility.

The causes of the increase in women working are:
- greater availability of jobs for women (they are jobs 'for women' because they are often part time and low paid), as there is a shift towards post-Fordist styles of production (see p. 84);
- women are more willing (because of the domestic responsibilities) than men to work part time and are therefore flexible and cheap labour for employers;
- it is culturally normal for women to work today, whereas in the first part of the twentieth century women were discouraged from working in paid employment;
- the desire of women to return to work as soon as possible, usually after the birth of the last child. This is aided by the fact that women are having fewer children, compressed into a shorter space of time.

Race and the labour market

(For a fuller discussion please see Chapter 8 Race, ethnicity and migration)

Overall, the ethnic minorities are more likely to:
- have lower status occupations;
- receive lower wages;
- have significantly higher levels of unemployment;
- be discriminated against in obtaining a job in the first place, and then in gaining promotion.

However, the overall category hides clear differences between the various groups. Those of Afro-Caribbean origin, for example, are most likely to be in semi-skilled and skilled employment. Those of African Asian backgrounds are likely to be over represented in the professions and management. Those from Bangladeshi backgrounds are concentrated in the unskilled jobs. The reasons for this are:
- **Racism** There is still evidence of racial discrimination in employment and promotion.
- **Institutional racism** This means that there is no direct racist beliefs by employers and managers, but other obstacles are placed in the way of job applicants. This could include such things as requirement to have a certain accent or style of dress or concern that clients/subordinates may not accept a member of the ethnic or religious minorities in a senior position.
- **Qualifications** Although a significant number of members of the ethnic minorities have high levels of qualifications, a higher proportion of Afro-Caribbean origin and Bangladeshi origin people have lower qualifications.

Globalisation

In the past twenty years there has been an increasing concentration of companies so that a few large multi-national companies have gained enormous economic power. The development of this **world economy** has seriously affected Britain in the field of manufacturing, as

- companies search for the cheapest labour costs and then import to Britain, rather than produce here. This means that production costs have to be kept low to keep Britain competitive in industrial production;
- large companies do set up production facilities in Britain, but in times of trading difficulty these are most likely to be closed down as the company seeks to lower costs;
- national governments have limited power to control the activities of multi-nationals;
- British companies choose to invest abroad, as they expect higher profits. In the mid 1990s, investment abroad, and investment out of Britain by British companies was actually higher than investment into the country by foreign multi-nationals. The effect of this outward investment is the loss of jobs in Britain, although the profits return to the companies' shareholders.

Post-Fordism

Linked to the de-industrialisation of Britain, and the growth of the global economy, there has been a move towards different methods of production in order to make higher quality and cheaper goods. Most writers agree that this style of production has been adapted from the Japanese model, and is known as Japanisation of production, or more commonly as post-Fordism (because it is very different from Henry Ford's idea of producing identical goods in one factory on a production line).

There are four elements to post-Fordism

- **Technology** The use of computerised control of manufacture, and computer aided design, robots to undertake particularly repetitive or tedious work.
- **Products** The ability to use the robotics and high technology to produce small numbers of different designs as opposed to the mass manufacture of identical items.
- **Jobs** There is a need for versatility, and possible more highly skilled workers, as opposed to the unskilled production line worker. All workers should be able to do all jobs.
- **Contracts** Post-Fordism methods of production mean that workers can be moved around the factory at any one time, or that more part-time workers are employed in order that they can be brought in at times of peak output and sent home when not needed. Finally, work may be contracted out to other companies and even to homeworkers.

9.3 Changing technology

British society is based upon industry, that is the mass production by factories of objects for our use. Britain was the first country in the world to move from a society based upon agriculture and manufacture in the home to one based upon industry. It began to industrialise in the middle of the eighteenth century. The process of moving from agriculture to large-scale factory production is known as **industrialisation**. Today most countries of the western world including Europe, the USA and Russia and parts of South-East Asia, notably Japan, have industrialised.

The main characteristics of an industrialised society are:

- Production is based upon complex machinery in factories (mechanisation) as opposed to home working;
- The majority of the population live in towns near the factories (urbanisation), as opposed to being dispersed throughout the country;
- The majority of the population work for an employer and receive fixed wages, rather than working for themselves;

- In order to gain higher wages and better working conditions, workers have banded together in trade unions to argue their case against employers and industrial conflict is common;
- Goods produced by the factories on such a large scale become cheap and available to the mass population who are able to achieve a much higher standard of living than before;
- An ever-evolving technology with the movement from mechanisation to automation;
- A division of labour in society, such that people produce only one part of the complete finished product.

Some of these characteristics need examining in further detail.

The division of labour

The most efficient means of producing good is by dividing the work into small, simple, repetitive tasks. The most famous example was the description given by the eighteenth-century economist Adam Smith of production in a pin factory. If each person had worked to make a whole pin, then each of the ten people working there would only have made twenty pins, but dividing the labour they actually made 48 000 a day. Today the division of labour is regarded as the normal factory way of producing; televisions, cars, washing machines, etc are all made in this way

Advantages
- More goods are produced at a lower price;
- More people can afford to purchase goods and so a higher standard of living is achieved;
- The low levels of skill required mean that many people who would be unable to cope with complex tasks find employment;
- Radical sociologists such as Henry Braverman suggest that the true advantage is that employers can earn greater profits from their workers by keeping control over the process of production. The workers in fact suffer.

Disadvantages
- The work is boring and repetitive;
- The worker therefore obtains little or no satisfaction from his or her job;
- The boredom and dissatisfaction can cause industrial disputes as the workers seek consolation in higher wages;
- Traditional skills and pride of craftsmanship are lost;
- Workers lose control over their work and the pace at which they work;
- Lack of pride in work leads to a lower quality of finished product.

Mechanisation to automation

Mechanisation and the consequent division of labour were the main changes brought about by industrialisation, but since then technological advances have occurred. These include:

Assembly line production
In this process operatives work on a line of part-manufactured products, with the product moving along a conveyor belt of some kind from one worker to the next. Each worker performs some simple repetitive task which adds another part or stage to the product. As the product moves along the line it nears completion. This is how most mass-produced cars are made.

Research
Goldthorpe and Lockwood in *The Affluent Worker* studied car assembly workers at the Vauxhall factory in Luton. They found that workers were bored and frustrated with their work. The conditions of work (noise and monotony) prevented close friendships being made. The workers were mainly concerned about obtaining as high a wage as possible and spending this on family and leisure pursuits. Relationship with employers tended to be hostile.

Process production

This method of production involves a continuous process in which products such as chemicals or petroleum enter one end as raw material and are refined into the finished product. Two types of workers are required (a) those who control the machinery, this being skilled, moderately interesting work and (b) those who load and maintain the production process.

Research

Nichols and Beynon in *Living with Capitalism* found that the work in process production was very different for the two groups of workers. Whereas those in control had relatively pleasant interesting work, those who maintained and loaded the processing plant were engaged in work not very different in lack of skill and amount of effort and unpleasantness from the production-line workers.

Automation

This is a general term to cover the use of machinery to perform tasks traditionally performed or at least controlled by workers. It varies from the very simplest form of automation where machines performing complex tasks are linked together by anther machine which eliminates the need for unskilled labourers carrying and lifting objects. A simple example is the way that bread is passed from the oven to the slicing machine and finally passed on to a packing machine.

However, with the growth of the new **microchip** technology, automation has taken a huge step forward; now skilled jobs that involve measurement and close quality control can be undertaken by machinery. Indeed, Fiat manufacturers most of its new cars almost entirely by computer-controlled machines. On a wider scale, microchips have radically changed service industries, so we have cash dispensers, word processors, pocket calculators, etc. This new form of technology has been called the **second industrial revolution**.

Advantages of automation include:
- Boring repetitive tasks can be eliminated.
- There is a demand for more highly educated workers to understand and control the machinery.
- The possibility exists of producing more goods for fewer hours of work. Therefore the working week could be shortened. There could be more opportunity for leisure.
- According to Blauner, automation brings the possibility of eliminating the divisions between production line workers and management. All could become involved in a team to solve work problems. This is because jobs would tend to be more responsible. They would involve responsibility for an area of production performed by machines.
- Work would become healthier and safer as the dangerous jobs would be eliminated.

Disadvantages of automation include:
- The major disadvantage of microchips is their very advantage for employers. That is they can perform a number of complex tasks which are the very essence of a person's skill. A simple example is the word processor, the use of which can be learned within a couple of hours and give a perfectly typed letter or document. Previously it took a skilled typist. The word processor has also taken away all the skills of printers – what once took up to five years to learn can now be learned in a day with the help of a word processor. Henry Braverman has called the process **deskilling**, whereby workers lose skills to machines. Employers use deskilling to cut the workforce and decrease wages.
- As a result of deskilling, a loss of pride and craftsmanship in virtually every form of employment will occur.
- Unemployment will increase (this is discussed in greater detail in Chapter 10).
- Wages will decrease.
- A decline will take place as people increasingly stay at home to work and to engage in leisure pursuits. This could alter the basis of our society which is dependent upon social mixing in shops, offices and factories.

9.4 Work satisfaction

As work forms one of the main activities of our lives, the degree of satisfaction obtained from work influences our whole life.

Alienation

Karl Marx has suggested the term **alienation** to describe the situation of people who gain no enjoyment from work. It has been suggested by Blauner that alienation includes the following elements:

- **Meaninglessness** A feeling that the job makes no sense. This occurs where the division of labour breaks work down into such small unrelated tasks that it becomes difficult to see what the point of the job really is;
- **Powerlessness** A belief that the worker has no power over the form his work takes, or the speed at which it is done. A car production line is a good example of this;
- **Normlessness** The worker feels that what his or her employer says he/she should feel about a job is not in fact how he/she himself sees it. It is difficult to feel pride and interest in the construction of a car if your job consists of putting on its wheels. This difference of opinion can lead to industrial conflict;
- **Isolation** Workers are cut off from each other by the noise and discomfort of the workplace; on a wider scale they are cut off by their work from feeling part of society. The work produces a desire only to better themselves and to forget the needs of others;
- **Self-estrangement** Ideally any job ought to use the abilities and intelligence of the worker, so that his or her work fulfils him. If the job fails to do this then the worker gradually loses his or her own personality and tries to express him/herself in leisure activities.

What factors influence the degree of alienation and work satisfaction?

- **The division of labour** Extreme division of labour makes the individual's task irrelevant and small;
- **Repetition** This leads to boredom and monotony as a variety of tasks is needed to keep people interested;
- **Noisy, unpleasant work conditions** These cut off workers from communicating with each other.
- **Low levels of skill** According to Baldamus the greater the level of skill the greater the degree of work satisfaction;
- **Control over production** When workers have some degree of say in the pace and form of the production process, the degree of commitment increases.

As we can see, people engaged in non-routine work in pleasant conditions, such as professional, managerial and skilled manual workers, gain far more work satisfaction and are less alienated than those engaged in routine unskilled work such as car assembly workers.

9.5 Attempts to make work more fulfilling

There has been two types of attempts to make work more fulfilling: on the one hand the actions of the employers and on the other the activities of the workers.

Employers' attempts

- **Making a pleasant work environment** Modern factory machines are designed to be less noisy so that workers can talk. Cleanliness and safety are now encouraged in modern factories;

- **Increase in welfare provisions** Firms give subsidised canteens, welfare and recreational facilities;
- **Workers' representatives in the management** Elected representatives of workers sit on the board of the company and are consulted over pace of work, etc;
- **Workers complete the whole task instead of the division of labour** Volvo in its Swedish plant divided its workers into groups to build complete cars. This encouraged workers into feeling responsible for the individual car they had built;
- **Higher wages or bonuses** Given to compensate for the boredom and difficulty of work.

Employees' attempts

Employees have devised their own 'unofficial' ways of resisting the conditions of work.
Limiting output Workers agree on what they consider to be a reasonable amount of work and then impose informal sanctions on those who try to work too hard.

Research

In the 1920s Mayo studied a group of workers in 'The Hawthorn Studies'. Any worker who tried too hard was brought back to the agreed output by sarcastic comments, practical jokes and, if all else failed, being 'sent to Coventry'.

Daydreaming In order to pass the boring time away workers (and students!) fantasised about life, particularly about what they will do in their leisure time.

Research

Ditton studied bakery workers and found that they regularly passed the time in a series of fantasies.

Playing tricks and practical jokes Another way of passing the time is to play jokes on one another – this may be a way to ease the boredom, but it also serves to release tension by allowing disputes between individuals to be sorted out by practical jokes. Those who are most disliked are usually on the receiving end.

9.6 Industrial relations

British society is based upon the economic system of capitalism. In essence this means that industry and commerce are owned by groups of individuals who wish to make as much profit as is reasonable. In order to do this they must keep their costs, which include labour, as low as possible.

Employees, on the other hand, wish to earn as much money as possible in wages, and to have the shortest working hours combined with the best conditions. This may lead to conflict.

Forms of conflict

- **Strike** – where the trade union supports the workers.
- **Work to rule** – where the workers stick rigidly to the conditions and regulations of their employment. This often has a serious effect on production.
- **Refusal to work overtime** – where the workers only do the minimum hours required of them. This is only effective where there is a demand for overtime from the employers.
- **Sit in/work in** – in extreme situations workers sometimes occupy their factories. This is less common in Britain than in continental Europe.
- **Sabotage** – if striking is illegal and there is no other way to show their frustration and anger, workers may engage in sabotage.

Strike patterns

The numbers of strikes diminished in the 1980s and 1990s. This was the result of:
- laws which outlawed some forms of industrial action including mass picketing and unofficial strikes;

- unemployment, which meant that employers could threaten workers with redundancy or the sack if there was industrial action. This is particularly true of multi-national companies which could set up elsewhere;
- new forms of industrial relations, particularly those associated with Japanese companies, which led to discussion rather than confrontation.

Trade unions

Trade unions represent large sections of the workforce – over 10 million people in 1997. There have been three main changes in the past twenty years.
- An overall decline, during which period they have lost more than 2.5 million members.
- The majority of the decline has been from the loss of manual workers.
- There has been a very significant growth in the new members who are in white-collar work and who are female.

The professions

Today, approximately 14% of the British workforce is employed in some form of 'profession'. The professions are divided into:
- the older established ones, in areas such as the law and medicine;
- the newer (sometimes called the 'marginal') professions such as in teaching, nursing and social work.

This is the fastest growing area of employment in the British occupational structure, alongside the increase in white-collar workers.

The **older professions** developed in the nineteenth century, when a number of occupations managed to gain royal charters giving them monopolies over their area of work. Thus solicitors, barristers and doctors all gained the title and status of professions, and effectively pushed aside competing practitioners in their areas of employment, such as homeopaths, etc. The professionals were overwhelmingly self-employed, or at least employed in private practices, and they charged fees for their activities.

The modern development of the professions however, comes from the massive growth in the state in its various forms. In particular the NHS, social work, teaching and local government, all created new posts in areas of technical expertise.

The **new 'professionals'** differed from their established counterparts in that they were employed primarily by the state, or by local authorities, and in large bureaucratic organisations.

The result of this process of 'professionalisation' is that the new professions occupy a slightly ambiguous or 'marginal' position with regard to the older established professions, as the marginal professions are:
- worse paid;
- subject to the authority and the salary levels of the state or large organisations;
- have lower status.

Millerson in *The Qualifying Associations* has suggested that professions have the following characteristics that distinguish them from trade unions:
- A high level of skill involving theoretical knowledge. A mechanic may know how to repair a car while the engineer understands the theory behind the internal combustion engine;
- An extensive education. The highest educational standards and training are needed;
- The professional works for the general good of the public, not just to make money. The doctor is primarily a healer not a businessman or businesswoman;
- A code of ethics which is of a high standard and regulate the behaviour of members of the professions;
- Self-regulation – the profession has the legal right to control and discipline its own members;
- Control of entry. Nobody can join a profession unless accepted by that profession's own governing body which controls the standard of entrants.

Millerson paints a rather rosy picture of professions; however, they have not gone uncriticised.

Criticism has come from Johnson *(Professions and Power)* who has suggested that professions are really middle-class trade unions which are primarily concerned to look after their own interests and factors such as control of entry, do not primarily test competence, but instead restrict the inflow of new members, so keeping wages and fees high.

Professions have been so successful in attaining high fees and high status for their members that many other middle-class workers have tried to have their employment known as a profession. Some, such as teachers and nurses, have not really succeeded and are **marginal professions**; some, such as architects have succeeded. Groups such as estate agents are in the process of claiming professional status for themselves. The proof of success is the number of Millerson's characteristics which a group of workers can attain.

Summary

1 No particular tasks can be described as **work** or **leisure**. Instead the definition of what is work and leisure varies from one person/situation to another.

2 In pre-industrialised societies, work and leisure were inextricably mixed together. It was not until industrialisation came that the clear-cut division between time at work and time at leisure came about.

3 The occupational structure is the term used to describe the nature of all jobs that people do and the way the industry is organised.

4 The occupational structure of Britain has changed considerably over the past 50 years. Changes include: (a) a move away from manual to non-manual work; (b) a move towards service industries; (c) an increase in the number of women working; (d) a growth in unemployment.

5 Different groups of people have very different chances of being successful in the occupational structure. There are significant differences between manual and non-manual workers, males and females, whites and the ethnic minorities, and different age groups.

6 Britain is a post-industrial society, with most people working in service and financial industries, and the bulk of the population live in towns and are paid employees rather than working for themselves.

7 The division of labour is a characteristic of industrial and post-industrial societies. Each person performs only a small task in the making of articles and the providing of services. This has very many drawbacks, the main one being that people find work less satisfying.

8 Industrialisation has gone through a number of stages in the development of technology. The most important in terms of its social consequences is automation and, particularly, the development of the microchip.

9 Alienation is the state where people feel that their jobs and also their lives are pointless. It is influenced by the degree of freedom and power the person has in the workplace.

10 The number of strikes in Britain has declined greatly in the last twenty years – Britain has a very low level of strike action.

11 This has been due to government policy, the world depression and new working practices.

12 The main causes of strikes are wage demands and conditions of work, and they usually reflect a general dissatisfaction with work.

13 Employers and employees both form organisations to look after their interests.

14 Unions have been declining in size since 1981, although there has been a significant growth in white-collar unions.

15 Professional organisations look after the interests of the middle-class workers. They seem to be the most effective means of protecting personal interests.

16 In pre-industrial societies, work was different from industrial societies in the following ways. Work and social lives were unified; work roles were ascribed or inherited; work as measured by time did not exist; there was no separate place for work.

17 In Japan, for instance, the process of industrialisation was greatly helped by the government and it was carefully built up. The differing cultures of the two nations has left considerable differences in the organisation of work.

18 Work influences our lives outside in a considerable number of ways. It influences family life, the type of local community, leisure patterns and health.

Self-test questions

1 What are the most common characteristics of work?
2 List the trends that have been apparent in the British occupational structure throughout the twentieth century.
3 What are the differences between the 'core' and 'periphery' sectors of employment?
4 What further changes in society are likely to result from this 'second industrial revolution'?
5 Define the term 'alienation' and mention the elements associated with it.
6 What is meant by 'industrial conflict'?
7 Give a brief account of the four major differences between work in industrial and pre-industrial society.
8 Identify the main points of comparison between the process of industrialisation in Japan and that in Britain.
9 Give four ways in which work influences our lives outside work.

Chapter 10
Unemployment

10.1 The extent and types of unemployment

The extent of unemployment

There is considerable dispute about the extent of unemployment. Government figures are based on the numbers of people claiming benefit and suggest that there are less than 2.5 million unemployed.

The official statistics of the number of people unemployed have been criticised by those who claim they are inaccurate for various reasons.

The figures are exaggerated

Some sociologists point to the extent of the informal economy, and how significant numbers of people are engaged in cash-in-hand employment. Estimates suggest that anything up to 15% of the unemployed have other earnings, which are not declared.

Underestimate

The figures are based on benefit claimants able and willing to work. This excludes:

- women not eligible for benefits, but who may wish to work;
- those on government training schemes;
- all those under 18 years of age (many of whom are officially supposed to be on training schemes);
- those over 60.

Types of unemployment

There are two main types of unemployment:

- **Short-term** (or frictional) unemployment – which lasts up to six months approximately, before a person obtains another job. This is not regarded as particularly significant as an indicator of the economic 'health' of a country.
- **Long-term** (or structural) unemployment. This is unemployment which continues for a longer period than six months. If this is the most common form of unemployment, it suggests that the economy is in difficulties, as it means that there are no jobs available in the economy for those seeking work, or there are jobs but they require different skills from the ones that the unemployed have to offer.

10.2 Differences in unemployment between groups

Not all groups of employees are likely to face the same risks of unemployment. The following groups are more likely to face unemployment.

The young and old

The two age groups on the extremes of the working age range have higher than average unemployment levels: 28% of those under 24 have experienced at least one period of unemployment, for instance.

The **reasons** are (a) the older workers are usually the ones most likely to be laid off by employers, who prefer younger workers with experience; (b) the young are also likely to be unemployed, because there are few new vacancies and because they do not have the experience for the vacancies that do arise.

However, it appears that young people are likely to have shorter periods of unemployment than older workers who, once made unemployed, are likely to remain so.

Ethnic minorities

It appears that unemployment among the ethnic minorities is higher than among whites: 29% of people from these groups have experienced some period of unemployment compared to 15% of whites.

The **reasons** are: (a) discrimination by employers; (b) the fact that in general the ethnic minorities perform less well in the education system; and (c) the fact that they are disproportionately represented in the younger age groups, which have higher rates of unemployment anyway.

Manual workers and the less skilled

Of every 10 workers registered unemployed, seven are manual workers, although manual workers now account for less than 50% of the workforce. The less skilled manual workers have the highest rates of unemployment. For instances, 28% of semi and unskilled manual workers have experienced some period of unemployment, compared to only 7% of professional employees.

The **reasons** are: (a) that unskilled jobs are being lost to automation; (b) that the shift in jobs generally is away from manufacturing towards white-collar and service industry employment; (c) areas of production that use mainly unskilled workers are being shifted abroad where wages are much lower.

10.3 Unemployment by region

Not all areas of the country have the same levels of unemployment (see Fig.10.2).
- The highest levels of unemployment in mainland Britain are in the North with 18% followed by Wales and the North-West by 16%.
- The lowest rates of unemployment are in the South East (9.5%) and East Anglia (10%).

The reasons for variations in unemployment by region

- The industries with the greatest levels of decline, such as heavy engineering are mainly in the North;
- The new light industries have developed near to the affluent markets of the South East, around London;

Fig.10.1 Unemployment by region, 1994

- There has been an overall move towards the South with the increase in trading with the countries of the European Union.
- The service industries grow to serve affluent areas. Their presence creates more jobs and so the area becomes more affluent which leads to the development of more service industries. This is happening in the South East and the reverse is happening in the North.

10.4 The causes of unemployment

- A change from the manufacturing industry to service industries. There has been a massive loss of jobs in the British manufacturing industry in the last twenty-five years – with over 3 million jobs disappearing. The new manufacturing industries (sometimes called 'sunrise industries'), which are involved in electronics, need far fewer employees.

  There has been a compensating increase in service jobs, but the people employed in this sector are not the same as those who are being made unemployed from the manufacturing sector.

- There has been no real overall increase in full-time employment since 1980 (although there has been an increase in part-time work). At the same time, there is a constant inflow of new, young workers, seeking work.
- Automation has been introduced into factories and increasingly into offices. In factories it has been used mainly to replace semi-skilled workers in such jobs as car assembly-line production. In offices it is being used to replace routine clerical work, such as recording accounts and sending out bills. Increasingly, microchip technology is allowing more skilled work to be done by machine.
- Foreign competition in manufactured goods has made considerable in-roads into traditional British markets, both in Britain itself and abroad. This has had the effect of making some British companies go out of business; others have laid off workers in order to reduce labour costs; and yet others have shifted their manufacturing operations to countries where wage rates are considerably lower.

10.5 The implications of unemployment for society and individuals

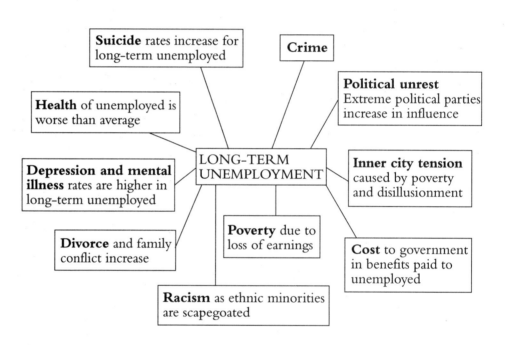

Fig.10.2 Implications of long-term unemployment

10.6 The experience of unemployment

The effects of unemployment are felt differently by different groups in society. Differences are noticeable between (a) the young; (b) the middle-aged and the over 55s; (c) women.

The young

There has been some disagreement over how the young experience unemployment.

- Young people have no experience of work and do not see their **identity** in terms of their jobs as older people do.

- They do not have any major financial responsibilities, such as a family and mortgage, etc. Unemployment need not be as serious a problem to them as to the middle aged and older groups. They receive social security and help from the wider family.
- It seems that the young are caught in a period of *drift* between childhood and adulthood (as marked by full-time employment). There is a greater stress on the values and importance of the youth culture.
- There is relatively little stigma attached to being unemployed as half of all young people are in this situation.
- Spare time is spent with friends from school who are also unemployed.

Research

Simon Frith has argued that inner city youth have adapted themselves quite well to this period of unemployment and have developed various means of 'getting by', with short bouts of irregular employment and some petty theft, etc. Unemployed youth are actually better off than when they were at school, as they receive social security. He sees a definite development of a new style of youth culture to cope with long-term unemployment.

A more **pessimistic** view of youth unemployment comes from Paul Willis in his research on unemployment in the Midlands. Willis argues that it is a normal part of a person's development in Britain to: (a) get a job, (b) with the earnings buy smart clothes and consumer goods, such as a car, (c) leave home, and (d) probably get married. Unemployment prevents many of these stages happening. Young people are stuck at home with little prospect of escape. This causes considerable tension.

According to Willis, the identities that older people gain through their jobs, and to a lesser extent through the things they own, are gained entirely through possession of status goods among the young. It is important to have a motorbike or a car, the right clothing, to be able to afford to pay for drinks in pubs, etc. Unable to afford these things, the young person loses his or her identity. Willis argues that this has, for example, led girls to become pregnant just to get a council flat.

Willis also points out that young people congregate in city centres where they can see and be seen. Their large numbers and high visibility, due to their styles of dress, make them a menace for the police who see them as potential threats to law and order. There develops therefore greater dislike and tension.

Middle age and unemployment

- The identity of the middle-aged is closely bound up with their jobs. When asked 'what are you?', the reply is 'I am a teacher/nurse', etc. Loss of employment means partial loss of identity.
- It also brings financial problems, with payment of bills, such as gas, electricity, instalments on the consumer durables, etc, becoming very difficult. Gradually the luxuries are taken away and there is a shift to essentials.
- Apart from the discomfort this brings, it also means that the social life and the friends that went with it have to be abandoned. There is therefore a withdrawal from contact. This leads to a degree of loneliness.
- The reasons for unemployment are generally seen as personal, in that the unemployed persons ask what is wrong with them that they were made unemployed. This problem becomes worse as the period of unemployment lengthens. Indeed, it has been pointed out that the unemployed are more likely to become mentally ill and be depressed than the employed.
- The unemployed are likely to feel bored, useless and frustrated.
- Within the family, the presence of the depressed and frustrated father/mother at home all day can lead to family tension.

Women and unemployment

- Official statistics indicate that women have not been as badly hit by unemployment as men. There are a number of reasons for this: (i) women are more likely to be in part-time work (which men do not want); (ii) they are likely to be in low-pay work anyway, so employers are happy to keep them on; (iii) they are employed mainly in the service industries which have not had such a decline in employment.

- However, it is known that the unemployment statistics do not tell the full story and the number of women recorded as unemployed is below the true figure (see Unit 10.1).
- The effects upon women are not so very different from those on men although there is a ready-made and socially acceptable role for unemployed women, as mothers and housewives which is not open to men.
- However, as women go to work for two reasons – (i) because the money is needed in the home, and (ii) to make some form of social contact outside the home – the effects on them are generally just as severe as on men.
- There is considerable loss of income to the family and therefore financial problems arise, even when the husband is still working. This can lead to a similar pattern of social withdrawal by a husband and wife from their circle of friends and a change in leisure patterns.
- The wife feels a loss of independence and must rely on her husband's salary.
- The traditional view of the female worker as someone who goes out to work for pin money fails to take into account single women, lone parents, divorcees and those who are supporting elderly relatives. These are often in the lowest earning categories anyway.

Research

Angela Coyle in *Redundant Women* studied the effects of unemployment on two groups of women laid off in the early 1890s from the garments industry in Yorkshire. She concluded that unemployment was a particularly harsh blow for these women as they has seen their job as an escape from the routine of family. The 'compensation' of the role of mother and housewife was not true for them.

Summary

1 There is some dispute over the true extent of unemployment. The official figures exclude certain categories of person.

2 In 1986 there were approximately 3 million unemployed in Britain. This was the highest figure ever.

3 There are two types of unemployment: short-term and long-term. Long-term has more social consequences.

4 Certain groups are more likely to be unemployed than others. In particular, the young and older workers, the ethnic minorities and the lower skilled.

5 Unemployment rates are much higher in the north of Britain than the South.

6 Unemployment is caused not by personal defects in the unemployed, but mainly by automation and by foreign competition. The government's attitude to unemployment is also crucial.

7 There are a number of possible consequences for British society. This could include the weakening of trade unions' and employees' rights; a lowering of wages; a growing gap between the lives of the rich and the poor; an increase in crime and the growth of politically extreme groups.

8 Unemployment hits different groups in the population in different ways. Older people may find it affects their identities more, while younger people may be able to cope better. However, it has been argued that the effects are just as bad on young people.

9 Women appear to suffer just as much as men from the consequences of unemployment.

Self-test questions

1   Which groups are more likely to suffer unemployment than others?
2   In general, what are the causes of unemployment?
3   Give a brief summary of the effects of unemployment for British society.
4   How are the middle-aged affected by unemployment?
5   In what ways are women likely to be affected by unemployment?

Chapter 11
Population

11.1 What is demography?

The study of population, more correctly known as **demography**, concentrates on studying changes in:

1. The size of the population;
2. The proportions in each age group;
3. The geographical distribution of the population;
4. The balance of the sexes;

11.2 The importance of demography

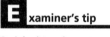

The demographic information collected is extremely useful, as it gives the government (a) a detailed picture of the British population at any one time; (b) a forecast of likely trends in the future. This allows the government to plan future policies.

Here are just four examples of the use of demographic information.

Education

It is important to know the numbers of children attending school in the future, so that schools can be expanded or closed, new teachers trained or excess teachers offered early retirement. It is also important to know in which area of the country they are likely to live, so that schools can be located in the right areas: it is no good building schools in Scotland if the growth of population is in the south-east of England! If the government knows the number of children born in a particular year, then it also knows that five years later those children will enter primary school and eleven years later will enter secondary school.

Health

Knowledge of the age of the population and where they live now and in the future, can help decide: (a) the numbers of doctors and nurses needed; (b) the number and location of hospitals; and (c) the type of health care needed. For example, a young population would need a lot of maternity services, as they would be likely to have many babies; an ageing population would need geriatric hospitals, specially adapted to care for the needs of old people.

Housing and town planning

Long-term trends can be predicted so that just the right number of houses of the right type, in the right place, can be built, with appropriate roads and services.

Social services

Knowing the trends in the size and age of the population allows the correct social services to be provided. For example, the current growth in the numbers of old people means that more money is needed for pensions and welfare services for the old.

11.3 Population size

The population of Britain rose steadily this century until 1961 but then it has hardly grown at all. This is illustrated in Fig.11.1

Fig.11.1 The population of the UK, 1961–1995
(Source: *Social Trends 27*, 1997)

				Thousands
1961	1971	1981	1991	1995
52,807	55,928	56,352	57,808	58,606

The size of the population at any one time is the result of three causes:
1. The number of births;
2. The number of deaths;
3. The movement of people into, or out of, a country.

Changes in the number of births

The **(crude) birthrate** is the number of live births each year for every 1000 people in the population and is the measure usually employed by sociologists when they discuss changes in the size of population. The higher the birthrate the more children are being born in a particular year.

Sometimes sociologists use the term the **fertility rate**, which refers to the number of children born for every 1000 women of childbearing age each year. This is more accurate as it relates births to the proportion of the population who could have children.

In the twentieth century, there has been an overall fall in the birthrate and this has accelerated sharply since 1967. Today the figure is 1.7 million. However, it has not been a constant decline as there have been three periods when the birthrate has risen: (a) 1919–21; (b) 1945–48; and (c) 1957–66.

Factors affecting the number of births

- Knowledge of and use of contraceptives. There has been an increasing use of methods of birth control throughout this century.
- The financial costs and benefits of having children. If children are useful, then it is likely that most people will try to have large families. At present children are seen as a burden, at least in economic terms.
- Cultural stress on the correct number of children. Society's view of a *normal* size of family varies over time and people will tend to conform to the average.
- Women's attitude to childbearing. Women are increasingly rejecting the idea that they should spend most of their lives having children.
- The patterns of births (and deaths) are illustrated in Fig.11.2.

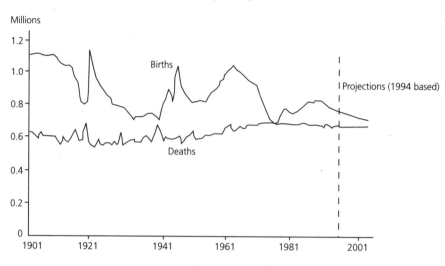

Fig.11.2 Birth and death rates in the UK, 1901–2001
(Source: *Social Trends 27*, 1997)

A description and explanation of the changes in the twentieth century

Before the beginning of the Industrial Revolution (1760), the British population grew very quickly. The improvements brought by industrialisation led to a massive reduction in the death rates, while the high birth rate continued. This led to a population explosion which continued until the turn of the century.

From the turn of the century until 1919, the birthrate was falling rapidly. This was because:

- Children had become an economic burden. This had happened as a result of the introduction of compulsory schooling in 1870, and the increasingly strict enforcement of it, which prevented children going out to work at 14. In previous times, the children's financial contribution to working-class households had been considerable. This was also true for the better-off middle class, who found that the wages demanded by servants (and in particular nannies), were too high for them. The result was that they had to look after their own children and so restricted the size of families.

- Throughout most of this period, there were serious problems in the British economy, with low wages and high unemployment, so people were reluctant to have large families.

- The numbers of children dying at or near birth had fallen dramatically in the 50 years prior to this period, therefore there was no need to have a large number of children in order to ensure that a few survived.

- The beginnings of pension schemes were developed in this period, so people realised that it was no longer necessary to have large families to ensure there would be someone to care for them when they were old.

- The restriction of family size was only possible because of the growing awareness of methods of birth control – at first among the middle class and later among the working class. The average family in this period was about 3.4 children.

From 1919 to the early 1920s, the birthrate rose steeply because of the return of soldiers after the First World War and their desire to start families.

From the early 1920s to the mid-1940s, the birthrate continued to decline because:

- Mass unemployment and low wages meant that people could not afford to have children.

- There was a growing belief in the virtues of small families, particularly among the middle class. This was linked to a change in attitudes to children as people began to believe that children needed love and affection.

- The use of contraceptives was gaining favour rapidly among the middle class. The average family size in this period was about 2.5 children.

From 1945 to 1948, the birth rate rose steeply once again because of the return of soldiers at the end of the Second World War and their desire to start families.

From the late 1940s to the late 1950s, the birthrate continued its overall decline because:

- There was by now widespread use of contraceptives among all social classes.
- There was a strong emphasis on having fewer children and giving them far higher standards of care and affection than in the pre-war period.
- Married couples were more interested in having a high standard of living than having large families. The average family size in this period was about 2.4 children.

From the late 1950s to the mid-1960s, the birthrate rose because:

- People were marrying younger and having children earlier.
- This was a period of considerable affluence and people felt that they could have both a larger family and high standard of living.
- The children born in the 'baby boom' after the Second World War were having their children. The average family size in this period was about 2.7 children.

From the mid-1960s until the present, the birth rate has declined, apart from a brief rise in the late 1970s, because:

- There has been a change in the role of women in society. They are less likely to accept the role of 'housewife' and more likely to demand the right to a career of their own. This means that they wish to limit the number of children they have (ideally to two) and to have them when they are in their mid- to late twenties.
- The 'pill' is widely used and highly reliable as a contraceptive, although a scare over the safety of the pill in the late 1970s led to women refusing to use it and a rise in the number of births.
- The *ideal* family in British culture is now regarded as husband/wife and two children, with great affection and care lavished on the children. The average family size is now 1.7 children.

Social class and fertility

Historically, the poorer groups in society have always had larger families as a form of insurance against old age, and as a means of increasing the breadwinners in he family. The richer groups had less need for children and so tended to have smaller families. By the turn of the century, the middle class had begun to restrict the size of their families using contraceptive devices, because of the economic factors described above. The working class eventually followed the lead of the middle class about twenty years later. This time-lag was caused by: (a) ignorance of contraception; (b) cultural patterns that emphasised the importance of large families; (c) the security that a large family provided. Over the twentieth century, the patterns of contraceptive use and family sizes of the middle and working classes have become increasingly similar.

Changes in the number of deaths

The **death (or mortality) rate** is the number of deaths for every 1000 people in the population.

The patterns of death can be seen in Fig.11.3.

Fig.11.3 Death rates

Year	1901	1921	1931	1951	1961	1971	1981	1991	1995
Deaths per 1000 of the population	17.1	12.4	12.5	12.6	12.0	11.6	11.8	11.2	11.0

Overall the death rate declined throughout the twentieth century, although there has been no fall in the last ten years. It rose sharply during the two world wars, 1914–18 and 1939–45.

The decline in the death rate has been explained by the following facts:

- **Improvements in public hygiene and sanitation** Modern sewage and refuse collection systems have drastically improved the standards of public cleanliness, which has prevented many of the killer diseases such as typhoid and cholera.
- **Advances in medicine** Medical advances, such as vaccinations against diseases, and improvements in medical care generally.

● **Higher standards of living** This is probably the most important influence on the falling death rate. As people have generally become better off, so their diets, type of food and housing conditions have improved. The result is a much healthier population.

The infant mortality rate A most important element in the overall decline in the death rate has been the decline in the infant mortality rate, which is the number of deaths of infants under one-year-old for every 1000 babies born alive.

The infant mortality rate has been dropping sharply for the whole of the twentieth century, as can be seen in Fig.11.4.

Fig.11.4   The infant mortality rate

Year	1891	1921	1951	1971	1981	1995
Infant deaths for every 1000 live births	153	72	30	17	10	9.7

Factors affecting the infant mortality rate (which forms part of the death rate) are the same as for the death rate in general. However, the following additional points are important:

● The NHS has provided an increasingly higher standard of health service for childbirth. These include highly trained midwives and clinics for advice and health care before and after the birth. These are free of course. In countries where these facilities are only for the better off, as they have to be paid for, the mortality rate is much higher, e.g. in Italy the infant mortality rate is 25, compared to our 10.

● Boys have a higher mortality rate than girls.

● Class differences are still very noticeable, with the infant mortality rate for children of the poorest groups in society twice as high as those of the upper middle class. Working-class mothers are also more likely to give birth to premature (and therefore weaker) babies. The causes of these class differences lie in lower standards of care, poorer diets and greater risks of accidents.

● Differences in ethnic groups exist, with children of Bangladeshi origin having higher mortality rates for instance.

11.4 Changes in migration

Immigration means the movement of people into a particular place or country. **Emigration** means the movement of people out of a particular place or country. Both words are based on the term *migration* which, in demography, means the movement of people.

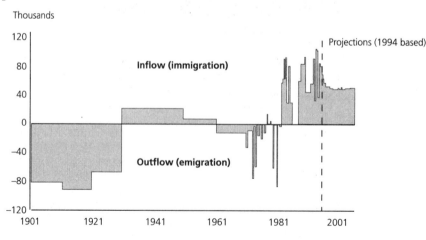

Fig.11.5 Numbers of people migrating to and from the UK, 1901–2001
(Source: *Social Trends 27*, 1997)

Britain has had a constant flow of emigration and immigration throughout its history. Fig.11.5 illustrates the general pattern of migration in the twentieth century. As you can see in only three periods, 1931–51, 1955–62 and the 1980s–90s has immigration been greater than emigration.

Emigration

Throughout the nineteenth century and right up to 1930, the British Empire provided a place for those British people who wished to emigrate. The total number of people who emigrated from Britain in the 100 years up to 1930 totalled about 20 million people. During the 1950s and early 1960s, the levels of emigration were fairly low because of the number of jobs available in Britain. By the 1970s the lack of jobs in Britain had led to a significant increase in emigration. The level of emigration depends upon the availability of work in Britain compared to abroad and whether other countries are willing to accept our emigrants.

Immigration

The pattern of immigration to Britain resembles a series of waves. Usually the high point of a particular wave of immigrants reflects serious economic or political problems in the home country of emigrants.

In the nineteenth century, Irish immigrants settled into Britain as a result of the dreadful economic conditions in Ireland. Today, the single largest group of immigrants are still those from the Irish Republic. Jewish refugees also came to escape persecution; they were still doing so in the 1930s to escape the Nazis.

In the early 1950s and 1960s, Commonwealth immigrants were recruited to come to Britain to fill job vacancies. In all, 620 000 immigrants came from Asian and Caribbean countries between 1955 and 1967. Since then there has been a considerable decline in the numbers of immigrants.

Immigration in the 1990s was formed from two main sources:

- marriage;
- applications for asylum.

Marriage
About half of those who come to live in Britain are the wives of migrants already settled here. These are generally marriages between Asians.

Applications for asylum
In 1995 there were 44 000 applications for asylum, an increase of 30% over 1994. The majority of these were from Nigeria, followed by Somalia. However, only a small proportion are granted refugee status – in 1995 it was just under 2000. The majority of those who obtained refugee status were from Iraq, Iran and the former Yugoslavia.

11.5 The gender balance

There are more males, up to the age of 50 than females; there are then more females then males. This is partly because, although more males are born than females, they are more likely to die through sickness and injury.

Fig.11.6. illustrates the proportions of males and females, by age

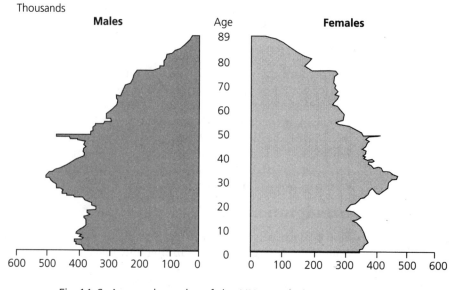

Fig.11.6 Age and gender of the UK population, 1995
(Source: *Social Trends 27*, 1997)

11.6 Changes in population

People live longer and healthier lives. In 1901, the average life expectancy (the typical length of life) at birth was about 48 for men and 52 for women. Today a person in their thirties can expect to live to 79 if a woman, and 76 if a man. However, someone of retiring age can reasonably expect to live into his or her late seventies.

In 1902 only 6.2% of the population was over 65; today the figure is 18% comprising 10 million people in all. People live longer because of better housing conditions, healthier diets and higher standards of medical care (all the same reasons that the death rate has declined).

Women are more likely to live longer than men and the vast majority of those over 75 years of age are women. Women live longer because:

- They are less likely to work in dangerous occupations such as mining or construction.
- Most combatants in wars are males.
- Men are more likely to smoke and drink heavily then women.
- A greater proportion of young men are likely to be killed in motorcycle and car accidents.

Consequences of an ageing population

The consequences of an ageing population can be divided into two:
- consequences for society;
- consequences for individuals.

Consequences for society
- The most important consequence is an increase in the **burden of dependency** – this means the proportion of the population who are two young or old to work compared to those of working age. The proportion of dependent people is currently very high at about 65%. This means that 35% of the population have to support the remaining 65%. This can mean higher levels of taxation.
- The elderly need more money spent on medical care than younger groups and therefore more has to be spent on geriatric wards in hospitals, on old people's homes and on increased medical care at home.
- There needs to be an increase in social services for the elderly.
- Government expenditure on the elderly in pensions and rent and council tax rebates (provided by local government) must increase.

Consequences for individuals
- As individuals grow older and receive only their pensions they experience poverty.
- Families must care for the elderly if they are unable to cope. This places tremendous pressure on married daughters (on whom the burden usually falls) who must look after their own families plus their ageing parents. Often this means giving up paid employment.
- As friends and partners die, the elderly may become increasingly isolated and lonely. This is particularly true for women, who generally live longer then men.

11.7 Consequences of population changes

An **increase** in population can lead to a number of problems, including the following:
- Pressure on health services as more medical staff are needed.
- Education – more teachers are needed and more schools need to be built.
- Employment – there is an ever-increasing demand for jobs and unless the economy can generate them a rise in unemployment takes place, with all the social problems related to it.
- Housing – the numbers of houses must be constantly increased just to cope with the demand. At the same time, older houses may become unfit to live in and need to be replaced or modernised.
- Environment – (a) the need for new houses, roads and services creates pressure on the countryside and developers will want to use the **green belt** (land set aside from building around cities in order to keep some countryside) and so **urban sprawl** (endless housing developments that link one town to another) may develop; (b) pollution increases with the increase in industry and waste disposal.

A **decrease** in the population can also lead to problems:
- Ageing – normally a decreasing or stable population (like Britain today) goes hand in hand with an ageing population. The problems associated with an ageing population are discussed in Unit 7.5.
- Lack of youthful ideas – there is likely to be a decline in new ideas and society will suffer from the lack of young, dynamic people.
- Decline in consumer demand – the decline in the number of people will mean a decline in the demand for consumer goods which could lead to unemployment.
- Education – schools will have to close and teachers be made redundant.

11.8 Changes in the distribution of the population in Britain

The geographical distribution of the population refers to the way that the population is distributed in: different areas of Britain, and in cities or the countryside.

Areas

- There has been a shift in the population away from living in the north of England, Wales and Scotland to living in the south of England.
- The main growth area of Britain is the South East, particularly East Anglia.

Cities or countryside?

- Throughout the 100 years before 1950 there was a move away from the countryside to the towns and cities. This was known as **urbanisation**.
- Since the 1950s, there has been a move away from living in city centres, to living in the suburbs. This is known as **suburbanisation**.
- Since the 1950s there has also been a shift towards living in **new towns,** such as Milton Keynes. (See Chapter 12 for a full discussion.)

Summary

1 Demography is the study of population patterns and changes.

2 It is important as it can help us to plan ahead.

3 Information on the population is found in the census and the registration of births, marriages and deaths.

4 The size of the population is determined by the numbers of (a) births, (b) deaths and (c) the numbers of people who move in or out of the country.

5 The birthrate is the number of babies born for every 1000 people in the population.

6 The birthrate has been falling throughout most of the twentieth century except for periods after the two world wars and from the late 1950s to the mid-1960s.

7 The fall in the birthrate is largely due to the increasing use of contraception, motivated by changing attitudes of women to their role and the increased costs of having children.

8 The death rate is the number of deaths for every 1000 people in the population.

9 The death rate fell in the early part of the twentieth century, but has been steady for a number of years.

10 The infant mortality rate is the number of babies that die under one-year-old for every 1000 babies born alive.

11 The infant mortality rate has been falling throughout the twentieth century.

12 There are increasing numbers of elderly people in Britain as life expectancy increases.

13 The increase in the elderly will cause a number of problems for society in providing adequate social services for them and for individuals (usually the daughters) who will have to sacrifice part of their own lives to care for them. There may also be the problems of loneliness and poverty for the aged.

14 People are moving out of the cities to the suburbs and smaller towns.

15 World population is growing rapidly and this is leading to desperate problems of poverty and starvation.

Self-test questions

1 What does the term 'demography' mean?
2 Why is all this demographic information of such importance to the government?
3 What factors affect the birthrate at any time?
4 What factors have influenced the changes in the death rate?
5 What three factors influence the size of the population?
6 What does the term 'an ageing population' mean?
7 What problems does it cause?
8 Why do women live longer then men?
9 Describe the main patterns of immigration and emigration during the twentieth century.

Chapter 12
Urbanisation and community

12.1 Urbanisation and industrialisation

In 1801, about 17% of the population of Britain lived in towns, by 1851 it had increased to 50% and 100 years later in 1951, it had reached its peak of 81%. Since about 1960, however, there has been a change with people moving out of the big cities, and about 78% of the population now live in large towns and cities.

- The process whereby people move into cities from the countryside is known as **urbanisation**. Urbanisation occurred at its most rapid pace in Britain in the nineteenth century.
- The process, whereby people move into cities from the countryside is known as **de-urbanisation**. This is now happening in Britain.

Urbanisation

There is a very close link between the processes of urbanisation and de-urbanisation and industrialisation. Links between urbanisation and industrialisation include:

- The changes in agriculture, which include:
  - the **enclosure movement**, in which the peasants were driven off the land.
  - the introduction of new agricultural machinery, which mean that far fewer workers were needed in agriculture.
- Industrialisation itself, which:
  - switched manufacture away from isolated communities, to towns;
  - introduced production by machine on a large scale, which meant that a large number of workers were needed in the factories.
- The conditions of the workers in the towns were dreadful. Housing was of extremely poor quality. Houses were built in terraces, often also back to back.
- The existence of large centres of population attracted traders and so shops developed on a large scale.
- The growth in complexity of industry meant that administrative services were needed and this led to the development of offices, separate from factories.
- As the towns developed, various areas became dominated by different social classes. The better areas of the town were taken by the middle class and the rich, while the workers lived next to the factories.

De-urbanisation

During the twentieth century, changes have taken place that led to a gradual withdrawal of people from the cities. This became a 'flight from the cities' from the 1970s onwards.

- The development of means of transport meant that people did not have to live next door to their workplace. At first it was mainly public transport and then later came the development and increasing ownership of private cars.
- The result of the development of transport was that the middle class moved out to the suburbs, or to 'commuter' towns near to the city, and would travel in to work. This development first took place in the 1930s.
- This linked with the growth of large-scale housing schemes, both private (such as Stevenage in Hertfordshire) and public (such as West Derby in Liverpool).
- Gradually the new developments and the transport links connected the large cities with surrounding towns. This led to a process of **metropolitanisation**, in which large cities swallowed up smaller towns around them.
- Local authorities in the 1950s engaged in massive redevelopments of the slum areas of the inner cities and moved much of the population out into large council estates (for example Dagenham in London). In the 1960s, instead of large estates, people were moved to 'New Towns', such as Basildon in Essex.
- Industry began to move out of the cities:
  - rates were lower and so was the price of land;
  - better communications, such as motorways and fast rail links, meant that products could be quickly transported to the centres of population;
  - this caused more people to move out of towns and cities.
- The inner city districts have become problem areas, as the working-class community has disappeared.

12.2 Community and association

Sociologists have been interested in the way that the move from a rural-based society to an urban-based one has altered the way people act towards each other.

The idea that the move from living in a rural situation to living in urban areas has influenced the nature of social life has been most thoroughly explored by (a) Tonnies and (b) Durkheim, both of whom were writing about one hundred years ago when the process of urbanisation had just completed its most rapid phase.

Tonnies distinguished between two types of society: **Gemeinschaft** (community) and **Gesellschaft** (association). Sociologists use either the English or German words. Durkheim agreed with this distinction, using the terms **mechanical** (in Tonnies' terms **community**) and **organic** (in Tonnie's terms **association**).

What both writers were pointing out was that there are two fundamentally different ways in which people can organise their social life. One way stresses close, personal ties between people, the other, impersonal, formal relationships. They argue that these different forms of social networks are directly related to rural and urban society.

Community (mechanical society – found in rural areas)

- Relationships are very close between people and are based on personal acquaintance between them. This form of relationship is known as **primary relationship**.
- People living in rural areas feel that they have interests in common and are united by these feelings.
- In rural society the social network is composed of fewer people, who are close-knit.
- People tend to play many different roles (e.g. father, shopkeeper, parish councillor, etc).
- These roles sometimes come into conflict with each other, e.g. as a parish councillor, advising on parking restrictions and as a shopkeeper who wants cars to be able to park outside his or her shop.
- A simple economy, usually based on agriculture.
- Little division of labour; workers cover a whole range of tasks, e.g. farm labourers.
- Mechanical society – most people are very alike in attitudes and behaviour.

- Ascribed status – the status of parents influences how people treat you.
- Locals – rural society is dominated by people who are born and bred there and reflect certain local values.

Association (organic society – found in urban areas)

- Relationships are generally impersonal and rather formal. It is rare that people are personally acquainted. Relationships tend to be rather shallow and transient. This form of social relationship is known as **secondary**.
- People living in urban areas feel little in common.
- The social network is large and dispersed. So urban dwellers meet many different people in daily life.
- People play fewer **multiple roles**, that is they generally play one role to one group of people, e.g. shopkeeper to his or her customers, but drinking companion in the pub with a different group of people.
- There is little role conflict because of the point above.
- The economy is complex, based on commerce, industry and personal services.
- Complex division of labour, with most people engaged in a specific task in a wide range of occupations.
- Organic society, with a great variety of types of people held together by mutual need.
- Achieved status – you are treated according to your personal merits, heavily influenced by your occupation and income.
- Cosmopolitans – the place is dominated by people who only stay for a short time and who have little commitment to that specific town.

Reasons for differences

Another sociologist, Wirth, has suggested three major differences between rural and urban societies which help to explain the differences between the community life in these areas.

Size

Towns and cities cover a large geographical area, unlike villages. This has many consequences, including the need for public transport and wide roads and the division of the town into areas often divided along class or race lines. Also the sheer size of the population prevents people from knowing each other.

Density of population

Towns have far more people per hectare than do rural areas. This concentration of people causes problems such as housing shortages and heavy traffic, as well as pollution. It also causes traders to provide many services, so there are shops, pubs, restaurants, etc.

Social heterogeneity

This means that people from many different backgrounds, divided for instances by race, class and education, all live together. This creates tensions in some cases as the groups may be antagonistic to each other. It also accounts for the **cosmopolitan** nature of social life in cities, that is the exhilarating mixture of ideas and people that makes cities so lively.

Community in the city: association in the village

The idea that rural and urban life are so different from each other has been strongly criticised by a number of sociologists. Studies of city and village life have not shown there to be such clear-cut differences between the social relationships.

Research

- Pahl in *Patterns of Urban Life* studied Swansea and found that it was in fact divided into quite clear **neighbourhoods**. This formed separate communities, each having an individual identity in which the people exhibited a pattern of social relationships very similar to Tonnies' **community** – which it has been claimed could only be found in rural areas. Pahl explains that communities exist in Swansea because it grew in the nineteenth century as a tinplating town, attracting people from the surrounding rural areas to live and work. These new arrivals settled in specific neighbourhoods in the town depending upon their origins and associated themselves with that neighbourhood. The following generations retained these individual communities.

- Young and Willmott in *Family and Kinship in East London* conducted an in-depth study of East London in the early 1950s. They found a strong community in the city with strong family ties and a sense of identity grounded in the locality and web of social relationships. When the area was redeveloped and many families were moved to new housing estates, it took a number of years for a new sense of community to develop among those re-housed.
- In another study *(Urbs in Rure)* Pahl studied 'commuter villages' in Hertfordshire on the fringe of the London commuting area. He found that village life was not as described in the idea of 'community'. There were deep divisions among those who lived in villages. So the description of village life painted by researchers such as Tonnies was incorrect.
- Raymond Williams in *The Country and the City* took an historical perspective and found that life in the medieval village, so often painted as idyllic, was just the opposite. The peasantry shared one important condition – they were exploited and oppressed by the landlords. He describes their situation as the **mutuality of the oppressed**.

Conclusion

The point to draw from these studies is not the *place* in which a group of people live that necessarily determines their relationships, but other things such as **social class, affluence** and **ethnicity**, for example.

12.3 Housing zones

In the 1920s and 1930s sociologists of the University of Chicago studied the housing and social patterns of the city. The results of the studies of Shaw and McKay suggested that levels of crime and of social problems in general were different in various parts of the city. They also noticed that people of similar social class and racial backgrounds settled in the same area of the city

As a result of these observations, Burgess developed a theory (based on Chicago) that there were five **concentric zones** (that is zones in the shape of rings) in cities, as illustrated in Fig.12.1.

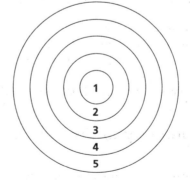

Fig.12.1 The concentric zone model

Zone 1 is the inner business district with the shops, civic buildings and commercial enterprises.

Zone 2 is the older residential area of large, once imposing houses. These were originally owned by affluent tradesmen, but they had long since moved away. The houses had fallen into disrepair, were divided and rented out to poorer people; in particular newly arrived immigrants, and those with irregular sources of income.

Zone 3 has a stable population of respectable working-class people, with a sense of community.

Zone 4 is lived in by the middle class and is the typical suburban area.

Zone 5 is the wealthy district in which the rich live in expensive houses with large gardens.

These zones were called **natural areas** by Chicago sociologists as they were not deliberately created, but arose from the social patterns of migration.

Burgess's explanation, based upon the history of Chicago, for the pattern of concentric zones forming natural areas, was in terms of the waves of immigration that occur in cities as they grow. He argued that initially the rich people lived in exclusive areas in the inner cities and the poorer groups lived further out. Gradually the richer people moved further out, living the inner city properties empty. The houses were too expensive for the lower class groups to maintain, and they were prepared to let out rooms within the houses. When new poor immigrants moved into the city they rented properties in this increasingly run-down area. The more successful immigrants eventually moved out, and as they did so the next wave of immigrants arrived to take lodgings in the inner city areas. The history of the city was one of wave after wave of immigration with the few successful immigrants moving out. As all this took place in Zone 2, it was called the **zone of transition**.

The constant changing of the population in the zone of transition and the poverty of the people led to numerous social problems such as delinquency, mental illness, prostitution and alcoholism. In Britain research has indicated that inner city areas do indeed have many more social problems than outer areas.

Research

Rex and Moore *(Race, Community and Conflict)*, studied **Sparkbrook**, an inner city area of Birmingham. They found that the description of the zone of transition was appropriate. The area consisted of large dilapidated houses which were divided into rented accommodation. As this was one of the few areas in Birmingham in which immigrants could find and afford lodgings, it had a very high proportion of black and Irish families. These co-existed uneasily together and with the poorer local families who were unable to move out. They found that conflict over housing was one of the main reasons for different groups coming into conflict with each other and this prevented integration.

Criticism of this **concentric zone** pattern of city development has been on the grounds that it is true only for certain cities. In Britain a number of other factors have influenced the way that zones have developed.

- Council overspill estates have been built at a considerable distance from the city centre; these are inhabited by working-class people.
- In recent years middle-class people have been moving back into certain areas in the centre of big cities; for example, into the London dockland region. This is the opposite of the trends described by the Chicago sociologists. It is called **gentrification**.

12.4 Patterns of life

Earlier we saw that one of the characteristics of the city is **social heterogeneity**, which means that there is a considerable number of different styles of life and groups within cities.

To illustrate this we can look at the different styles of life to be found in:

- the inner city,
- the suburbs.

The inner city

The diversity of the inner cities

The inner city areas have undergone major changes as the population has moved out to the suburbs, overspill estates and new towns. Inner cities now have a wide variety of groups living there, replacing the traditional working class. Gans has suggested that the following groups can be found in inner city areas:

- Bohemians: students and ex-students clinging to the student way of life. These move into the lower city area for the low rents and the nearness to cultural life;
- The ethnic minorities: these move here in the first place because it is the only area where they can find accommodation and because it is near to the available employment;
- The deprived and the poor; usually these people who are unable to work and have nowhere to go. They include the physically and mentally ill, tramps, the long-term unemployed;
- The trapped: these are people who came before the decline of the inner city, but because of investments in a house or shop or local loyalty, or because they have no alternative, remain in the inner city. These are the elderly and the poor generally.

Problems of the inner cities

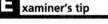
It can be seen then that to talk about the inner cities as if they contained one population would be wrong. However, the inner cities do have considerably greater problems than the rest of Britain.

A sociological study of the inner cities reported that they had:

- 7% of the population but 14% of the unskilled workers;
- considerable racial tension;
- at least twice the national rate of unemployment;
- up to ten times the proportion of people living below the supplementary benefit line;
- four times the average number of overcrowded households;
- twice the national average of one-parent families;
- half the national rate of car ownership;

It should also be added that the inner city crime rate is the highest of any area in the country.

The inner city riots

In 1981 and 1985 there were serious disturbances in inner city areas in Bristol, London, Manchester and Liverpool.

The reasons why the riots exploded in each specific case was different. For instance, in Southall, London in 1981 it was a battle between white skinheads and Asians who were defending their area, as they saw it, from racist attacks by the skinheads. In 1985 in Brixton it was young West Indians (and some whites) who felt they were being pressured too greatly by the police. However, there are certain underlying causes that create conditions and tensions leading to rioting:

- the extent of inner city deprivation;
- the high rates of unemployment;
- racism;
- different policing tactics in the inner city areas.

All of these cause a feeling of hopelessness, a belief in the strength of racism and a sense of bitterness among the ethnic minorities in the inner city areas.

Research

Phil Cohen studied the changes that had taken place in East London during the 1960s. he found that the traditional working-class East London community had been held together by:

- The extended family structure: this has been fully described by Young and Willmott, and was the traditional working-class extended family, which was based on the mother who kept all the members in regular contact with each other.
- The density of population: a large number of people lived in the relatively small area of East London, in small terraced houses. People were thrown very much together. Because of the number of people to each house, much of the social life was outdoors in the streets.
- All the jobs were local: most men worked on the docks and so homes and jobs were close to each other.

In the 1950s and 1960s changes took place that effectively dismantled the local community. Most important of all was the rehousing of large numbers of people in the new towns and in overspill estates. The density of population declined and the extended family was broken up.

The second important change was the decline in the London docks so that men had to go elsewhere for work.

Thirdly, redevelopment drove out the traditional local traders and craftsmen who could no longer afford the high rents.

The result was the breakdown of the traditional working-class East London community. As people were re-housed out of East London, there was an influx of Asian immigrants who now form a large part of the population of that area.

The suburbs

The suburbs developed with the growth of transport in the early part of the twentieth century. They tend to be more affluent in character than the inner city areas, with more middle-class people.

Life in the suburbs is less centred on the family, or the locality, but more on specific interests. People are friendly through activity at the local primary school parent/teacher association or the golf club. It appears that people are more likely to be measured on their possessions than their personalities. There is very little employment locally and so people who live in suburbs tend to commute to work.

In the past twenty years there has been a significant growth in home ownership among all groups of the population so that the stereotype of the suburb as being necessarily middle class is now out of date. Affluence among the working class and a decline in rented property means that it is now normal for working-class couples to move to the suburbs in search of housing.

Research

Willmott and Young *(Family and Class in a London Suburb)* studied life in the London suburb of Woodford. They found that family life was much looser than the close-knit kinship network they had found in their earlier study of the working-class inner London area of Bethnal Green. Suburban people were: 'on the whole friendly, neighbourly and helpful to each other. They attend clubs and churches together, they entertain friends and neighbours in their homes, they like (or at any rate prefer to like) their fellow residents'. They suggest that middle-class people have greater skill than working-class people at **making friends**, as long as people conform to the middle-class standards.

Summary

1 Urbanisation is the process by which towns develop and the bulk of the population of a country come to live in the city.

2 De-urbanisation describes the move away from living in cities. People move to small towns, distant suburbs and the countryside.

3 The process of urbanisation began in the early nineteenth century and reached its peak in the 1950s, since when Britain has been de-urbanising.

4 Urbanisation and industrialisation are closely linked. It was industrialisation and the growth of factories that created towns and cities as we know them now in Britain.

5 There has been a distinction made between the form of life in rural areas and the form of life in urban areas. This distinction has often been described as *Gemeinschaft* (community) and *Gesellschaft* (association).

6   The main differences between *Gemeinschaft* (rural) and *Gesellschaft* (urban) forms of community life lie in the close personal ties to be found in the rural areas. In the city life is far more impersonal.

7   The differences have been put down to size, density of population and cultural mix of people.

8   There has been strong criticism of the idea that a place can influence the social relationships of people. Research has shown that there are close communities in the cities and there are major divisions in the village and rural areas.

9   Cities have been divided into zones which have clear-cut social characteristics. In some of these areas, particularly in the zone of transition in the inner city, there are much higher crime rates.

10 The inner areas of the cities are suffering from a considerable number of problems, such as overcrowding, poverty, high crime rates and unemployment.

11 The new towns and overspill estates that were built in the 1950s have not fully re-created the traditional working-class communities of the inner cities.

12 Increasingly, there has been a move out of the inner cities to the countryside. This has been mainly due to the growth of transport links – such as fast trains and motorways – and the move out of inner city areas of new employment opportunities. House prices too are lower out of the cities.

Self-test questions

1   Explain what is meant by the terms (a) 'urbanisation'; (b) 'de-urbanisation'.
2   Briefly explain the relationship between industrialisation and urbanisation.
3   Explain the difference between 'community and 'association'.
4   Why are simple contrasts between life in rural and urban societies sometimes misleading?
5   What groups of people tend to live in the inner cities?

Chapter 13
Poverty and the Welfare State

13.1 Definitions of poverty

There are three ways of defining poverty, these are:
- **1** absolute definitions;
- **2** relative definitions;
- **3** consensual definitions.

13.2 Absolute poverty

One of the founders of sociological research into poverty was Seebohm Rowntree, who studied poverty in York in three different pieces of research published in 1899, 1936 and 1950. Rowntree believed that he could define a **poverty line** below which people were clearly in poverty, and above which they escaped from poverty. The line was drawn at the level of **'the minimum of provision needed to maintain health and working efficiency'**. Rowntree's initial aim was to shock people into awareness of the huge extent of poverty in Britain. In order to achieve this, he had to select an unambiguous poverty line which everybody would agree represented a true minimum level of existence.

Rowntree argued that there were three elements to a person's essential expenditure: (a) food, (b) clothing, (c) housing.

By finding the minimum costs of these three and adding them together, Rowntree believed he could construct the poverty line.

- **Food** He asked a panel of doctors to work out a basic diet that would just keep a person healthy;
- **Clothing** He calculated the minimum necessary clothing that a person needed to be reasonably warm and dry;
- **Housing** Rowntree took the average rents paid by working-class people for their housing. People had to pay the rents asked by landlords, so the average represented the minimum.

Rowntree's definition has been influential and was actually used by the Beveridge Committee who created the basis of our present social security system.

There are criticisms of this **absolute** definition of poverty, however:

- How can the poor be expected to know what the best diet is?
- Rowntree assumed that they would always buy at the lowest possible prices, yet the lowest prices are usually obtained when buying in bulk, or at least the largest size packets and jars. Poor people cannot afford at any one time to pay out for the largest size containers. The poor therefore end up paying the highest prices.
- Rowntree did not allow for any **luxuries**, e.g. cigarettes or alcohol, however. It is unreasonable to exclude any spending on leisure or minor luxury items. (In the 1950 study he did allow a tiny amount for luxuries.)
- It is not possible to fix a line of poverty since what is considered to be poverty varies with time and society. This is the criticism that has led to the **relative** definition of poverty.

13.3 Relative poverty

The relative definition suggests that it is not possible to isolate what is considered poverty from the general expectations of people in society, and their everyday living standards. Expectations change over time within societies, and vary from one society to another.

The measurement of poverty in relative definitions

Within this approach there are three methods used to measure relative poverty:
- low income family statistics;
- relative income;
- disposable income.

LIFS (Low Income Family Statistics)
The first way to measure poverty is to take the government's own level of income support, plus an allowance for housing and other expenses which are given through the welfare system. The amount added up to approximately 140% of the basic government benefit allowance (currently Income Support/Jobseeker's Allowance). The reasoning behind this is that this minimum level of income the government itself believes it is possible to live on.

Relative income
The average income is worked out and then a certain percentage is arrived at which researchers regard so below average that it must be poverty. The two lines most commonly used are 50% or 80% of average income.

Spending power or disposable income
This is the measurement used in European Commission studies of comparative poverty across the European Union. According to this definition, having less than 50% of average spending power is an approximate guide to poverty.

Fig. 13.1 The advantages and disadvantages of the relative approaches to measuring poverty

Advantages	Disadvantages
It relates the poverty to the expectations of society. It gives a realistic picture of deprivation within a society. It broadens the idea of what poverty is, from necessities to a range of other needs that people have in a society, and which make life bearable.	Taken to its extreme, this approach means that as long as there is inequality there is poverty. It might be claimed that because a person does not have the extras which most people have come to expect in contemporary Britain, they are poor. An alternative argument could be that as long as they are fed, housed and clothed then they are not truly poor. Poverty is destitution. The relative approach can lead to people ignoring the differences across societies, thus the approach seems to say that in a Third World society, as long as a person is not starving they are not poor – because expectations are so much lower in that society. If income support is used as the measure of poverty, the absurd situation occurs that the higher the level of income support the more the numbers of people there are in 'poverty'!

13.4 Consensual definitions of poverty

In this approach people were asked to rank, in order of importance, what they considered to be necessities. These were then put together, and as a result a group of necessities were found which were agreed to by a large majority of the people questioned. Using these agreed (hence **consensual**) necessities, they were then able to work out a level of deprivation which the majority of the population felt unacceptable.

Measurement of the poverty line according to the consensual approach

In 1985 and 1991, Mack and Lansley asked over 1000 people what they thought 'necessities' were, and then from their replies made a list of what the most commonly agreed necessities were.

Fig. 13.2 An example of a consensual poverty line
(Source: C. Oppenheim, *Poverty: The Facts*, Child Poverty Action Group, 1993)

Examples of items included	Examples of items excluded
Basic designs, mass manufactured furniture, textiles and hardware	Antiques, handmade or precious household durables
Prescription charges, dental care, sight test	Spectacles, private health care
Fridge-freezer, washing machine, microwave oven, food-mixer, sewing machine	Tumble-dryer, shower, electric blankets
Basic clothing, sensible designs	Second-hand, designer and high fashion clothing
TV, video hire, basic music system and camera	Children's TVs, compact discs, camcorders
Second-hand 5-year-old car, second-hand adult bicycle, new children's bikes	A second car, caravan, camping equipment, mountain bikes
Basic jewellery, watch	Precious jewellery
Basic cosmetics, haircuts	Perfume, hair perm
Alcohol – men 14 units, women 10 units	Smoking
One-week annual holiday	Holiday abroad
Walking, swimming, cycling, football, cinema, panto every two years, youth club, scouts/guides	Fishing, water sports, horse-riding, creative or educational classes children's ballet/music lessons

13.5 The significance of definitions of poverty

The variety of definitions of poverty given here is at first rather confusing and possibly appears to be pointless.

- Different definitions, however, give substantially different estimates of the numbers living in poverty. For instance, an **absolute** definition would suggest that there are very few people in poverty in Britain. Any of the **relative** or **consensual** ones would put the estimate at a minimum of 10 million people in poverty.
- Different definitions draw the line of poverty so that whole groups of people are placed in or out of poverty depending on the definition. For example, if the definition of poverty is everybody with an income below that of income support payments, then all those in receipt of social security are out of poverty; raise the definition to 140% of social security and millions of people immediately become 'poor'.
- The different definitions will then have important implications for government policy. If the definition suggests that large numbers of people are in poverty, then clearly the government needs to act, for instance, by raising state benefits.

13.6 The poverty line

All the definitions discussed so far have aimed at producing a line of poverty that can distinguish the poor from the rest of the population. However, we must be cautious in stating that these are poor people who are somehow distinct from the rest of the population. It is more accurate to say that at certain periods in their lives (such as in the periods of dependent children and old àge) and under certain conditions (such as illness, temporary unemployment) people may decline into poverty. At other periods they may move out of poverty. So we should see people moving in and out of poverty, rather than a clear group of poor people.

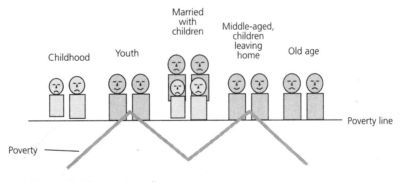

Fig.13.3 The poverty line

13.7 Who are the poor?

The following groups are most likely to have the highest proportion of their members living in poverty:

- the unemployed;
- low paid;

- lone-parent families;
- sick and disabled;
- older people;
- women;
- the ethnic minorities.

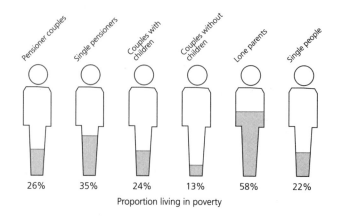

Fig. 13.4 The risk of poverty by family status
(Source: C. Oppenheim, *Poverty: The Facts,* Child Poverty Action Group, 1996)

The unemployed

About 60% of the unemployed have incomes below 50% average income. Official statistics indicate that after three months of unemployment, the average disposable income of a family drops by 59%.

The numbers of people who are out of work change with the economy. However, certain groups in the population are more likely than others to be made unemployed. These include:

- the least skilled – as automated machinery has replaced them. Unemployment levels for unskilled manual workers can be as high as six times that of professional workers.
- those living away from the south/south east of England. The south east of England has a number of advantages for employers, including a skilled workforce, proximity to Europe, and a large, affluent population to purchase the goods or products.
- Ethnic minorities. Partly as a result of racism, and partly because skill levels are lower overall amongst Afro-Caribbeans and some of the Asian communities, there are significantly higher levels of unemployment amongst the ethnic minorities. It is estimated that twice as many blacks and Asians are unemployed as whites.

The low paid

According to British statistics, about 80% of all full-time workers were living in poverty as a result of having incomes of 50% below the average; 71% of women in all forms of employment were on low pay, which is defined as two-thirds of the average male wage.

Low paid workers are particularly often caught in the poverty trap, whereby an increase in earnings results in the loss of means tested benefits. In 1990, over 400 000 people in Britain were caught in this poverty trap.

Over half of all those living in poverty comprise the low paid and their **children**. The income earned from employment is inadequate to pay for the extra costs of having children.

Lone-parent families

Single parents are likely to be the poorest of the poor, with six out of ten single parents living in poverty. The main reasons are the high costs of having children, and the low income that can be earned because of limited earning opportunities. This means that lone-parent families are more likely to be on state benefits.

Sick and disabled

Fourteen per cent of all adults, and 33% of all children, suffer from one or more serious disability, and of these people with disabilities, 34% are living in poverty. There have been significant increases in the number of people with disabilities, as a result of:

- people living longer and therefore being more prone to disabilities in old age;
- improvements in medicine leading to higher rates of survival of younger people and infants with disabilities.

The average income for an adult, under retirement age, with a disability is 72% of non-disabled people. Those with disabilities are unable to work, or are limited to particular kinds of employment, usually that which is low paid. But not only is their income low, their expenditure is higher because of their disabilities. This lowers their standards of living further.

Older people

Approximately 18% of the population are over retirement age, numbering around 11 million people. Women form the majority of these. Approximately 25% of people of pensionable age have incomes below 50% of average incomes. Older people are generally dependent upon pensions for their income, and the state pension is so low that living in receipt of state pensions, means that older people will be in poverty. The state pension in 1990 was about 16.5% of the average male weekly earnings.

Women

About 4.5 million women are living in poverty. In virtually every category we have looked at above, women form the majority of people in the group. They are more likely to be low paid, to be sick or disabled, to live longer, and they form approximately 95% of all heads of lone-parent families on Income Support/Jobseeker's Allowance.

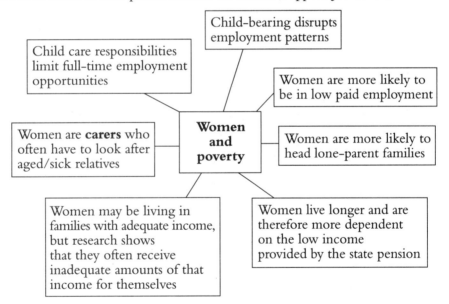

Fig. 13.5 Women and poverty: causes

Ethnic minorities

Ethnic minority families are significantly more likely to work in low paid industries, to be unemployed than the majority of the population. They are twice as likely to be in the poorest 20% of the population compared to white people.

13.8 The causes of poverty

There are two differing types of explanations for the causes of poverty:
- dependency;
- exclusion.

Dependency explanations

These approaches argue that people who are poor because of some deficiency in themselves or which is passed on in the group to which they belong in society. Within this overall approach to explaining the causes of poverty, we can distinguish approaches which have different emphases. These are:
- emphasising the underclass;
- emphasising the culture of poverty.

The underclass

Examiner's tip

Link this to the debate on whether the underclass actually exists.

This argument was first developed by an American, Charles Murray who claims that an underclass exists of people who are lazy and make no effort to work or look after themselves. They have come to believe that it is their right to receive benefits from the state and not have to work.

It is important to remember that the underclass refers only to those poor people who make no effort to help themselves – Murray accepts that there are many poor people who are in this state through no 'fault' of their own. Nevertheless, the bulk of poverty is caused by those who do not make the effort to earn a living, and/or squander what they do have.

Culture of poverty

The culture of poverty argument was first developed by Oscar Lewis when he studied very poor people in Central America. The values and behaviour (the **culture**) of these poor people was significantly different from the majority of the population. Lewis argued that this was because these particular values enabled the very poor to cope with circumstances which would otherwise lead to despair and hopelessness.

However, Lewis argues that these very values which help cope with poverty also trap the people in poverty. For example, one of the beliefs of the culture of poverty is to live for today and not worry about the future. This makes sense – where there is tremendous poverty, no one knows what the future holds. However, it also prevents them planning ahead and perhaps trying to break out of their poverty.

Exclusion approaches

The second set of explanations for poverty, is based on the idea of exclusion – meaning that the poor are in that situation because they are squeezed out of a decent standard of living by the actions of others. Another term for this process is **marginalisation**. Those who lose out – the disabled, older people, women, the ethnic minorities, and of course, children, are all those who have least power in society.

Marginalisation

According to this approach some groups of people lose out in complex industrial societies through no fault of their own. They are the casualties of industrial and social change. The victims include those such as the physically and mentally disabled, lone parents, the less skilled, older people and so on. It was this explanation for poverty that largely underlay the foundation of the Welfare State.

Economic system approach

A more radical explanation for the continuation of poverty comes from those who argue that society is a competition between various groups. Power and wealth generally go together, as do poverty and powerlessness. The groups in poverty are largely formed from the powerless, in particular women, children and the ethnic minorities. Low pay and poor state benefits are the result of the fact that to pay more would be harmful to the interests of those who are more affluent.

The poverty trap

The poverty trap occurs where a person (or family) receives a number of means tested benefits from the state when they are unable to obtain work. If the person then finds employment, it is possible that the gains in income from that employment may well be lost, because the Department of Social Security withdraws some or all of the means tested benefits.

13.9 Development of the Welfare State

The term Welfare State refers to a society in which the state actively intervenes to ensure that its citizens have adequate standards of income, housing, education and health services.

The origins of the Welfare State go back to the Liberal government of 1908. Booth's writings and Rowntree's research on poverty in York influenced the Liberal government to introduce old age pensions. The most important measure was the introduction of **National Insurance** in 1911. This is a scheme in which employers, employees and the state all make contributions to a fund to provide insurance against illness and disablement. By 1914 there were 14 million people contributing to the scheme.

Between 1906 and 1919 the Liberals introduced new services in the fields of social security, health, education, housing, employment and the treatment of offenders. Many of these services were then cut back between 1921 and 1939.

In 1945–50 the Labour government committed itself to a far wider and more radical reform than the Liberals had attempted. Nobody was to be allowed to live in poverty and everybody was to have proper health care and education regardless of their income. The difference between the Labour version of the Welfare State and the Liberal welfare provisions, was that the Welfare State was to be for everybody.

Most of the provisions of the Welfare State were based on the recommendations of a committee headed by Lord Beveridge. The scheme introduced the **social security system**, the comprehensive **National Health Service**, a **free secondary school system**, special **help for the disabled**, provision for **decent housing**, state intervention to maintain **full employment**, and a system of **family allowances**.

Although changes have been introduced in the system since it was initiated between 1945–50, it remains fundamentally the same. However, from 1979 to 1997 the Conservative government showed that it would like to see the system partially dismantled in favour of a two-tier scheme. For instance, in the sphere of medicine, it would like to have seen most people paying for **private** health care whilst only those who could not afford to pay would go to the National Health Service.

The reasons why the Labour government introduced a Welfare State have to be seen against:

- The background of twenty years of mass unemployment before the Second World War, when there was little help given to alleviate poverty;
- The previous measures introduced by the Liberal government were found to be totally inadequate;
- The wartime destruction of British cities gave the impetus for the construction of new, better-built houses in well-planned environments;
- There was an overwhelming desire shared by the mass of the British people never to return to pre-war conditions.

13.10 The debate on the Welfare State

Advantages of the Welfare State

- It has eliminated the worst excesses of poverty.
- It helps people who through no fault of their own (such as physical disability) are unable to work, and without financial aid would be reduced to begging or voluntary charity;
- It has given everybody access to decent medical treatment;
- Before the Second World War it was mainly the children of more affluent parents who could receive a secondary school education, as fees were charged. Today education is freely available.
- It has led to the elimination of the worst forms of slum housing that existed in Britain.
- It has provided elderly people with an income that allows them to live with some degree of dignity in their old age.

Disadvantages of the Welfare State

In recent years there has been a growth in criticism of the Welfare State.

- One group of critics argues that it does not provide enough help for the poor, disabled and elderly. They argue for an extension and a raising of the standards of the Welfare State.
- However, other groups argue that the Welfare State has gone too far and ought to be partially dismantled. They argue that the Welfare State:
  - Is wasteful: because the Welfare State is universal, that is it gives certain benefits to everybody, for example Child Benefit, many who do not actually need financial help receive it. This is seen as a waste of money. These people argue for more **selective** provision, that is giving to those who can prove they are in need;
  - Because of the enormous financial cost of the Welfare State the level of benefits is too low. They argue that by concentrating selectively, the same money could provide better services for fewer people;
  - The Welfare State is too bureaucratic and impersonal and increasingly controls our lives;
  - The provision of benefits to all, robs individuals of their desire to look after themselves. They do not have to worry about the future or try very hard to get employment, as they know that the Welfare State will always look after them. This criticism seems rather weak if one looks at the levels of benefit given for unemployed people for instance: they are so low that few people can truly wish to live permanently on them;
  - The provision of benefits and health care weakens the family, by taking away its functions. If there was less provision by the state, families would have to cope and this would strengthen the institution of the family.

Conclusion

The critics of the Welfare State may have some valid points, but a glance back to life for the working class in Britain before its existence shows a dreadful level of poverty, disease and misery, which the Welfare State has undoubtedly relieved.

13.11 Does the Welfare State redistribute wealth?

The Welfare State, it is claimed, is meant to redistribute benefits from the affluent to the poorer sections of society. Critics of the Welfare State have disputed this, and Tudor Hart coined the term the **inverse care law**, meaning that the Welfare State actually benefits the affluent at the cost of the poor. This is because the middle classes make better use of the health and welfare services, it is claimed. However, the evidence does point to a limited degree of redistribution caused by the effects of taxation and welfare provision.

However after taxes and welfare benefits have been taken into consideration, the top 20% of the population still retain more than twice the income of the average earners and four times that of the poorest 20%.

The Welfare State seems then to have only marginally redistributed wealth.

Explanations for this are targeting and means testing. There is considerable debate between those who argue that state benefits should be **targeted** – based on the technique of means testing, and those who argue that the only way to eradicate poverty is with **universal** provision.

Means testing and targeting

Targeting describes a system of welfare provision that delivers state benefits to *only* those most in need. An example of this is Incapacity Benefit, which replaced Invalidity Benefit, as the government reasoned that it was too easy to get Invalidity Benefit. People who are disabled or suffer from a long-standing illness can claim Incapacity Benefit, but they have to be severely disabled, and in case of doubt they are checked by a doctor.

Targeting is closely linked to **means testing**, which means that even if a person is eligible to receive a certain benefit, they can only do so if they have an income or savings below a certain level. Most government benefits are means tested today, for example Housing Benefit.

The advantages of means testing and targeting include:
- it targets help to the most needy, and does not give money or services to those who could afford to pay and who are currently being subsidised by the rest of the population. Some people may actually be worse off than those they are subsidising;
- targeting groups should cost less to the state as fewer people should receive benefits;
- the savings could go to providing better services for the recipients, or it could be used by the government to lower taxes.

Disadvantages include:
- means testing is complex and creates a large bureaucracy to administer it, so savings would not return to the government but would be used up in higher administration charges;
- as targeting is complex, it means that quite often mistakes are made;
- people are confused as to what they are entitled to claim, as the system is often complex;
- people often fail to take up the benefits because they feel embarrassed to ask (they feel 'stigmatised');
- as income rises, so state benefits decline – this can lead to the **poverty trap** (mentioned earlier), where many people actually lose more in state benefit than they gain from the increase in income they receive when they get a job.

Universalism

The alternative to targeting is to give benefits to everybody who falls into a particular category. For example, every family in Britain having a child receives Child Benefit, even though many families may not need it.

Other examples include: everybody over retirement age receives the state pension, even if they are rich; every British citizen receives free health care through the National Health Service.

When everyone in a particular category receives benefits, then it is known as universalism. Supporters of universalism claim they are defending the Welfare State, though few benefits available since the beginning of the Welfare State have been truly universal – the majority of state benefits are actually means tested.

Advantages of universalism include:
- it eradicates the poverty trap – because there is no decrease in benefits as income rises through employment;
- it ensures that everyone who is in need obtains the benefits, and no one is omitted through their ignorance of benefits available or through fear of stigma;
- it is cheap, because there is no expensive bureaucracy working out entitlement through means testing.

Disadvantages include:
- it is highly expensive because so many people unnecessarily receive benefits. Money is wasted, which could go to other more needy groups;
- giving people benefits which are not really needed encourages them to rely upon the state rather than on their own resources – this is known as **welfare dependency**.

13.12 Voluntary organisations

Apart from the welfare services provided by the state, there is a whole host of voluntary agencies which provide assistance. These have grown to complement the state services and fall into two main groupings.

Increasingly the mixture of provision of health and welfare by state and voluntary or private companies is known as the 'mixed economy of welfare'.

Formally organised groups and charities
Their object is to help others in need. Examples of these include:
- **Relate** counsels and helps with sexual and marital problems. Counsellors are unpaid but highly trained;
- **Mencap** helps mentally handicapped people;
- **Community Service Volunteers** CSV takes volunteers between 16 and 35 to perform one year of full-time service. They receive board and lodging and some small payment;
- **Shelter** This organisation is primarily concerned with housing issues and tries to help the ill-housed and homeless;
- **War on Want** This collects money for international help.

Self-help groups
These are organised to protect or promote their own interests. They include such organisations as:

Gingerbread This is an organisation looking after the interests of single parents;

Alcoholics Anonymous People who have alcohol problems are able to meet regularly to help themselves over their difficulties.

Voluntary services still exist in the Welfare State because:
- Small voluntary agencies are often better able to cope with specific problems which the state bureaucracy may find difficult to handle. The work of **Release** with drug addicts is a good example, as there is little state provision to help people with drug problems;
- Volunteers are far more flexible in the hours they are prepared to work, so the Samaritans who provide advice and friendship over the phone, have somebody on call 24 hours a day;
- Volunteers have often had similar problems themselves and can bring a degree of personal experience into their work. Alcoholics Anonymous is an example of this;
- Volunteers may help groups that are not generally popular. **PROP** is an organisation that looks after the rights of prisoners;

- Volunteer agencies sometimes exist to attack the state's complacency over certain problems. For instance, the Child Poverty Action Group actively criticises the government for leaving millions of children in poverty.

Summary

1   There are basically two competing definitions of poverty: (a) an absolute definition based on the minimum amount needed to keep someone clothed, fed and housed; and (b) a relative one based on the idea that poverty varies with the normal expectations of society.

2   Most modern studies are based on the relative definition.

3   It is not true to say that the poor consist of one separate group of people in poverty the whole of their lives. Many people move in and out of poverty at different periods of their lives. Poverty is therefore a very dynamic changing thing.

4   There is a minimum of $7\frac{1}{2}$ million people in poverty.

5   The groups in poverty are the low paid, the unemployed, the elderly, the single-parent families, the sick and disabled.

6   There is greater poverty in the north than south of Britain.

7   The reasons that have been suggested for the existence of poverty are: (a) the cycle of deprivation; (b) the culture of poverty; (c) lack of power; and (d) the very structure of society itself.

8   Once people are in poverty they are often trapped there with little means of escape.

9   Poor people suffer not just from lack of money but from such things as lack of educational provision, health care and decent housing.

10   British governments have intervened to try to limit poverty. There is now an educational system that is free up to 16, a health service, supplementary benefits and pensions, various allowances and a progressive taxation system.

11   The Welfare State was created at the end of the Second World War.

12   Its aims were to wipe out poverty, poor housing, low-standard education and inadequate health care for the masses.

13   The Welfare State has only partially been successful in its aims.

14   There has been a vigorous debate between those who argue for a cut-back in the Welfare State, claiming that it is no longer needed and that it is a waste of resources, and those who defend it pointing out that it is still desperately needed and that the alternative would be to turn the clock back to the 1930s, when health care depended on ability to pay, not degree of illness.

15   There are two ways to allocate benefits – targeting and universal methods.

16   The role of the voluntary services remains crucial to the running of welfare services in Britain, as the state is not able to provide everything.

Self-test questions

1   What is the difference between 'absolute' and 'relative' poverty?
2   Explain what is meant by the term 'the poverty line'.
3   Which groups are most commonly found among the poor?
4   Apart from the problems directly caused by having small incomes, what other problems are often faced by the poor?
5   Why does poverty continue to exist in Britain despite the introduction of the Welfare State?
6   In which areas of the social services does the Welfare State operate?
7   Name any three advantages and three disadvantages of the Welfare State.
8   Give examples of the kind of services provided by voluntary organisations.

Chapter 14
Politics and power

14.1 Power and authority

Max Weber distinguished between 'power' and 'authority'.

Power is the situation when a person forces his or her will on others that they do as they are ordered. The people may not agree with what they are told but they obey. Power is usually enforced by threats of one kind or another. This is the method by which many non-democratic societies are controlled.

Authority is when the people who are told to do something willingly obey. There is no threat. There are three types of authority:

- **Charismatic** A person is obeyed because of the sheer force of personality – as, for example, Jesus Christ.
- **Traditional** A person is obeyed because of his or her position. The person in that position has always been obeyed and it is customary to do so, e.g. tribal chiefs, parents.
- **Bureaucratic** In modern societies most places of work and most organisations have a bureaucracy, which consists of people doing different tasks with some having more important positions than others, and being able to tell others what to do.

  Authority here is related to the 'job' a person does, not the personality of the individual. Whoever fills the role in the organisation has the right to demand obedience. However, outside the specific requirement and rights of the job, the person has no authority, e.g. a teacher in school can tell pupils what to do. In the shopping centre on Saturday, however, the teacher has no such rights.

In reality, of course, the three types of authority get mixed together. However, the distinction between those who have power (based on threat) and those who have authority (based on agreement) is clear cut.

Most political systems spend a great deal of time and effort trying to persuade their people that they are fortunate to live in a society with a good political system, which they should obey willingly – this is termed **political socialisation.**

14.2 Voting behaviour

The following issues have been raised in sociological debates regarding voting:
- social class;
- class de-alignment;
- party images;
- geography and nationalism;
- factors of age, gender and ethnicity.

Social class

Social class has traditionally been one of the main influences on voting behaviour. However, over the last twenty years this influence has declined. Until the late 1970s it was generally true to say that over two-thirds of working-class people voted Labour, and a slightly higher proportion of middle-class people voted Conservative.

Today, there is still a relationship, with the majority of working-class people voting Labour and the majority of middle-class people voting Conservative. However, the difference is that they do not automatically vote along class as they once did. Voters are more likely to change their voting patterns depending upon which party is more likely to benefit them.

Class de-alignment

This move away from strong loyalty to a particular political party depending upon the social class to which a person belongs, to a more fluid voting pattern, has been called class de-alignment.

Reasons for class de-alignment in voting
- The changing nature of employment from a clear division between manual work/white-collar work, to the situation where more people are in white-collar and professional jobs, has broken many of the traditional class divisions.
- People are less likely to identify themselves as working class or middle class today.
- The trade unions used to be closely associated with the Labour Party, and helped to deliver the votes of its members. Today, the trade unions are much weaker, have fewer members and are less closely identified with the Labour Party.
- Housing is more likely to be mixed today rather than having the traditional divisions between the working class who lived in inner city areas or in large local state housing estates. This has helped break down divisions.
- The political parties have attempted to produce policies which are attractive to both of the main social classes, not just one.

Party images

A relatively small proportion of the electorate has a clear idea of what the exact policies of the political parties are. Instead, they tend to vote for an image of what they imagine the party stands for. Traditionally, the Labour Party was regarded as the party of the working class, which was good for the party when the majority of the electorate was working class, but not so good once employment changes dismembered the working class.

Political parties therefore seek to portray an image about themselves which attracts voters' support. An example of this was the Labour Party winning the 1997 General Election. They achieved this by altering their image.

Old Labour Party image	New Labour Party image
For the working class	For the whole nation
Close ties to trade unions	No special links with the unions
High taxes	Low taxes
High spending on health and welfare	Prudent levels of spending
Against business	Supports business
Soft on criminals	Tough on crime
Believes in socialism	Believes in capitalism

Geographical location and nationalism

If class has declined as an indicator of voting preference, geography has increased:
- the inner cities are more likely to vote Labour (because these have a higher proportion of poorer people, who are still loyal to Labour);
- wealthy commuter and suburban areas are less likely to vote Labour;
- rural areas in England are more likely to vote Conservative;
- voting patterns in Wales, Scotland and Northern Ireland tend to differ from voting patterns in England.

Wales is the most like England, but has a significant nationalist vote. Rural areas are likely to vote nationalist or Labour.

Scotland has a majority of Labour MPs, but has significant votes for a nationalist party (SDP). Rural areas also tend to vote Liberal Democrat.

Northern Ireland is split between parties who wish it to unite with Eire and parties which wish to remain an integral part of the UK.

Reasons for the growth of nationalism include:

- the interests of Britain being neglected for the interests of England;
- the identities of Wales and Scotland being lost;
- a revival of nationalism across Europe, as people search for 'identities';
- a perception that government spending is unfairly biased towards London;
- a belief that decision making was being made in London without Scotland and Wales having a chance to be influential;
- the fact that the European Commission encourages regions and smaller 'nations' to express their identities;
- in Northern Ireland a belief that Northern Ireland is a part of the country of Ireland and should be reunited with it.

Age, gender and ethnicity

- **Age** is not a particularly significant factor, although young people are the least likely to vote.
- **Gender** Historically women have been more likely than men to vote Conservative. This seems no longer to be the case, and voting by women is influenced by the factors we discussed earlier under class de-alignment.
- **Ethnic group** Traditionally, the Conservatives had an image of being anti-immigrant and later, less supportive of the ethnic minorities. Labour had the image of being more supportive. Ethnic minorities are still more likely to vote Labour.

14.3 Types of voter

The loyal voter

This type of voter stays with a particular party most of his or her life; most often he/she is a working-class Labour supporter or middle-class Conservative supporter.

Non-voters

In general elections, approximately 27% of the electorate do not vote. It appears that (i) poorer people, (ii) older people, (iii) women, (iv) younger voters, and (v) the least educated tend to abstain (not vote) more often than the national average.

People abstain for either positive or negative reasons:

Positive reasons include:

- No candidate standing for the party the person would normally choose;
- The candidate standing for the party of his or her normal choice may be objectionable to the person;
- There may be an aspect of his or her normal party's policy with which he/she disagrees, but he/she cannot bring him/herself to vote for another;
- The person may regard the result as so obvious (a safe seat) that he/she may not bother to vote;
- The individual disagrees with the political system or with all of the political parties providing candidates.

Negative reasons include:

- Apathy (cannot be bothered to vote);
- Illness;
- Does not have any faith in politicians;
- Fails to understand the policies of the parties.

Abstaining from voting is important because it can influence the result of an election, especially in a seat with a very small majority for the sitting Member of Parliament (a marginal seat).

Floating voters

Floating voters are people who regularly switch votes. This group is the main target for political propaganda. As class de-alignment increases, floating voters become more important.

Tactical voting

When people realise that the candidate of their first choice has absolutely no chance of winning, they may switch to a second choice candidate of another party in order to defeat the likely winner whom they deeply dislike. It has been suggested that the Liberal Democratic Party receives many of its votes through tactical voting, as Conservatives voting switch to the Liberal Democratic Party in safe Labour seats and Labour supporters do the same in safe Conservative seats. In the 1997 election tactical voting was regarded as extremely influential in the Labour victory.

14.4 Voting and opinion polls

Opinion polls and surveys that find out the voting intentions or political opinions of the electors. Gallup Poll Ltd was the first to use them in Britain as long ago as 1938. Since 1974 they have predicted accurately (within 2%) the voting figures for the general elections. Before then, however, they were slightly erratic; indeed in the 1970 election all the polls except one (four out of five) predicted a Labour victory, yet the result was a win for the Conservatives.

The accuracy of the polls depends on:

- The accuracy of the sample – it must be a true mirror of those voting.
- The quality of the questions asked – poorly framed questions can lead the person questioned to misunderstand the meaning of the question and so give a wrong, or inappropriate, answer.
- The nearer the election, the more accurate the results as people will have made up their minds by then.
- Polls should avoid asking questions on voting intentions after sensational political events as people may temporarily change their views.

Opinion polls are a form of sociological survey. The discussion in Chapter 2 considers the problems of surveys in detail.

The influence of opinion polls on voters

In some European countries, for example Germany, the publication of polls near elections is banned because it is felt they could influence voting patterns. They could do this in two ways:

- If the polls predict a substantial win for one party, its supporters may be lulled into a false sense of security and they may not bother voting, as they think victory is certain. The numbers of people who do this may be so great that their party actually loses.
- A party may be appearing to win by such a large margin that people who are undecided may vote for the 'weaker' of the two (or more) parties, just to make sure that no one party has too great a majority and introduces 'radical' policies.

In the 1997 British General Election it seemed that a considerable number of voters used information from the opinion polls to vote tactically.

The influence of opinion polls on politicians

Polls are also used to test public opinion on certain issues and may be used by pressure groups to influence politicians. Obviously a government following very unpopular policies would be silly not to take notice of opinion polls telling them so. However, most senior politicians argue that it is the job of governments to **lead opinion** not just to **follow it**.

14.5 Politics and the mass media

Newspapers in Britain have generally been more sympathetic to the Conservatives than Labour. The only daily newspaper that regularly supported the Labour Party before 1997 was the *Daily Mirror*. *The Guardian* also presented the Labour case sympathetically. Patterns of ownership and attitudes of a newspaper's journalists will often influence decisions as to what line to take on a particular political issue.

Broadcasting (radio and television) is legally obliged to present a political debate **impartially**, which means the programmes cannot be biased against one party or another. Research evidence on change in political attitudes as a result of exposure to the media's influence, suggests that they do not change existing attitudes but **reinforce attitudes** already held. This is because readers and viewers select the message which they want and which fits the attitudes they already hold.

However, it is important to remember, as Stuart Hall points out, that newspapers **set the agenda** in defining what is regarded as important. If stories are not prominently covered by the media, they are not noticed or discussed. Only information and stories regarded as newsworthy by journalists appear. If journalists consistently, if unintentionally, present only one side of the story, then in the long run they will influence political attitudes.

When the Labour Party decided to change its image in the early 1990s, and become New Labour, it spent a considerable amount of effort in trying to persuade important media owners (in particular the owner of *The Times*, the *Sun* and *Sky Broadcasting*) to become sympathetic to its new views. Its campaign was successful and it received the support of most newspapers.

14.6 Pressure groups (interest groups)

Political parties try to persuade electors to vote for them, so that they can form a government. They usually have policies on a wide range of issues.

Pressure groups (often also called interest groups) differ in that they are groups formed to defend or promote one specific cause only. They do not try to win seats in Parliament, but instead attempt to influence the policies of political parties,

An example of a political party is the Labour Party. An example of a pressure group is the Campaign for Nuclear Disarmament (CND).

There are two types of pressure group:

Promotional pressure groups
These put forward a particular view point which they believe is socially or morally for the good of the community. An example of this type of pressure group is **Friends of the Earth**, which tries to oppose the destruction of the environment by governments (French nuclear bombs in the Pacific) and by industry (the dumping of nuclear waste in the Irish Sea).

Defensive pressure groups
These attempt to defend the specific interests of their members. An example of this sort of group is a trade union, which concerns itself with the wages and conditions of work of its members. The division between promotional and protective groups is not hard and fast. Very often groups are both protective and promotional. For example the RAC and AA look after the interests of their members and promote the interests of car owners in general.

The importance of pressure groups in a democracy

Pressure groups are absolutely essential in a democracy. Whereas political parties deal with broad areas of policy, pressure groups represent particular causes. Political parties are constantly being approached by different groups seeking support. It is through this that political parties are able to keep in touch with people and can respond to their wishes. A vote every five years is not an adequate way for people to tell politicians what specific policies they ought to follow in certain areas. In effect, pressure groups prevent the political parties from becoming too remote from the electors, by constantly channelling opinions to them. This approach has been called **pluralism** (the term comes from the word 'plural', meaning 'more than one', so it indicates 'more than one centre of power').

Criticism

It ought to be remembered that not all groups of people have the same ability to influence decisions. Which group has more power, the unemployed or the employers organisation, the CBI? Richer, better organised groups are more likely to influence the government than poorer ones – even if these poorer groups are more representative of public opinion.

The methods used by pressure groups to influence decisions

Consultantships

Many Conservative MPs are paid by industries or individual companies to keep an eye on possible parliamentary actions that might influence their activities.

Sponsorship

MPs have either secretarial or electoral expenses paid for them by trade unions and in return they speak for those unions in Parliament.

Block votes

A pressure group encourages its members to support a political party which agrees to support its aims.

Publicity

Pressure groups try to influence what appears in the newspapers and on television. They try to gain a large amount of media attention and to be portrayed sympathetically if possible. The anti-seal culling groups have been very successful in this, having television news film shown of the slaughter of seals in horrifying detail.

A less successful method of gaining publicity is to hand out leaflets and hold street protests, marches, etc.

Specialised knowledge

If a decision involves complex technical knowledge, then the decision makers turn to the experts. So, influencing the experts can eventually influence the final decision. Large construction companies and the Central Electricity Generating Board maintain close contact with nuclear power experts. In the debate on nuclear versus non-nuclear forms of power generating, they have the sympathy of many experts.

Key positions

In order to execute certain government policies, politicians may need the cooperation of the group actually carrying them out. If the group has a monopoly over the task it can influence the decision. The British Medical Association (BMA) has been very successful in looking after the interests of doctors.

Civil disobedience

If all else fails then pressure groups turn to civil disobedience. They may block roads or stage illegal protests. An example of this is the activities of the road protesters who tried to prevent the building of the Newbury bypass in Berkshire by occupying the site where the road was going to be built. In the extreme, some groups turn to criminal activities. An example of this is the Animal Liberation Movement, which breaks into factory farms and experimental laboratories and frees the animals.

New social movements

These are groups of people who share views on a range of issues but who do not seek to create organised pressure groups for change. They may engage in a variety of different types of actions without any formal organisational structure. There is no single issue on which they unite, but in general they share a different type of view of how the world should be. An example of a new social movement is New Age Travellers.

14.7 The state

The state is a political organisation that dominates and controls society; it consists of the elected parliament, the legal system and the Civil Service. In democratic societies the state ought to reflect the beliefs of the population in general and ultimately be under their control. In a totalitarian society it generally reflects the will of only a few rich and powerful people who control it.

Control of the state: the theories

Sociologists have disagreed on the extent to which the state in Britain really does reflect the will of the people. Indeed, some writers influenced mainly by the writing of Karl Marx, have argued that the state in Britain really operates to the benefit of a small number of rich and powerful people comprising less than 5% of the population.

Two clear views have therefore been expressed:

- That the state represents the interests of the people and that power is widely spread among the people. This is known as the **pluralist model**.
- That only a small group of people rule. This is known as a **ruling class model.**

Pluralism

This is the model of the political system that sees the state firmly under the control of the people. They are in control in two ways: first through elections. Every five years the electors choose the political party they prefer. Second, in between elections, the political parties are kept informed by pressure groups which arise from specific concerns of the people.

The strength and amount of activity of pressure groups reflect their following in the population as a whole. By responding to pressure groups the politicians are responding to the popular will.

This has been criticised by those who argue that the power of pressure groups reflects how much money and how many political connections they have rather than popular support.

Ruling class model

Marxists argue that a small, unrepresentative group rules. The basis of its power is the ownership of the major manufacturing and commercial institutions. The rich ensure that they retain their wealth by creating a political system that effectively rules out any fundamental change, and by funding political parties that look after their interests. They point out that only 10% of the British population own almost 50% of the wealth.

This approach can be criticised as it fails to realise the extent to which ordinary people can engage in pressure group activity and influence government decisions.

The Civil Service

This is the **executive** of the government, carrying out its policies. Like the **legislature** (that is the Houses of Parliament and the government itself), it has been the centre of tremendous debate over the nature of its power. It is supposed to carry out the decisions of the legislature. However, many sociologists see it as being a power in its own right.

Its senior staff are recruited overwhelmingly from public schools and the universities of Oxford and Cambridge. Furthermore, most of the top civil servants come from the highest social classes in British society – particularly those working in the Foreign Office. Those who do not are socialised into a special 'civil service culture', which gives them a particular set of values. Left-wing politicians who have gained power have all commented on how efficient the Civil Service is, but also how it obstructs any radical left-wing changes. It is basically a conservative force therefore. In recent years, fears have been expressed about the very close relationship that has developed between top civil servants and industry. It has now become common for top civil servants to 'retire' into high positions in industries related to their Civil Service experience. For instance, a top Ministry of Defence civil servant left the Civil Service for a senior post with United Scientific Holdings, a major weapons producer.

Summary

1 The way people vote is influenced by: (a) social class; (b) party images, and (c) geographical location.

2 The changes in the class structure have been very great in recent years and this has meant that class is slowly weakening as a predictor of voting preferences. This is known as **class de-alignment**.

3 Tactical voting is when people prefer to switch their vote to a party other than the one of their first choice in order to prevent the candidate of another party winning.

4 Opinion polls are surveys to find out the political preferences of the electorate, in particular to predict how they will vote in an election. It is sometimes argued that the opinion polls can influence the outcome of elections by providing enough information for people to engage in tactical voting.

5 The mass media do not seem to have any powerful effect on how people choose to vote in the short term, but only over time they create a 'climate of opinion'.

6 Pressure (or interest) groups are organisations that try to persuade those in power to act in particular ways which they see as beneficial to themselves in the community. Their members do not seek political office themselves. They influence MPs in a number of ways, including: (a) consultations and sponsorships, (b) block votes, (c) publicity, (d) providing or influencing those with specialised knowledge, (e) withholding cooperation if they are in key positions, (f) public demonstrations and civil disobedience.

7 The state refers to the government, its Civil Service and its legal system. There are two views: (a) the pluralist model, which sees the British state as reflecting the will of the people, (b) the ruling class model, which sees the state operating in the interests of a small minority.

Self-test questions

1 Explain the differences between democracy and totalitarianism.
2 What is a pressure group?
3 How is a pressure group different from a political party?
4 How could opinion polls possibly influence the outcome of an election?
5 Explain the part played by the mass media in influencing how people vote.
6 Give two reasons why people may not vote in elections.
7 What is the relationship between geographical location and voting behaviour?
8 Explain the term 'pluralism'.

Chapter 15
Social control

15.1 The meaning of social control

Through your study of sociology you will have discovered that in order for society to exist there must be order and predictability. Any group of people living together must have common expectations if they are to engage in any form of social life. If I cannot predict how you are going to act, how is it possible for us to act jointly? Indeed, those who act in an unpredictable way are defined as **eccentric** or even **mad**. People in society need to share a common set of **values** and **beliefs** about social behaviour. These commonly held beliefs, however, are only very general guides to action, they are not specific in telling us how to behave. Sociologists suggest that there are specific guides to action, which we call norms. '**Norms**' simply means normal ways of behaving. Sometimes these are referred to as **mores**.

In order to persuade people to follow these norms, societies have developed two methods of ensuring conformity: informal and formal control.

15.2 Informal control

Link the issues raised in this chapter to the chapters on socialisation, gender and crime.

This is the most common form of control and is based upon the socialisation process, which we experience as we grow up. Socialisation and social control are mixed together so it is difficult to distinguish one clearly from the other. However, at its simplest, we can say that socialisation consists of learning the values of society, while social control consists of reinforcing those values we once learned.

Primary socialisation
This is the process of learning the values of society directly from contact with people around us who are very close to us, such as our family and friends. This occurs first in the family, where we are taught the expected patterns of behaviour. If we conform we are praised, but if we behave against the accepted values then we are punished – punishment may take various forms, from being smacked through to our parents simply telling us off. Most importantly, however, we learn to believe that certain behaviour is correct or preferable. This **internalised** guide to behaviour is what we commonly call our **conscience**. This process of learning the rules and values is reinforced by our friends. As a person moves from childhood through to adulthood, the **peer group** becomes particularly important, modifying the values of childhood and preparing the youth for adulthood.

Secondary socialisation

This is the process by which the fundamental patterns of behaviour learned in childhood in the family and from friends are strengthened by institutions such as the school, the mass media and the church.

These institutions consistently put forward a set of values which support the society as it is, guiding our behaviour towards conformity.

The result of informal control through primary and secondary socialisation is to create within people's minds an acceptance of the correctness, normality and 'naturalness' of society as it is. Sometimes sociologists refer to this process as one of **ideological control**.

Changes in informal control

Informal control has changed over time. Since the end of the nineteenth century the power of religion has declined and that of the education system and the mass media have increased.

Up until the nineteenth century, the simplest way of making people conform was to stress the existence of God, who would punish people after their death if they acted against the values of society. As no one comes back after death to talk about their experiences, then there is no way to contradict this threat. However, with the growth of secularisation, the use of a threat of a punishing god declined. The education system and the mass media developed effectively to replace religion.

The education system operates at two levels. First there is the choice of material that is taught in schools – this usually reinforces the values of society. For example, in most schools Orwell's book *Animal Farm* is studied and is generally used as a warning against the evils of totalitarianism and communism. the choice of the book in effect strengthens the claim that our form of society is the best.

Second, there are the comments and expectations of the teachers, the so-called **hidden curriculum**. Teachers often have expectations of pupils based on their own values: the appropriate behaviour for girls, for instance. If children do not conform, the teachers may not punish them, but show disapproval.

The mass media portray a version of events in the world which strongly supports accepted values, while criticising the activities of criminals and political 'extremists'.

The variety of values within the main culture

Although we learn to share a common set of values, beliefs and norms called the culture, we also learn alternative variations of this culture (which, however, still exist *within* the dominant culture). These are known as **subcultures**, which usually vary with such things as age, social class and ethnic group.

15.3 Formal control

Informal control is based on rewards and encouragement for correct behaviour and sanctions such as ridicule, gossip and comment for incorrect behaviour.

Formal control refers to the public, legal forms of controlling the population. Certain activities are regarded as dangerous to society, by those who hold power, and are therefore forbidden.

Formal social controls are enforced by special agents appointed for that purpose, the most formal are the police, courts and prisons who catch, judge and punish anyone who breaks the law; they attempt to deter others from doing the same thing.

When the normal mechanisms breakdown, then the army may be called in, as occurred in Northern Ireland.

Although they appear to be the strongest forms of social control, formal controls and the legal rules they underpin are in fact much weaker than the informal controls based upon commonly held values and internalised in individuals' consciences.

15.4 The nature of social control

Few dispute the fact that some form of social control is necessary in order to ensure that people conform to the rules of society. However, there is a major dispute about *who benefits* from the rules of society,

There are two views on this: the pluralist position and the Marxist-influence approach.

The pluralist option

This approach stresses that rules generally reflect the true feelings of the population of any society. The law, the media, the education system all reflect the needs and the wishes of the people. (The term 'pluralist' comes from the word 'plural' and simply means that decision making is in the hands of many people.)

The Marxist-influenced approach

This approach states that social control in most of its forms (especially the formal ones) is part of a system in which the ruling class composed of the rich and the powerful maintains its own power and influence.

Force is only used in the last resort, for it is far more effective to control the population by persuading them to accept the society as it is.

Examples of social control

Throughout this book, social control has been dealt with in some detail as it relates to particular topics.

Social control and the family: Chapter 3
Social control and education: Chapter 4
Social control and gender: Chapter 6
Social control at work: Chapter 9
Social control and politics: Chapter 14
Social control and the media: Chapter 17

15.5 Social control in other societies

In simple, tribal societies there are no such things as agencies of formal control. All social control is informal. Among the Bushmen of the Kalahari Desert in Africa, for example, there is no chief or leader. The group travels the desert in search of food, and decisions are made more by common sense and by custom rather than any person taking the active role of leader. Clearly there are some in the group whose opinion is considered of more worth than others, but that is all.

Social order is maintained very much by informal methods, such as gossip, publicly voiced complaints against someone in order to bring shame on him or her, people refusing to talk to someone else. In very serious cases of dispute, then the offender may be rejected by the tribe, or if an offender has harmed another member of the tribe, it may be that a relative of the dead or injured person has the right to take revenge.

However, it is important to realise that conflict and deviance such as we know them were extremely rare in simple societies. Some of the reasons why include:

- **Small groups** The groups in simple societies were very small, as food was in such short supply that rarely could more than a few dozen find enough food in one area to survive. Social harmony is easier to create in small groups.
- **The uncertainty** In simple societies, there was only ever just enough food to go around. No one could be sure of finding food or remaining well enough to go out to look for themselves. By cooperating with others and stressing this cooperation, there was a greater chance of survival. Hunters cooperated in finding food and the kill was brought back and divided between the whole group. Even if one person

failed to obtain food on a particular day, he/she would still eat.

- **The gift relationship** One of the most important methods of maintaining cooperation in simple societies was the giving of gifts. If a person needed to help build a shelter, for example, then another would offer to help. The individual was obliged to accept the offer of help and was obliged to offer some form of thanks, either by giving help or a gift on another occasion.

- **Intermarriage** Because of the small size of societies, there was considerable intermarriage, so that most people were related. These kinship ties also helped to pull people together.

- **Age ties** In a number of simple societies, such as the Turkana of the Sudan, there are ties among all those of the same age. They go through the **rites of passage** of entry from childhood into adulthood together and swear allegiance to others of the same age. In this way, when the tribe fragments into smaller bands, separately herding their cattle, the bonds formed by the age ties cross over the suspicions and differences that emerge over time.

- **Religion** This is possibly the most important of the forms of social control. Among the Turkana, for instance, murder is virtually unknown as their religion tells them that murder prevents rain. As they live in semi-desert conditions, this is obviously an extremely important rule.

  Usually the basic values of society are contained in the religion of society and failure to observe religious instruction is believed to lead to some form of natural disaster.

Summary

1 Social control consists of the forms of pressure that are put on people to conform to the accepted patterns of behaviour in society.

2 Formal control consists of the official rules and laws of society that are enforced by specially created agencies such as the policy, the judiciary and the prisons.

3 Informal control relates to the many expectations of behaviour made by society which are not enforced by the law. The agencies that enforce these unofficial rules of society are the family, the peer group, the media, etc.

4 Without social control society would not exist, for order and predictability are absolutely necessary for every society.

5 However, every industrial society has a number of different sets of values within it which provide a slightly different form of social control. These varieties are known as subcultures.

6 There are two different views on the nature of social control. The first is that social rules are applied for the benefit of everyone and that the law is a reflection of the feelings of the people.

  The alternative approach is that the laws reflect the interests of the most powerful groups in society and that they have also managed to impose their way of thinking on the population through agencies of social control.

7 In simpler societies there are no agencies of formal control. However, informal control is much more important and much stricter.

Self-test questions

1 What is the difference between 'formal' and 'informal' control?
2 What is the distinction between socialisation and social control?
3 Give two examples of 'agencies' that enforce social control.
4 It has been suggested that religion plays a part in social control. Briefly explain this.
5 Do 'simple' societies have any form of formal control? Explain the reasons for your answer.

Chapter 16
Crime and deviance

16.1 Reasons why some deviant acts are criminal

In the distinction between formal and informal social control, discussed in the previous unit, it can be clearly seen that **illegal** acts and **socially incorrect** acts may not be the same thing. For instance it may be viewed as morally bad by certain groups in the community to be homosexual, but it is not necessarily illegal. As sociologists study social rules and social actions, the more important distinction for them is not between legal and illegal acts, but rather the difference between **socially acceptable** acts and **socially stigmatised** acts. Acts that are regarded in some way as socially wrong are labelled by sociologists as deviant. Deviant acts, therefore, are all acts that are regarded as rule (norm) breaking whether they are legal or illegal.

Why are some deviant acts **illegal** and others not? The following explanations have been suggested:

- reflects majority view that a particular act is extremely deviant;
- moral crusades;
- suits the interests of the powerful.

Reflects the majority view

This explanation sees certain deviant acts as being so extreme that the majority of the population agree to ban them and so a law is passed. Durkheim is associated with this approach.

Moral crusade

This approach stresses the activities of a particular pressure group, who manage to have a law passed making particular acts which they disapprove of (for moral reasons or for their own gain) illegal.

An example of a moral crusade is the activities of the National Viewers and Listeners Association which is trying to have much stricter controls on the level of sex and violence on television.

The interests of the powerful

Marxist-influenced writers argue that the law reflects the interest of powerful groups in society and it benefits them. They point to the way that white collar 'crime' – that is, theft by middle-class people, such as tax evasion, is seldom prosecuted; and how the law basically protects the property of the better off.

16.2 Patterns of crime

- Crime rose steadily until the early 1990s after which time there has been a decline.
- The two most common offences for which people are prosecuted are (i) theft and handling stolen goods, and (ii) burglary.
- Violent crime comprises only about 5% of all offences recorded by the police.
- Sexual offences comprise only about 1% of offences recorded (though, as we shall see later, this is an underestimate as many women are reluctant to report sexual offences committed against them).

Who commits crime?

The statistics indicate that:
- males are far more likely to commit crime than females, the proportion is approximately 5 to 1;
- that the peak age for committing crime for males is between 16 and 19;
- the peak age for committing crime for females is between 13 and 15.

Crime is therefore more likely to be committed by young males. Approximately one-third of all men under 30 have been prosecuted or cautioned for a criminal offence.

16.3 Sociological explanations of crime and delinquency

Sociologists have suggested a number of possible explanations for criminal behaviour. These include:
- the subcultural approach;
- anomie;
- the Marxist approach;
- Left Realism;
- Control theory.

The subcultural approach

This approach has a number of variations, some of which are mentioned below. However, they all share the basic belief that those who commit a crime share a set of values which is different from the values of society as a whole That is, they have a **subculture**. Generally, the explanation is that they were brought up by their parents to have values sympathetic to crime.

Research

David Downes *(The Delinquent Solution)* studied a group of youths in East London. He could find no evidence of a distinctive set of values which could be called a subculture. Instead he found that the youths passed their time, trying to get as much fun out of life as possible. Sometimes this brought them into conflict with the law.

Anomie

Robert Merton has suggested that all societies in order to motivate people, provide them with some aim which they can achieve through hard work. However, in certain times the aim (which is usually to be financially well off) becomes impossible for the majority of the population, and especially for the working class to attain, e.g. in periods of high unemployment. Merton argues that this leads to an increase in the level of crime, as people turn to illegal means to achieve financial success. Merton calls this situation when the goals of society are not possible by conventional means **anomie**.

The Marxist approach

Sociologists following the tradition of Karl Marx have suggested that the true causes of crime lie in the type of society we have in Britain. In our **capitalist** society, the ownership of most industry and commerce is in the hands of a few people – at most 10% of the population. (This is an economic explanation of crime.) According to Marxists, (a) **the values** and (b) **the laws** of society area heavily influenced by the wishes of this powerful group.

The laws

Laws largely reflect the wishes of the powerful, according to Marxists. Thus the criminal law looks after *their* interests, stressing as it does the importance of private property, for example, of which they have the most. The laws therefore make the activities of other groups criminal, and justify the activities of the powerful.

The groups whose behaviour is made criminal therefore are those who have less power.

Left Realism

New Left Realism was the name given to the form of left-wing analysis of crime developed by Lea, Young and Mathews amongst others. They modified the subculture approach to develop frameworks which help explain why groups of young people are more likely to commit crime.

Crimes are committed by young males who live in a society in which they see high levels of income and expenditure by certain groups. These young males aspire to have the same goods and services, so they develop subcultures which allow them to commit crime. Left Realists argue that it is not poverty that causes them to turn to crime, but **relative deprivation** – their lack of goods relative to others around them. Left Realists point out that in committing crime to get goods and money, they help to destroy communities in which they live – creating fear and distrust.

Control theory

Control theories do not ask why people *break* the rules of society, but why they *follow* any rules in the first place. In *The Causes of Delinquency*, Hirshi argues that individuals are linked to society by four bonds. These are:
- **Attachment** – the extent to which people care about others' wishes and opinions.
- **Commitment** – the amount of personal investment that people put into their life in terms of education, hard work, career moves, etc.
- **Involvement** – this concerns activities, thus a busy person with a wide range of interests and activities may be too busy to engage in deviant activities.
- **Belief** – this concerns the intensity or degree of belief of someone in the rules of society.

The extent to which a person conforms to the four elements above represents the extent to which that person is likely to engage in criminal activities.

16.4 Labelling

In order to simplify and make sense of the world, we *classify* objects and people. For example, we talk about 'flowers', naming a whole variety of plants, or 'houses' a term that covers hundreds of different styles of dwelling. When it comes to people we also clarify or apply labels such as 'troublemaker', a 'homosexual', a 'fool', or a 'saint'. Each label carries with it a complete package of images and prejudices. The result is that we treat people very differently according to the label.

The **consequences** of labelling can be very great for a person – altering his or her whole life. The results of labelling have been called **a deviant career** by sociologists, meaning that if a person is given the label of being a deviant, then he/she will find him/herself treated very differently by others and this, in turn, will influence his or her own behaviour. For example, let us take the example of two people, both of whom steal some money.

Person A This person is caught and labelled a thief, friends desert her, others gossip and comment about her, and if she is arrested and sent to prison, she loses her job. On release from prison she will find it difficult to obtain other employment and so may have to resort to crime in order to survive.

Person A's perception of herself is also changed as she may now view herself as a thief and a criminal.

Person B This person is not caught and life continues as before.

It can be seen then that it is not the committing of a deviant act that is important, but the labelling of someone as having committed the act.

16.5 Labelling and deviancy amplification

It has been argued that in certain circumstances the labelling of some groups as deviant by agencies such as the media and the police can actually generate more deviance. This idea is known as **deviancy amplification**. We will examine two examples of deviancy amplification here: the role of the mass media and the role of the police.

The mass media

The mass media are very powerful in their ability to label certain groups as deviant. As most people may never meet the labelled groups themselves, the description of the group of individuals given by the media will be the image they hold of them. As the media tend to sensationalise issues in order to attract readers and viewers, it is likely that the labels attached to groups will be exaggerated in order to generate interest.

It has been suggested that newspapers and television create **folk devils** – that is people who are supposedly the source of tremendous disruption to society. The interest created by the media in these folk devils makes good news, but also causes **moral panics**. A moral panic is the situation where a group of folk devils (such as football hooligans or drug addicts) is presented so often in the media as evil and troublesome, that the public and the police become obsessed with eliminating it. Greater police resources are allocated to the control of this group and as a consequence more arrests are made.

The point is that the creation of the labels by the media and the moral panic that follows are based on great exaggeration of the true amount of trouble caused by the labelled group.

The police

The activities of the police are guided by ideas of which groups constitute the most likely to cause trouble to society and how they ought to be handled. In particular working-class and black youths are seen to be potential troublemakers. The police therefore tend to stop and search working-class and black youths far more often than any other group in the population. The result is that they are more likely to uncover crime among this group. And this, of course, proves to them that they are right to pick on this group in the first place. The police therefore will put greater resources into controlling this group and there is a corresponding rise in criminality which is uncovered.

Research
Jock Young *(The Drugtakers)* studied the activities of the police in Notting Hill, London. He found that when the police decided to crack down on drug taking, they did so by having an intensive period of stopping and searching people who they thought looked 'the drug-taking type'. They uncovered an amount of drugs and this encouraged them to crack down harder on the same type of person.

As a result of the police activities and prosecutions of those who sold drugs on a casual basis, the supply of drugs declined. In stepped professional criminals who were prepared to take the risks, but who demanded much higher prices. They were also prepared to add other ingredients into the drugs to cheat on the weight, which could cause serious illness or even death. To pay for the drugs, the drug takers were tempted into crime. Furthermore, the isolation of drug takers into small, secretive groups had the effect of making these people define themselves as drug takers and experiment with stronger, physically addictive drugs. So police activity actually made the situation worse.

16.6 Gender and crime

Female crime is very low compared to male crime, with five male offenders for every one female offender known to the police, and with women forming only 1500 of the 55 000 people in prison.

Explanations for female crime

There are three types of explanations centring on:
- differential socialisation;
- social control;
- lack of opportunity.

Differential socialisation

Females are generally socialised into a pattern of values and actions which stress that women are less aggressive and violent. These roles are taught through parents, schools, the media, etc. Socialisation is into the roles such as parent/carer, which rely upon responsibility and awareness of the needs of others.

Social control

Women are not only socialised differently, they are more strictly controlled in their attitudes and activities.
- Women are expected to base themselves and their lives in the home. There are **two spheres of life** – that dominated by men (streets after dark, pubs, the workplace) and those by women (homes, shops during the day). Women are restricted from the male sphere in which crime takes place.
- **Male monopoly of violence** Women are strongly discouraged from violence, whereas the potential for its use remains an element of masculinity.
- **Reputation** Women have to be careful of their public displays of behaviour for fear of being labelled as promiscuous, etc. Lees' study of schoolgirls (*Losing Out*), shows how girls label other girls, and this constrains behaviour.

Opportunity to commit crime

Throughout their lives females are shielded from opportunities to commit crime. Socialisation does not equip them with the aggressive male attitudes to violence.

Social control keeps them under the surveillance of parents, their peer group and male partners.

Career opportunities for women are more limited and they are rarely in the position to commit fraud or other forms of white-collar crime.

16.7 Understanding criminal statistics

Examiner's tip

Emphasise the fact that official crime statistics are unreliable and victimisation surveys are far more useful.

Official statistics need to be treated with considerable caution. In 1993, only about 4% of crimes were reported to the police.

Failure to report crimes to the police

The British Crime Survey revealed that people failed to report crime to the police because:

- They regarded the matter as too trivial, e.g. only a small amount of money stolen;
- They felt the police would be unable to do anything about the offence, e.g. a theft from a busy shop which could have been committed by anyone;
- They felt it was private matter they could deal with themselves, e.g. theft between friends;
- They feared or disliked the police, e.g. drug user who has been tricked into parting with his money for a 'bad deal';
- We can add to these that in the case of sexual offences, women who have been sexually assaulted often feel too embarrassed and humiliated to report it to the police.

Failure of police to record crime

Police may not record crime where:

- They regard the complainant of too low a status or too unreliable to take seriously, e.g. a complaint by a tramp or a drunk.
- They may regard the crime as too trivial to waste their time on, e.g. theft of a few pence;
- They may regard the matter as having nothing to do with them, even though it is technically an illegal act, e.g. less serious marital violence as a result of a quarrel between husband and wife.
- The decision to define an act as illegal and to respond to it as such is dependent on the policeman or policewoman's **discretion**.

Police activity

According to Stanley Cohen, police may become **sensitised** (strongly aware) towards certain types of crime or category of offender. In this case they will take notice of this offence. As a consequence the figures for this crime rise.

Policies

Certain police forces tend to pursue certain crimes more than others. Jarvis points out that Nottinghamshire has particularly high rates of motoring offences, not because of bad driving, but because of strong police emphasis on motoring law in that county.

Distribution of police

According to Box, more police officers are sent to patrol working-class areas of cities than middle-class suburbs, therefore crime rates in the working-class areas are higher, simply because there are more police to **notice** criminal acts.

Increase in police

Between 1970 and 1995 the police force in Britain increased by over 30%. There may be more crime observed and recorded as a result of this.

Changes in the law

Categories of crime are sometimes changed as a result of changes in the law. For instance, the figures of crime before and after 1977 are not strictly comparable because of a change in the categorisation of crimes that year.

Categorisation of crimes by the police

Different police forces categorise crimes differently, and this leads to complications in giving national figures.

16.8 Victims of crime

Victimisation surveys

Increasingly, sociologists have wanted to know about the victim as much as the criminal. As a result there has been the development of 'Victimisation surveys'. Victimisation surveys are usually of two types:

- **national surveys** of a whole country in which people are asked to provide information on crimes which have been perpetrated against them;
- **area or neighbourhood surveys** where a specific, usually inner city, neighbourhood is targeted and sociologists engage in a more detailed study of the same issues.

The national study – the British Crime Survey

The British Crime Survey (BCS) conducted by the Home Office shows that only one in four crimes of property offences and one in five offences of violence were recorded in the official statistics. Interestingly, and perhaps alarmingly as well, over the time of the surveys the *actual number* of crimes reported to the police has risen, while a smaller *proportion* of crimes (out of all those committed) are reported to the police (see Fig. 16.1).

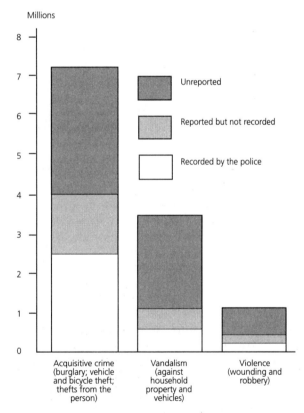

Fig. 16.1   Reported and unreported crimes
(Source: British Crime Survey, Home Office Research Findings, 1994)

The BCS found that the risk of being a victim of minor offences was high, but of suffering a serious offence was very small. Theft was the most common crime, and particularly theft linked to vehicles in some way. A staggering 36% of all offences recorded involved thefts from or of vehicles.

Burglaries made up 9% of the crimes, violent offences, such as wounding and robbery made up 5%, and common assaults comprised a further 12%.

Once BCS information was broken down, the differences in *experiences* of crime were quite dramatic.

The **risk of being a victim** is closely related to:
- geographical area,
- an individual's age,
- sex, and
- pattern of leisure activities, such as drinking alcohol and going out in the evening.

Examples of the striking **differences** include:
- robbery is twice as likely to occur to those under 45 than over;
- robbery is twice as likely to occur to men than to women;
- 80% of the victims of assault are men;
- the most common victim of an assault is a single male, under the age of 30, who goes out to pubs more than twice a week, to drink fairly heavily, and who himself assaults others!
- the risk of being burgled is five times higher for those living in urban areas.

Those of Afro-Caribbean origin and Asian origin were more likely to be the victims of crimes. Those of Asian origin in particular were more likely to suffer higher levels of loss or damage, and greater levels of violence against them. Over 24% of Asian origin victims believed that the offence was primarily racist in character, compared to 15% of those of Afro-Caribbean origins.

Local crime surveys

A number of local crime surveys have been carried out. The best known are the Merseyside and Islington (north London) crime surveys.

The biggest difference between national and local statistics were in sexual and domestic assaults with extremely few emerging from national surveys and many more from local ones. One British Crime Survey, for example, found a level of 4.2% of women experiencing domestic violence, while the Islington survey in 1992 claimed that 12% of its female respondents had suffered domestic violence. The figures for sexual offences were as low as 0.3% for the national survey and as high as 6% for the Islington survey.

Women as the victims of crime

The extent of crime against women

The British Crime Survey shows that 35% of women (aged 30–60) feel unsafe going out in the dark, compared to only 4% of males. Yet women seem to have very slightly lower levels of attacks on them than males, with 1.4% of women and 1.6% of males in that age group.

The Islington Crime Survey indicated that female victims are concentrated in certain age groups and areas of cities. We also know that sexual assaults have the lowest levels of reporting to the police (and possibly to social science surveys) because of embarrassment. The figures for sexual assault are therefore much higher than recorded.

Sexual assaults
- **Relationship of attacker to victim** The majority of sexual attacks involve people who are known to each other, including family members.
- **Place of attack** About one-third of sexual assaults take place in the homes of the victims, approximately the same as in the street or in an isolated spot.

Sociologists largely reject the biological argument that sexual assaults are motivated by uncontrollable sexual desire on the part of men. The following explanations have been suggested:
- **Rape as control** Brownmiller suggests that rape is a means of controlling women which has been used historically by men to keep women in an inferior position.
- **Rape as an extension of 'normal' male behaviour** Smart suggests that rape is merely an extension of normal sexual bargaining which occurs in British society. Socialisation of women is to stress their allure to men. On the other hand men are expected to initiate sexual encounters and women to at least make a show of 'resistance'. Therefore rape can be seen not as freakish deviance regarding the values of our society, but as an *extension* of them.

Marital violence

Under-reporting takes place here, as with rape. The police will only arrest where the case seems sufficiently serious. Therefore this is left to the discretion of the police.

Explanations for marital violence fall under two headings:

- **Individual explanations** These stress precipitating factors, such as violence in the childhood experiences of the male; high levels of alcohol intake; mental illness.
- **Structural (or feminist) explanations** Dobash and Dobash (*Violence against Wives*) argue that violence against female partners is embedded in our culture. Throughout history the use of a limited degree of violence by husbands has been culturally (and legally) acceptable.

    Culturally the values of family life are of a dominant male and a submissive wife who should perform her duties to a very high level. Women who fail to do so can be reasonably coerced.

Summary

1 Deviant acts are all acts that are regarded as rule breaking, whether they are legal or illegal.

2 The actions that are defined as deviant vary according to time, society and who it is that commits the act.

3 The reasons why an act is deviant in one situation but not in another are related to (a) the power and status of the person committing the act, (b) the values that deviance is measured against, which change over time, and (c) the different sets of values that exist at the same time in one society (so that one person's acts may be defined as deviant by others from a different subculture).

4 Deviant acts can be distinguished from illegal acts. Only some deviant acts are classified as illegal.

5 Deviant acts are illegal in one situation but not in another, because (a) they reflect a generally held view that these particular acts are very bad, (b) there is a 'moral crusade' to make an act illegal, and (c) those with power influence the creation of the law and they wish certain acts to be illegal.

6 There are certain groups in the population which, according to the official statistics commit higher than average levels of crime.
   - Males commit more crime than females – about 5 to 1 in proportion.
   - Younger people are most likely to commit crime: for males the most common age of committing crime is 18.
   - Levels of crime are much higher in the inner city areas.
   - Working-class youth have higher rates of crime than middle-class youth – about 4 to 1.

7 It has been suggested that part of the reason for the claimed higher levels of crime among certain groups compared to the population in general is related to (a) the different attitudes of the police and (b) defects in the official statistics.

8 There have been a number of explanations for crime and delinquency. They include:

   (a) the subcultural approach, which is based on the idea that the person who commits the crime has different values from the rest of the population.

   (b) Anomie – where people feel that they want the material possessions of society and are encouraged to possess them by advertising and the whole culture. When they cannot get them legally, they turn to illegal methods.

(c) New Left Realism – this, too, stresses the importance of the desire to possess and suggests this causes subcultures.

9 Social control theorists argue that it is more important to understand why people do *not* commit crime than why they do.

10 There have been a number of alternative explanations for crime, stressing the psychological and physical differences between criminals and the majority of the population.

11 Labelling means to place particular people in a category and then to act towards them in a particular way. For instance, if a person is labelled as a hero(ine) then he/she is treated with great respect; if labelled a coward he/she is treated equally with disrespect.

12 Labelling is very important in its consequences for people. Those who are labelled as deviant (even if they are not) are treated very differently, and this can affect their whole lives.

13 The activities of the police and the mass media are very important in their ability to label people.

14 Sometimes the media can create the idea that society is under threat from certain groups (such as 'football hooligans') and a 'moral panic' occurs which actually raises the level of the crime. This process is known as deviancy amplification.

15 The official statistics on crime need to be treated with great caution. It appears that many people do not report crimes to the police and that the police sometimes do not record acts which have been reported to them as crimes.

16 People are most likely to report crime when they can benefit themselves by it – for example, by reporting burglary and car theft because they have insurance. They are least likely to report it when they may be harmed themselves or regard the matter as private.

17 Victims of crime are usually the least powerful in society.

Self-test questions

1 Explain the differences between deviant acts and illegal acts.
2 Are deviant acts always defined the same in every society?
3 Do females commit the same amount of crime as males? Explain your answer.
4 What does the term 'labelling' mean?
5 What are 'moral panics'?
6 Why do official statistics of crime need to be treated cautiously?

Chapter 17
Media

17.1 Types and characteristics of the media

The **media** is the term used to cover the following forms of communication: TV, radio, newspapers, magazines, books, films and recordings.

- All these are one-way systems of communication from a single source to a large number of people (a 'mass' of people).
- The audience receiving the information has little or no chance of responding to the source.
- Mass media always involve the technology of broadcasting or print and distribution.
- The mass media are usually operated for profit (although not the BBC and many other national broadcasting systems).
- The mass media present information or entertainment in a specific format. Television for example has many half-hour programmes divided into categories such as 'news' or 'light entertainment'.

Two-way communication

The communication of the media is in contrast to two-way, face-to-face communication where two people exchange ideas or messages, such as in conversation.

- The communication is highly personal.
- Either of the people may interrupt the other and present an alternative viewpoint.
- The communication is started and finished according to the desires of people to communicate, not a fixed schedule.
- Much personal communication is conducted without any technology being involved – although of course telephones, the Internet, faxes, and CB radio are used.

By contrast, mass communication is based on the use of technology. Generally, the words or images are broadcast or printed and distributed.

17.2 Socialisation, social control and the media

(For detailed discussion of socialisation see Chapter 1; for social control see Chapter 15.)

The mass media play an extremely important role in **secondary socialisation,** which is the form of socialisation that reinforces the basic **primary socialisation** learned in childhood. They are able to do this in a number of ways:

- They are the most important source of information about the wider world, beyond the personal experience of most people. We only know about politics, crimes and sporting events through the media, unless we are actually present.
- Attitudes and opinions about the world are therefore formed by the media.
- How the media present information is crucial. They do not simply show the facts or the situation as they are, but put an interpretation on them.
- This interpretation consists of stressing the basic values of society in their contents, emphasising the difference between the normal and the deviant.
- This emphasis is achieved in two ways: (a) by **selection** of material. A typical news story consists of a shocking event such as a violent crime which highlights what society disapproves of – normal everyday behaviour is not regarded as news; (b) by **presentation,** reporting deviant events in a way that shows they are not approved of – newspapers generally present their news on criminals, drugtakers, etc in such a way as to show their disapproval.
- Once formed, people's views of the world are constantly **reinforced** by the media.

There is considerable dispute between those who argue (a) that the media are owned and controlled by a few of the rich and powerful who then impose their values on the population and (b) those who argue that the media reflect the views and attitudes of most of the population, and if they did not they would not survive in a fiercely competitive market. They also point out the role of the press in uncovering corruption and wrong-doing among the powerful.

17.3 The media and social control

Women and the media

The media help to perpetuate the division of roles between males and females. Some daily newspapers, for example, include photographs of semi-naked women. The contents of specialised magazines for women reaffirm that the accepted role for women is to make themselves attractive, to be good mothers and housewives. Different magazines may act for different age groups and interests, but these themes remain, merely being adjusted in tune with the age groups. Female youth magazines, for instance, stress the need to get a boyfriend and the importance of romance in girls' lives.

Male magazines on the other hand tend to be concerned with specialist hobbies, such as cars, motorbikes or wind surfing. There are some that consist almost entirely of female nudes.

On the wider issues of images of males and females presented in the media, research has shown that the roles of the main heroes and the other dominant characters in most plays, films and television programmes are written for men, with women playing their assistants. It is the man's role to provide excitement and the woman's to provide attractiveness.

The process by which the media reinforce and maintain the gender divisions in society begins as soon as a person can read. The first reading books tend to have very clear-cut male and female roles. Virtually all books, until a few years ago, automatically used male examples (e.g. if a student studies hard, *he* will pass the sociology exam).

Research

Majorie Ferguson in *Forever Feminine* studied the three best-selling women's magazines between 1949 and 1974: *Woman, Woman's Own* and *Woman's Weekly*. She found certain themes running through all those years. They included: women's need for emotion; feminine unpredictability; the importance of being young; love and marriage; and the theme of self-improvement. When she came to study the magazines for 1979–80, Ferguson found a change in that there was a greater stress on women being independent and not just being housewives – showing that women's magazines are changing to reflect the changing role of women. Nevertheless she still found that the key message of the magazine is that women are different from men and have different needs.

Angela McRobbie in *Jackie, an Ideology of Adolescent Femininity* examined the stories in the girls' magazine *Jackie*. She found that the main message of the stories was that a girl was someone to be looked at and appreciated, rather than someone who went out and about doing things. The main theme of the magazines was romance and love. McRobbie argues that the magazines encourage girls to be passive and to regard only romance as truly important in their lives.

Suzanne Czaplinski's *Sexism in Award-Winning Picture Books* is an American study of children's illustrated books. She found that (a) there was a very strict division of roles between males and females – even though the roles were often outdated, (b) there were far more male then female characters; (c) the roles that women were given were as mothers and aunts, rather than as the main characters of the story.

The **stereotype** of what are female characteristics is constantly reinforced by the media. In terms of **social control** women who challenge the stereotype are regarded as being odd in some way or deviant.

Race and the media

The British population is 95% white. Blacks and Asians are a small minority, over half of whom were born here. The impression given by the media, however, is that there is still an immigration problem and that there are far more blacks and Asians than actually exist. The stress of media coverage is on the conflict caused by so many immigrants in Britain, rather than on blacks' and Asians' difficulties in the fields of work, housing and education.

The differences between blacks and whites are constantly referred to and thus in reality reinforced.

Research

Troyna in *Public Awareness and the Media: A Study of Reporting Race* found that between 1976 and 1978 the reporting of race in the media was based upon the theme of the outsiders who were living among us. The second biggest topic of race was the issue of immigration – even though there has been a very sharp decline in the numbers of black and Asian immigrants in the last twenty-five years.

In a survey he carried out, he concluded that the media did encourage people to believe that black people were a source of trouble.

Criticism

The argument that the media actually encourage racial prejudice has been criticised by Braham, who argues that the British press merely reflect racist feeling already held by the population.

The result of the media treatment of blacks is, however, to strengthen a stereotype of them.

Criminals and the media

The media are commercial institutions trying to earn profits from attracting as many viewers, listeners or readers as possible (and the BBC has to work in this commercial environment). The result is that some crimes which are of greater 'human interest' are grossly over-reported compared to others. For example, crimes of violence are over-reported by 36 times their actual occurrence and crimes of indecency by 34 times. The result is that people receive a highly distorted view of the sorts of crimes taking place, and thereby people's fears are greatly increased.

The media creates a stereotype of the 'typical' sort of crime, and creates public fear about it – which can lead to moral panic. When this occurs people get so worried about certain crimes as a result of media coverage that all the forces of law and order are thrown against the stereotyped deviants, while other forms of crime are left alone.

Research
Stuart Hall, in *Policing the Crisis*, argued that in the early 1970s there was a sudden upsurge in the reporting of crime dubbed as 'mugging', in which a person or small group was attacked and robbed in the streets. The coverage in the media was intense, even though the actual number of muggings formed a small proportion of all crimes. As a response to press coverage, a huge number of police were drafted to Brixton, the area regarded as the centre of mugging in London, A stereotype of the mugger became the black youth. The police, who had been looking for a justification of heavy policing in Brixton, used the mugging crisis as the reason for swamping the district. The **stereotype** criminal becomes the inner city delinquent and the **social control** element is that the factors causing the problems of inner city youth are ignored and the spotlight taken off the multi-million-pound swindles in the City of London.

17.4 The media, labelling and moral panics

The media are the providers of information on deviance for most people, including politicians and, to some extent, the police. The image projected about deviance and crime by newspapers and television can affect the activities of the police and the attitudes of the public.

Labelling or stereotyping is when a person or group is described as having certain characteristics and then responded to in a way that seems appropriate for people with these particular characteristics. For example, if a person is described as 'mad' then, *whether it is true or not*, he/she will be treated as mad, even if his or her behaviour is perfectly normal.

The media have the power to label certain groups and their actions in this way and sometimes to create great public concern about them.

This process of defining a group and then providing media coverage in such a way as to sensationalise a problem, and possibly make an imaginary problem by exaggeration and distortion has the following elements.

The activity
A group of people are performing an act which is regarded as anti-social by more powerful groups in society, for example social security 'scroungers'.

Defined as newsworthy by the media
The media in some way or other finds out about the group's activities and regards these as newsworthy because
- there may be a lack of 'news' at the time and the story may help sell papers;
- they may act to the benefit of influential groups who have the power to get their version of events placed in the media.

Competition of media
Once a story appears in one paper or on television, competitors will attempt to out-do that original story, resulting in exaggeration and distortion.

Moral panic
The audience have become so concerned or 'sensitised' to the particular issue they are almost actively seeking these problems out. Every activity which can vaguely be put into the stereotyped category is placed there. People are distressed and fascinated.

The moral panic finishes
It will gradually die out as the media lose their interest and turn to a subject with greater novelty.

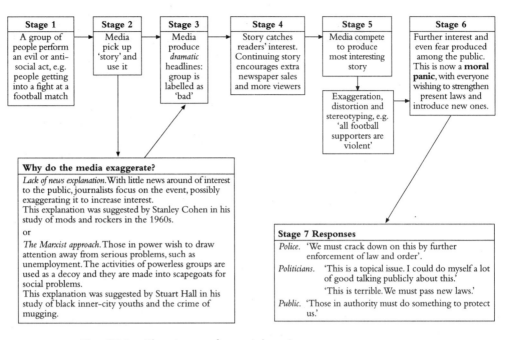

Fig. 17.1   The stages of a moral panic
(Source: Adapted from Stephen Moore, *Sociology Alive!*,
Stanley Thornes, 2nd edition, 1996)

Research

In the mid–1960s, Stanley Cohen, in *Folk Devils and Moral Panics*, studied the way that the media helped to create an image concerning the original mods and rockers.

Cohen claims that as a result of a sparcity of news the media fastened their attention on the activities of youths in seaside resorts over an Easter Bank Holiday Weekend. The media classified the youths into two groups – mods and rockers, a distinction that had not been made clearly by the youths themselves.

Cohen shows how the exaggeration and distortion of the media concerning what happened there meant that youths identified themselves with the images portrayed, and 'became' mods or rockers.

The policy were highly sensitised to the possible problems that these youths were likely to cause and so introduced a much higher level of policing. This inevitably brought about higher arrest rates. The 'trouble' the media had first reported (and largely invented) thus occurred. According to Cohen the results of the media's activities were:

- **The label** For young people a certain style of dress came to symbolise being a mod – and the behaviour of mods was to go to seaside resorts on bank holidays and to look for trouble with the rockers. The police and public, too, saw a style of dress signifying 'trouble'. So *anybody* dressed liked this was a possible troublemaker.

- **A moral panic** The activities of the media created such an irrational fear among the police, the public and the politicians that there was effectively a panic to introduce measures against the perceived troublemakers.

- **The amplification of deviance** The result was a greater increase in actual deviance as a result of the media's activities than there would have been without them.

The example given earlier of Stuart Hall's study of 'mugging', is a second example of stereotyping by the media.

Hall argues that in the 1970s there was a breakdown in social control in the inner cities as a result of increasing unemployment and social problems, and an excuse was sought for heavier policing. The media's mugging 'campaign' provided the justification.

17.5 Explanation of media influence on behaviour

It is generally believed that the mass media influence behaviour, and much of the discussion on socialisation in this chapter rests upon this assumption. However, sociologists are not in agreement on the *extent* to which the media influence our behaviour and *how* they influence our behaviour.

The behaviour (or hypodermic syringe) model

The first attempts to explain the influence of the media were based on the common-sense approach that if it was true that the media influence our behaviour, then watching a violent or sexually stimulating film would alter a person's behaviour.

Research
In the 1960s Bandura showed a film of children being violent to dolls to another group of children, who were then given dolls themselves. He found that children tended to imitate the violence on the screen.

Criticism
The idea that people watch a television programme or film and are so influenced by it that they abandon their normal behaviour to go out to attack people, seems too naive. It treats people as if they have no mind or views of their own.

Audience selection

The model just described has been replaced by a greater understanding that people choose what programmes they wish to watch and which newspapers they buy. Instead of being passive, the audience in this approach is seen as actively interpreting the information given.

In order for something to influence our behaviour we must first have a receptive attitude towards it. An **attitude** is a firmly held belief which causes a person to respond in a particular way to a stimulus or event. Attitudes are necessary in order for us to make sense of our world. They form a **code** (or cultural map) which allows us to respond with consistency to similar types of situation. The mass media can **reinforce** attitudes already held, but it is difficult for them fundamentally to change people's attitudes. This is because people tend to select the information they want to hear or read. Thus:

- People select the type of newspaper they wish to read, usually one that confirms their political attitudes;
- People view events through their particular bias and select the elements of the **facts** that reinforce their existing attitudes;
- People remember information that confirms their opinions and forget the rest.

The effect of the information upon our attitudes is also influenced by (i) the origins of the information: a prestigious source is more likely to be believed than an unknown one; (ii) the situation in which the information is received – whether it **fits** in and helps to make sense of the situation in which the audience find themselves.

Research
David Morley, in *The Nationwide Audience,* studied the responses of different groups of people to a popular BBC 6 o'clock 'magazine' show. He found that the different groups approached the material presented in the programme in different ways, reflecting the particular background and values they held. For instance bank managers saw the programme's treatment of the 1977 budget in a very different light from a group of shop stewards.

The cultural approach

This approach derives from the **audience selection** approach, but sees the influence of the media as being more powerful, *over a long time,* in that they create a culture or climate of thought, within which people hold opinions. In other words, the media define the range of acceptable options on any matter. The first two approaches, then, stress that the media have an influence after a short time. The third approach stresses less the direct effect, rather than the creation of a climate of opinion.

The best known piece of research using this approach is of the Glasgow University Media Group, which analysed news bulletins in the 1980s. It argued that the language and the settings of interviews and the presentation of the information all led to a strong bias against the unions in industrial matters. The unions are presented as the trouble makers and the assumption underlying strike reporting was that the unions were the cause of the problem.

The Glasgow University Media Group argues that the bias derives from the uncritical acceptance of the journalists of a hierarchy of credibility in which the views of the powerful are regarded as the ones which 'set the framework' for the reporting.

Troyna (*Public Awareness and the Media: Reporting of Race*) examined the press between 1976 and 78 and found that the central theme was of 'outsiders living amongst us'. The impression given was of far more members of the ethnic minorities in the UK population than actually exist here and the media stressed the 'problems' they caused.

17.6 Violence and the media

Much research has been centred on the role of the media (particularly television) in encouraging violence. But the research has not been conclusive.

Research

In *Violence in Television* (1972), a report prepared for the BBC by Katz et al, a questionnaire was completed by a minimum of 600 households on 12 evenings of television viewing. Further to this, individuals and 50 families were also interviewed. The results indicated that as most violence seen was so obviously fictitious and unrelated from real life, it had little influence on the viewers. The authorities found that the viewers were, however, becoming **desensitised** by so much violence, so that they were becoming less alarmed by it in real life. However, violence on television did not incite people to violent acts in real life.

In *Television Violence and the Adolescent Boy* (1978), which is based upon interviews of over 1500 boys aged 12–17 in London, Belson found that **high exposure** to violence on television does increase the amount of serious violence in adolescent boys.

Halloran, who was heavily involved in a study commissioned by the Independent Broadcasting Authority, *The Portrayal of Violence on TV* (1978), argues that it is a mistake to try to form a **direct** link between violence and television viewing. Although the study found that violence on television could **reinforce** existing aggressive attitudes, it also argued that television is only one of many influences on people's behaviour. So violent adolescents may be drawn to watching violence on television, but television is not the **cause** of the tendency to violence.

We can see that the answer to the different survey results lies in the fact that the mass media's influence on our behaviour must be balanced against the importance of family socialisation, the strength of the legal system and the wide cultural values of our society, all of which abhor violence.

17.7 Mass media and political opinion

Sociologists are generally of the opinion that in the short term the mass media do little to change people's voting intentions. However, exposure over a long period of time to a political message can change people's opinions towards it. Therefore, party political broadcasts and the mass media's election coverage may influence only the **floating** voter; the rest have already made up their minds who they are going to vote for. Over a number of years the mass media's coverage of certain political events can cause a change in attitude.

Most people read a particular paper for reasons other than its political slant – for example for its arts or sports coverage. However, for whatever reason a particular newspaper is bought, the fact remains that it is supporting the policies of one or other political party. This party is usually, but not always, the one favoured by the paper's proprietors.

Interestingly, television is seen as being independent and providing more reliable news than newspapers. The BBC is a public corporation, while the **independent** channels are controlled by the Independent Broadcasting Authority who combined to form the Independent Television Authority. The television companies are therefore seen to be less influenced by any one person. However, as the next section will show, television's presentation of news and information can be as misleading as that of the newspapers.

Whereas a newspaper owner may deliberately influence the paper's support of certain policies, journalists are often guilty of **unwitting bias**. What becomes news, both in newspapers and on radio and television is shaped, not only by commercial pressures and the constraint to act within in the law, but also by organisational pressures from within the mass media. Golding and Elliott have pointed out that the content of news portrays a very particular one-sided view of the world. This is not the result of a **conspiracy**, however, but is a necessary consequence of how events are regarded as news in the first place, and are then selected and presented to an audience. Journalists emphasis the more interesting, colourful areas of social life at the expense of the more mundane. A result of this is that those in powerful and privileged positions are more often consulted for information and opinion. Howard Becker has called this the **hierarchy of credibility**, whereby those in powerful positions in society are more likely to be believed than a member of the public.

(Further discussion on politics and the media can be found in Chapter 15.)

Examiner's tip

Emphasise the close link between the media and the wider culture.

17.8 Contents of the media

Newspapers

The **contents** vary according to readership.
- 'Popular' papers like the *Sun* concentrate on: (i) human interest stories, such as the lives of TV celebrities, pop stars and royalty; (ii) mainstream sport, such as football, snooker and cricket; (iii) 'sexy' or 'spicy' stories; (iv) sensational happenings, usually in Britain.
- The 'quality' newspapers usually concentrate on: (i) political events; (ii) economic problems; (iii) in-depth coverage of a particular topic, possibly on a weekly rota basis (for instance the *Guardian's* weekly section devoted to education); (iv) sport.

The **presentation** varies with the type of newspaper.
- Popular papers: (i) have very short articles; (ii) they are written in extremely simple English; (iii) the information given is very simple and viewpoints (if included at all) are presented in black-and-white; (iv) there is great sensationalism – with the attempt to excite the reader; (v) great use is made of photographs – particularly of attractive women.

- The quality papers: (i) have much longer articles, (ii) they are written in depth; (iii) the information is usually fairly complex and there is some attempt to give different viewpoints – although most of the papers are biased towards a conservative viewpoint; (iv) the presentation is usually fairly dull, with less exaggeration; (v) fewer photographs are used.

Television

In the past the BBC was far less sensational than ITV. However, the need to keep audiences high has led to adoption of the ITV style of broadcasting, which is to attract the biggest audience possible.

Both BBC and ITV have specialist channels where the programmes for minority tastes are shown: BBC2 and Channels 4 and 5. In some ways this division reflects the popular/quality divisions in newspapers.

There has been an expansion of television broadcasting from the five main channels which are 'terrestially' broadcast, to an increasing number of channels available by satellite transmission and cable. These have widened the range of choice. Some people argue that there has been growth in 'mass culture' as the stations vie for audience figures and the commercially based companies fight for advertising revenue.

The recording industry

The recording industry is dominated by a few large companies. It is in their interest to stabilise the market for recordings. The greater the diversity of music, of groups and of styles, the more complex the selling of recordings becomes. The result is that recording companies (as well as radio stations) push a relatively small number of musicians whose music is 'mainstream'. A good example of this has been the commercialisation of rap music which emerged as black inner city, US confrontational music and has gradually been incorporated whilst maintaining a sense of danger and confrontation within commercial limits. The wider diversity of styles is ignored. After a while, however, if this sound gets stale, the public will usually become attracted to another style of music of another group. At first these pose a threat to the established order, but gradually the new style is taken on by the recording companies, polished and becomes the new mainstream. This pattern of stagnation is particularly strong in the United States.

17.9 Reasons for the style of the media's contents

Profitability

The media, like other commercial institutions, needs to be profitable in order to survive. The exception is the BBC, which is funded by the government, who levy an annual licence fee on the use of television sets. However, the BBC exists in a commercial environment and has to compete against the private television stations in order to prove its popularity and its right to exist.

For broadcasting (i.e. television and radio) and newspapers, profitability involves:
- Having the maximum number of viewers/listeners or the maximum possible number of sales;
- Advertising – having large sales or viewing figures is not enough, what is also needed is advertising revenue. This is attracted by having large circulation/viewing figures of the right target group for advertisers. The better-off the audience, the smaller the numbers of people viewing/reading is necessary for the newspaper or television station to exist.

The biggest selling daily newspapers today, the *Sun* and the *Daily Mirror*, have mainly a working-class readership. The smallest selling, the *Guardian* and *The Independent*, have a middle-class readership. For the commercial television stations, the sheer size of the audience means that they are attractive to most types of advertisers.

Differences in audience/readership

Newspapers deliberately aim their contents to attract a particular sort of reader. The 'popular' dailies, such as the *Daily Mirror*, which are aimed at a largely working-class audience, tend to concentrate on what they regard the working class as wanting: which is basically sensational 'stories' with dollops of sex. The quality newspapers consider their middle-class audience wish to read about politics and money.

The ownership of the papers

Newspapers owners are relatively few in number in Britain. Rupert Murdoch, owner of *The Times* and the *Sun* is the best known. There is clear evidence from journalists that owners impose their views on the editors to ensure that the papers reflect their ideas.

The activities of journalists

Undoubtedly, journalists' activities are the most important influence on the content and presentation of the news. Journalists work with a concept of **newsworthiness**. Among the elements guiding journalists in the way they select and present their material are:

- **Frequency** Things that happen quickly and which are easily understood, fit into frequency of publication of daily newspapers – a big bank robbery, for example. Events that take a long time to unfold are not regarded as news. until the intervention of Bob Geldof, there was very little interest in the famines of Africa.
- **Threshold of importance** The assumed importance of an event. Something at local level will not be regarded as important enough for national news. The assumed importance affects the amount of coverage. A local car accident is not worthy of inclusion in national news, but a 50-car pile up on the M1 is. This also applies to people; some are more important than others;
- **Clarity** The simpler and clearer an event is – or at least the clearer it can be presented – affects its inclusion in the news. Problems with the economy are difficult to present, but a strike is easy and clear.
- **Meaningfulness** Events have to be culturally meaningful to the journalist and to his or her audience. So events in non-western countries receive little coverage.
- **Unexpectedness** Things that happen everyday or are entirely predictable are not news worthy – there needs to be an element of surprise. However, the news must also be culturally meaningful.
- **Composition** There is a belief that there ought to be a balance of types of news items. For example, there ought to be a mix of exciting and topical stories, balanced with 'human interest' items.
- **Personalisation** The stress is always on personalities, not on the political, economic, or social background from which they are drawn.

17.10 Patterns of ownership and control

Ownership

The debate between **pluralist** and **radical** writers is closely related to the patterns of media ownership. The more widespread the ownership of the media, the greater the diversity of views. On the other hand, concentration of ownership in a few hands tends to strengthen the radical writers' argument.

Concentration of control

The first characteristic of the mass media is **concentration of control**. One of the more successful companies in the newspaper business for example has been Rupert Murdoch's News International Corporation which now owns *The Times, The Sunday Times,* the *Sun,* the *News of the World* and Sky Broadcasting. The four newspapers account for 41% of all daily and 45% of all Sunday newspaper sales.

Diversification

The second largest characteristic of the mass media is **diversification**.

- Large commercial concerns with no previous experience of mass media ownership are now diversifying their interest and acquiring ownership of a range of media outlets. This has produced a tangled web of interlocking interests.
- Owners of a particular medium are buying into another to minimise the financial risks of specialising in one medium, where they may be stranded if there is a shift of popularity (e.g. from the cinema to the video). This means that new media reflect the format and values of the existing media.

Multi-nationalisation

The third characteristic is **multi-nationalisation** which means that the media have increasingly become international, e.g. Murdoch's News International is an important force in Australia and the United States as well as in Britain.

Control

The power of the owners

Ownership of the media rests in the hands of a few companies. Within the restraints of good taste and the need to be commercially successful, a newspaper's owner has a tremendous amount of power to shape its political direction. The day-to-day decisions are left to an editor who knows what his or her employers expect of him or her.

Influences running against the control of the owners alone

It is important to realise that the owners are not the only influence on the contents of the media, as we saw earlier. The following also influence the contents:

- Journalists' sense of news values (discussed in Unit 17.9). Journalists have certain ideas of what constitutes news – although the views of the owners will profoundly affect the content and viewpoint of the newspapers, there does exist a professional sense of what constitutes news values. The freedom of the journalists to decide on the content varies with the newspaper group.
- The need to be commercial. For a newspaper or television station, there is the need to have high readership or viewing figures. Clearly contents that are too far from public opinion and taste are therefore excluded.
- The need to attract advertising. Advertising revenue is crucial to the success of any newspaper or television/radio station (other than the BBC). The contents of the media must therefore (i) attract the right sort of audience to interest advertisers, and (ii) not offend the interests of advertisers.

Control and broadcasting

Control of radio and television is different from that of newspapers and the recording industry.

- The BBC is state owned and run with state subsidies;
- Commercial radio and television although private owned, are under the authority of the Independent Broadcasting Authority, which has considerable controlling powers.

However, it means that control still remains in the hands of very few people, who are usually chosen for their pro-Establishment views.

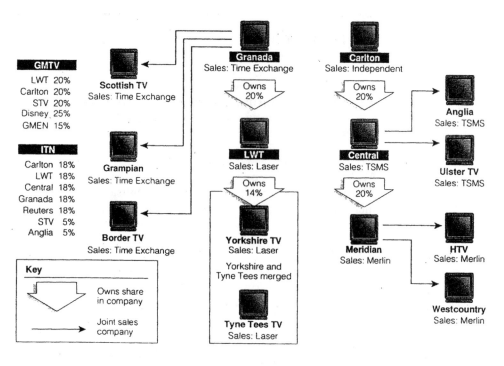

Fig.17.2 Who owns the ITV companies?
(Source: *The Guardian*, 20 November 1993)

The government's influence on the media

Licence fees are the means by which the BBC is financed. The licence fee is paid by the viewer to the government who passes it on to the BBC. The BBC is, by law, totally independent of the government. The government could not withdraw its finance because it did not agree with the content of the BBC's broadcasting.

Government subsidies are a different type of support from licence fees; subsidies are not provided for by law and can easily be withdrawn from media too critical of the established political and social order. Government support in this country is not so structured as in other nations. It is rather an informal system of aid and takes the following forms:

- for the BBC the government makes up the shortfall between the revenue from licence fees and the actual amount required. The BBC also receives a grant for its external services;

- for commercial television there is a reduction in the levy on advertising revenue. In 1971 the levy was substantially reduced and in 1973 was altered to apply to profits rather than revenue;

- Britain has no direct system for aid for newspapers, but government advertising is a significant form of indirect support. Like private advertising, however, its distribution is uneven, favouring the more popular papers.

Conclusion: patterns of ownership and control

- The mass media are dominated by a few companies, plus the BBC. On the surface this points to a close control of media output by their owners who can use it to express their own opinions.

- However, other factors heavily influence the content of the media. Hartley points out that the mass media operate in a competitive commercial environment and therefore need to be economically viable. This entails: (a) attracting advertising revenue, (b) maintaining a large audience.

- Commercial factors probably influence the decisions and attitudes of the owners of the media, rather than personal political preferences.

- In the actual **news-making** and **leisure-producing** activities of those employed in the media, the **informal methods of control** operate to limit the breadth of values and views expressed in the media.

Summary

1 The term **mass media** refers to the following forms of communication: television, radio, books and magazines, recordings and films.

2 All these share the characteristic that one source of information communicates with a large number of people who have no means of communicating back.

3 The development of the media has been linked to the changes in technology and growth of an affluent audience.

4 We are at the beginning of a revolution in mass communications with the introduction of word processors and satellites.

5 The media are an important part of the process of **secondary socialisation** (this includes other agencies such as the school and the church), which reinforces the activities of the family in its role of **primary socialisation**. They reinforce the values learned in the family which allow people to become full participating members of society.

6 The media perform an important role in society control, by helping to create attitudes to certain forms of behaviour and groups of people.

7 There is a dispute among sociologists as to whether the media, as agents of social control, benefit the rich and powerful, or the whole society.

8 There are certain images and stereotypes that are constantly being presented in the media. A stereotype is a simplified image of a supposedly typical member of a particular group, which distorts reality.

9 On example of this is the presentation of women in the media, which creates a particular image of women through the use of photographs and language.

10 The effect of the media on crime is important. The amount and type of coverage of an event can create an increase in crime, known as an **amplification of deviance**.

11 It has been argued that the media have been used to distort the extent of crime in inner cities in order to justify extra policing.

12 Explanations of the influence of the media fall into three groups: those that stress the powerful immediate response of people stimulating material – the **behaviourist model**; secondly, those that stress that audiences choose the information they want from what is presented to them – the **audience selection model** (therefore, for instance, only those already attracted to violence would be affected by a violent film); and thirdly, the **cultural approach**, which stresses that the influence of the media is much more long term creating an agenda of appropriate attitudes.

13 Violence and the media the evidence of the studies is contradictory, but would suggest that high exposure to violent films and TV programmes can reinforce violent values already held.

14 The effect of the media on political opinion is extremely complex. They do not appear to influence voting patterns directly as people tend to choose the facts they want. However, it can have a generally socialising affect by creating the general climate of opinion.

15 The contents and presentation of the media vary according to the type of audience that is aimed at. Newspapers do not simply report 'facts' that have happened, but choose what they consider to be interesting pieces of information for the particular readership they serve.

16 Their choice of material depends mainly upon the journalists' idea of what constitutes **newsworthy material.**

17 The media in Britain are owned and controlled by a very small number of people.

18 Over a period of time, three trends can be found: concentration; diversification and multi-nationalisation.

19 The owners' power to influence the contents is great, but other factors such as advertising and the need for a large audience are just as powerful.

20 Advertising has considerable influence on the contents of the media – as the advertisers are important economically to the media.

Self-test questions

1 What are the distinctive characteristics of the mass media as compared to other forms of communication?
2 In what ways do the media play a role in the process of socialisation?
3 With the help of examples, show how research has demonstrated the media's importance in perpetuating the division of roles between males and females.
4 What characteristics are commonly found in the way that the media deal with race?
5 How can the media give a distorted impression of the types of criminal activity found in Britain today?
6 How do the media's activities result in the amplification of 'deviance'?
7 It is often said that the media (especially television) encourage violence: what evidence is there for this?
8 To what extent do the media influence people's voting behaviour?
9 How does the presentation of 'popular' papers differ from that of 'quality' papers?
10 What factors are chiefly responsible for style of the contents of the media?

Chapter 18
Answers to self-test questions

Chapter 1 Socialisation

1 Socialisation means the process by which people are taught the values and behaviour expected of them in society.

2 Primary socialisation: this is the process by which people first learn the values and behaviour expected of them from people who are very close to them and important in their development. These people would include family and the peer group.
Secondary socialisation is the process by which we learn the values and ideas of the wider society, which build upon our previous socialisation in the family. Typical institutions that influence us are the school and the mass media.

3 Three of the following: the family, the peer group, schools, the mass media, the workplace.
In each of your three examples you ought to note that behaviour is modified in some way and that people are rewarded for acting in certain ways and punished for acting in other ways.
In the family people first learn how to behave and they are also given adult roles to copy. Very importantly they also learn gender roles.
In the peer group, wider roles are learned from friends and so the child moves slightly away from the influence of the family. Play is extremely important as children learn to play a wide variety of adult roles, and learn to put themselves in the places of other people through learning team games.
In schools the common expectations of the wider society are imposed upon all children. Those from certain class and ethnic backgrounds are introduced to the dominant values of society. Discipline is taught and there is the first introduction to the constraints of work.
The mass media convey messages concerning society's attitudes to a wide range of issues. People's attitudes are formed.
The workplace socialises people into very specific attitudes and forms of behaviour in order for them to cope with their day's work and to get on with colleagues.

4 Culture means the whole range of the knowledge, ideas and habits of society which are transmitted from one generation to the next.

5 Role conflict is when the different roles that people play in life come into conflict with each other. The example given in the text concerns a person who is a police officer catching a friend who is speeding – does the police officer book the friend or let him go?

Chapter 2 Research methods

1 (a) Cross-sectional studies are surveys of the population at a particular time – a good example would be an opinion poll.

(b) Case studies are in-depth studies of a particular place or event which help us to understand it. The information, however, is not necessarily helpful in understanding other situations.

(c) Longitudinal studies are those carried out on a particular group over a long period of time. Typically this involves following a group of children through their lives.

2 Secondary sources consist of information that are collected by people other than sociologists for various purposes. These include a wide variety of sources such as official statistics as in the Census, personal diaries and newspaper reports. They are useful to the sociologist as they generally provide information that he/she is unable to find out for him/herself. They provide background information and help confirm the research of the sociologist. They are always used where the sociologist has to delve into the past when there is no one available to question.

3 The sociologist would use a mail questionnaire in order to ask questions of a large number of people, who would probably be scattered over a wide area. The sociologist would use participant observation when he/she wanted to study a group of people in depth in order to understand their motives and behaviour in action. Generally the group under study would be in one place and would be the sort of group to which a questionnaire or formal interview could be given, for example, a group of delinquents.

4 In order to fully understand a group of people it may not be adequate just to ask them questions. It may also be important to observe them as they behave in normal circumstances. These people may not be able or willing to fill in questionnaires. By joining them, and in some cases actually becoming one of them, the sociologist can truly understand them.
The main problems of observational methods are that the researcher may become too influenced by the group and therefore may fail to analyse the information in an objective manner. Alternatively, the researcher may influence the group and so disturb the 'natural' activities of the group.

5 (a) Open-ended questions are those questions that do not require a specific choice of reply, such as 'yes' or 'no'. They allow the respondent free choice to express him/herself in his/her own words. Open-ended questions are generally used when discussing complex issues and the researcher is seeking some depth of reply.

(b) Interviewer bias occurs when the values of the interviewer influence the replies of the person interviewed. The interviewer may irritate the person interviewed so that he/she responds in an abrupt or misleading way. The interviewee may want to please the interviewer and so says what he/she thinks the interviewer wishes to hear. The interviewer may induce the person interviewed to reply in a certain way by asking' leading' questions, or by altering the tone of voice to show disapproval.

(c) Experiments: these are when people are placed in carefully controlled situations where their response can be closely observed. Sociologists do not use them too often as the situations are artificial and do not reflect real situations and therefore real responses.

Chapter 3 The family

1   Nuclear family – consists of two generations (parents and children)living together. This type of family is usually found in modern industrial societies such as Britain today.
Extended family – consists of three generations (grandparents, parents and children) living together. This type of family is usually found in pre-industrial societies such as the Bedouin of the Negev desert.

2   According to some sociologists (e.g. Talcott Parsons, McIver and Page), the family has now lost many of its functions, especially since the state provides so many services and the family is no longer an economic unit in the sense of all producing and working together. Other sociologists (e.g. Fletcher) have argued that many of the original functions remain, although perhaps in a changed form; and it can also be said that the modern family looks after its members to a higher standard than ever before.

3   It is argued that the family can be emotionally intense, involve the repression of women and lead to violence and psychological disorders. Marxists see the family as a purveyor of very conservative values and as a convenient unit in perpetuating the capitalist economic system.

4   At the beginning of this century the family was male dominated with the father being the 'breadwinner' and 'head of the household'. Women were regarded as inferior and spent their lives looking after their children, their husbands and their homes. The legal position of women reflected this.
More recently greater equality has been established between husbands and wives. Domestic tasks are shared, women are more likely to go out to work and contribute to the family budget. The husband and wife tend to spend their leisure time together.

5   Children are now treated more as responsible individuals and have more freedom than previously. At the same time, parents provide greater care of children and closer emotional bonds are formed. Treatment of boys and girls is much nearer to being equal, but differences still remain.

6   Depending upon their health, old people can play a useful part in family life. They can help to bring up children, especially when mothers go out to work, and often provide financial assistance.

7   Such families only represent about 23% of households in Britain, 29% are married couples with no children, 6% are couples living with non-dependent children. Furthermore, there has been a trend towards cohabitation rather than marriage. Finally, 7% of households with dependent children are headed by a lone parent.

8   Marriage is usually seen as characteristic of adulthood and the first stage in creating a family. It makes a decision to maintain sexual relations exclusively with one person. In terms of the social order, marriage gives us identity and status.

9   Divorce is not the only form of marital breakdown; there are also cases of separation and desertion, and unhappy marriages. For some of these categories, especially the last two, there are no reliable figures.

10   The number of people marrying has declined by 20% since 1971. Divorces have doubled in that time and over a third of babies are born outside marriage. The number of one parent families is increasing and people are more likely to exercise their right to separate if they are unhappy in a marriage.

Chapter 4 Education

1   Formal education takes place in a special institution such as a school or college, whereas informal education normally takes place in casual interaction between the members of families or between friends, etc.

Formal education usually consists of a specific, clearly defined skill or set of skills such as is taught in the school curriculum.

Informal education cannot be clearly defined in its aim except that the child learns the values, beliefs and daily knowledge necessary to act in a normal way.

Formal education usually only occurs for a set period of people's lives, whereas informal education occurs in both simple and technologically advanced societies.

2   (a) The hidden curriculum means the ideas and values that the pupils learn in the school from teachers and other pupils, which are not officially part of the lessons.

(b) Two of the following:
   (i)   Gender roles are learnt at school, through the comments of teachers, the contents of books and the attitudes of the peer group.
   (ii) Racial differences: through jokes, attitudes and book contents.
   (iii) Class differences: these are also learned through comments on accents, differences in spending patterns, comments about parents' jobs and teachers' expectations.
   (iv) Streaming and examinations not only grade children by ability, but also teach children to expect to be treated according to ability. This will later be reflected in different standards of pay and status in employment.
   (v)   Language: only middle-class English is seen as correct.
   (vi) Social control: children are taught to be obedient. By learning to obey teachers they are also learning to obey their supervisors and bosses later.

3   (a) Labelling: when a teacher believes a pupil to be a particular type of child and adjusts his/her responses accordingly. For instance he or she may label a boy as a troublemaker and be excessively harsh in his/her dealings with that boy. The boy then responds in some way to that label, perhaps even becoming a troublemaker out of resentment. It does not matter if the original label is correct or not as long as the teacher believes it to be so, and his/her belief influences the future behaviour of the boy.

(b) Social control: every society needs to control its members. If it does not do so then people will act in any way that they wish. This can lead to chaos. In our society there are a number of agencies of control, among them the school. Social control is taught both formally in the rules and discipline of the school, and informally in the ways that pupils learn from other pupils and the teachers the normal response to most social situations.

4   Modern societies are extremely complex, both culturally and technologically. It is impossible for the necessary values and skills to be passed on from one generation to the next by the family as in more simple societies.

The education system ensures that the basic needs of society are catered for. First it is necessary for a degree of order to exist, both culturally and politically. Without some order society would collapse in chaos. The first two functions of the education system ensure that a core set of beliefs and values are passed on from one generation to the next. This is the transmission of culture. The second function of social control ensures that people obey the norms of society and the laws.

The third and fourth functions are mainly concerned with the need of society to produce the food and products necessary for our survival. Economic training ensures that skills are taught so all jobs can be performed, at every level. This is particularly important in rapidly changing societies such as our own, where skills useful in one generation are obsolete in the next. Social selection by schools ensures that the most able children are chosen to perform the most difficult tasks. Examinations therefore sort out and grade children.

5   It introduced:
    - *local management of schools*, which gave greater control over budgets to schools, and reduced the role of local education authorities.
    - *grant maintained schools*, which could opt out completely of local education control, taking money directly from the government. This allowed selection.
    - *the national curriculum*, which stated exactly what schools had to teach, the pace of teaching and the targets that pupils had to have achieved at 7, 11 and 14 and 16 years of age. To measure attainment, assessments (SATs) are carried out nationally and the results published.

6   Vocational education means relating what is learned in schools and colleges much more closely to the types of skills needed in the work place. There has been the introduction of 'vocational qualifications' such as NVQs which are specific recognised skills for a particular job, and GNVQs which are a rather more general range of transferable skills, within broad vocational categories. Training Enterprise Councils (TECs) have been introduced to organise the running of skill-based training on behalf of local businesses. TECs often run programmes in competition with local colleges.

7   Benefits include:
    - If the UK is not to fall behind other countries, it must teach adequate job skills and how to compete.
    - It enables the newly skilled workers to find jobs.
    Criticisms include:
    - The things taught are less educational and more about learning the right attitudes of attendance, punctuality and acceptance of the power of employers.
    - Those on training courses have few employment rights.
    - The schemes don't really get people jobs at the end of them.
    - The training schemes are sexist, with females being socialised into taking low-paid, 'service' work.

8   Two of the following:
    Once in a class, pupils adjust themselves to the general academic and behaviour standards of that class.
    Pupils in lower streams feel failures compared to higher stream pupils. This can lead to feelings of frustration and so to rebellious behaviour against the school. The attitudes of teachers alter with the stream they are teaching. The lower the stream the less the teacher expects and this in turn can influence the motivation and self-respect of the pupils.

9   Females are more successful than males.
    Girls are more likely to be successful throughout the education system up to degree level, when both achieve equally.
    Females are more likely to choose to study social science, language and caring subjects than males, who are in turn, more likely proportionately to study science and engineering subjects.

The significance of subject choice is that it strongly influences the choice of further/higher education and the type of employment. The national curriculum means that for the younger school students both sexes follow the same subjects.

10 (a) No, the children of certain Asian groups, noticeably those of African Asians, do particularly well. Children of Afro-Caribbean origin and Bangladeshis appear to perform worst of all.

   (b) The explanations for the variations in performance appear to be linked to:
   (i) family background – that is levels of education and amount of encouragement/ expectations; (ii) the ability to reject racism – it seems that the cultural strength of Asian backgrounds helps them to reject the racism they experience; (iii) if the Asian children or those of Afro-Caribbean origin are from middle-class backgrounds, then they do particularly well in the education system.

Chapter 5 Social stratification

1 Caste, estates (feudalism), slavery.

2 Life chances are a person's chances of success or failure in life, which sociologists believe are strongly influenced in Britain by the social class into which we are born.

3 Weber argued that people could be divided by more than their ownership of wealth: economic factors such as wealth and income, status, and power needed to be added together in order to indicate a person's life chances. As people do not necessarily enjoy equal amounts of all these elements, society represents a complicated variety of divisions.

4 Occupation is often related to a range of other factors such as: differences in income; differences in prestige; differences in education; differences in life style, speech, dress, etc.
Problems involved in using this approach include the fact that some people in similar occupations may have very different backgrounds and resources, and in any case the same job title may mean very different things in different circumstances. Occupational classifications also ignore the unemployed.

5 (a) Greater affluence and wider availability of consumer goods.
(b) There are now at least 3 million unemployed and a real division is occurring between those in secure employment and the rest of the workforce. (c) More people now own their own homes and are moving from inner cities to outer city suburbs and new towns. (d) Greater opportunities exist within the educational system. (e) The occupational structure is changing considerably with the decline of manual occupations, also connected with the impact of new technology. There has also been a growth in professional and junior management job opportunities and more openings for people of working-class origins. (f) The number of women in employment has been increasing consistently.

6 This is a heavily disputed area. Supporters of the idea point to the undisputed existence of significant numbers of people who are the very poorest, primarily composed of the sick, the elderly, single parents and the long-term unemployed. However some sociologists point to the reason for this as lack of opportunity and the low levels of government benefits. Others, such as Charles Murray argue that these people have little or no interest in contributing to society. They have a distinctive set of values which justify crime, living off state benefits and are uninterested in finding employment.
Heath used material from British Attitude Surveys, and found

that there were few differences in values between what would be defined as the members of the underclass and the 'traditional' working class.

7   They argue that other divisions have now emerged which are at least as significant as social class.
    These include:
    (a) Ethnic divisions – 'race' plays as important a part in determining a person's lifestyle as social class.
    (b) Gender – affects types of employment, levels of salary and also family responsibilities.
    (c) The long-term unemployed – for these social class based upon employment divisions are irrelevant.
    (d) The division between people employed in the private sector and those employed by the state – they may be doing similar jobs, but conditions, wages and security are very different.

8   Wealth means the ownership of such assets as property and stocks and shares. Much wealth is owned by a relatively small proportion of Britain, the top 1% of the British population own 23% of marketable wealth.

9   (a) Social mobility means the movement of people up and down the social scale. The two types of social mobility are 'intragenerational' and 'intergenerational'.
    (b) Measurement of social mobility is difficult because occupational categories are not easy to define accurately and over time, the status and significance of jobs tends to change making comparisons complicated. Furthermore, at what point in a person's career do you measure his/her social mobility?

10 Research such as the Oxford Mobility Study has demonstrated that upward mobility has certainly increased. Evidence shows that the chances of going into higher occupational groups, e.g. the service class, has increased and that the class structure was more open in the middle of the twentieth century than at the beginning.
    It was also recognised, however, that there were significant differences in the relative chances of different social groups and that the changing occupational structure had given rise to a greater proportion of higher categories of employment, and this created more room at the top. It should also be noted that there have been few studies of the patterns of social mobility of women. Finally, there is much evidence to show that the top positions in society are still held by the elite (or ruling class).

Chapter 6 Gender

1   Gender role refers to the expectations of behaviour which we have of males and females. Typical gender roles are labourer (male) and housewife (female).

2   Traditional accounts of homosexuality treat it as deviant and abnormal, although as many as 6% of males and almost 4% of females have had at least one homosexual/lesbian experience in their lives. Sociologists have therefore suggested that sexual identities are not as clear cut as generally believed.
    It was not until the nineteenth century that the only accepted form of 'normal' sexuality was heterosexual sex. The term 'homosexuality' was first used in 1860. Foucault argues that the ability to impose a particular way of viewing sex reflects differences in power between social groups, so that the views on sexuality reflect the power of heterosexual males.

3   Choose two from the following:
    The family Parents exercise stricter control over daughters compared to sons. Husbands have expectations of wives

concerning appropriate behaviour.

The peer group Girls' behaviour is constrained as much by other girls as by males or parents. Research by Lees has pointed to their fear of gaining a 'reputation' (e.g. for being sexually available).

Public sphere Women are controlled in public (streets at night, pubs, etc) through fear of male harassment or even violence.

Employment Women are usually employed in least responsible positions, with male managers, so they are more likely to be controlled and supervised by men.

4   Legal equality and equal treatment in social life, employment and education are very different things. The attitudes that society holds towards women still mean that they are expected to do things, like rearing children and being good housewives, that effectively prevent them having a successful career. It is not by chance that women are trapped in low-paid, part time and low-status work. Men's attitudes have to be changed towards women if they are to achieve equality.

5   Sociologists have explained the position of women in the labour market in two ways.
   Dual labour market theory where there are two types of jobs:
   (a) secure, with the possibility of promotion;
   (b) insecure, with no definite future and no benefits such as pension, paid holidays, etc.
   Women are much more likely than men to be trapped in the second as they often have to work part time because of child care responsibilities.
   Reserve army of labour. A second approach is that they are treated as a cheap pool of labour which employers can draw on when they are short of workers. When employers no longer need them, women are laid off.

6   Women usually work part time because of family commitments. They are expected to look after the children and therefore have to arrange their work hours around the times of school. Twenty-eight per cent of women questioned gave child care as their main reason for not working.

7   Mainly because they are encouraged to see themselves primarily as mothers and housewives rather than career women. It is argued that this is because they are constantly encouraged to do so by the education system, the family and the media.

8   The main characteristics of housework are (a) that it is unpaid and supposedly done 'for love'; (b) that it is low status and not regarded as real work; (c) it is monotonous and boring like factory work; (d) housewives are very isolated, as they spend most of their day with young children and may only come into contact with other adults at the shops for instance.
   Housework is certainly work, merely performed at home and unpaid.

Chapter 7 Age

1   Sociologists are interested in age because people are treated differently from others of a different age. Expectations of behaviour vary according to society and are not directly linked to biological age.

2   Generally children are protected from the 'realities' of life because childhood is seen as a period of great innocence. Children are not allowed to partake in the same activities as adults (e.g. work activities, voting, drinking alcohol). It is believed that children are not sufficiently mature to make sensible choices. They must be moulded into the appropriate values through socialisation.

3   The tendency to treat the child as someone in need of care and protection only derives from the eighteenth century. Before this time children over the age of 5 were treated as little adults. Children worked with adults and did not have separate games, lengthy education, etc.

4   Youth culture is the distinctive set of beliefs, values and ways of acting which is associated with young people aged 13–19 years. There are a variety of youth cultures, depending on such things as social class, 'race', gender and even location.

5   Old people in Britain have low status and are regarded as having little to contribute to society. Because old people have retired this creates problems of self-identity, since a person's employment often gives him/her identity.

Chapter 8 Race and ethnicity

1   'Race' is taken to mean a group that shares certain biological characteristics. It is extremely difficult to divide people into clear racial groups as there are great overlaps. Ethnic groups are groups of people who share a common culture, often different from that of the majority of that society.

2   Most immigrants moved to West Yorkshire and the East of Lancashire, the West Midlands and the South-East, especially London. Within these areas they settled in inner-city districts of places such as Birmingham or London.
Immigrants moved to these areas because there were job vacancies in which British workers were not interested, mainly in low-paid unpleasant work in declining industries. It has been argued that without migrant labour many of the traditional British industries would have collapsed.

3   The reasons why migrants came to Britain after 1950 are (three of the following): firstly, because of poverty and unemployment at home, thus they were forced to look for work elsewhere. Secondly, because of persecution where the dominant groups in their 'home' society were persecuting the minority group, forcing them to flee to another country which would accept them. This happened in Uganda. Thirdly, migrants are attracted by the possibility of work. This often involves active recruitment from the 'host' country. In the case of Britain in the 1950s, the limits of the British working population had been reached and so workers were encouraged to come from abroad to fill vacancies. The final reason for immigration in Britain concerns the fact that once a member of the family has come to Britain, the rest of the family may wish to come to Britain in order to be reunited with the original immigrant. The original workers to come to Britain, especially among Indian, Pakistani and Bangladeshi people, were men, and later they sent for their wives and children. The system of arranged marriages also means that fiancées are brought over from their original homelands.

4   Among the main causes of prejudice are:
     (a) the tendency of people who are intolerant of others' beliefs and customs to be prejudiced against the minority groups;
     (b) stereotyping, which portrays racial groups as being inferior. Stereotypes of black people are often a result of our colonial past and involve the belief that black people are inferior, less intelligent and less dependable than whites. All blacks are regarded as having the same weaknesses;
     (c) scapegoating, which means that in periods of economic decline or social tension certain groups are blamed for the problems that exist. In Britain people are sometimes blamed for unemployment, inner-city problems and crime.

5   Discrimination in employment: all the immigrant groups tend to be over-represented in jobs requiring fairly low levels of skill. In particular, black people face discrimination in obtaining work, and unemployment among black people, especially youths, is much higher than the national average. Black people who have jobs are likely to experience poorer working conditions than whites and have far fewer chances of promotion.
Discrimination in housing: although reasonably high proportions of blacks and Asians own their own houses, a much smaller proportion are council tenants and research shows that they tend to wait longer on housing lists than white people. Generally they can face discrimination in renting private accommodation or when trying to buy property. They also tend to live in older, poorer quality housing, often with inadequate facilities.

6   Legislation has been passed to reduce racial discrimination. The Race Relations Act makes it illegal to discriminate in the provision of goods or services to the public, or in the areas of employment and housing. It is also illegal to incite racial hatred.
In 1976 the Commission of Racial Equality was established with the power to bring cases of discrimination to court and to encourage greater awareness of the need for racial harmony. There have also been moves to introduce changes in the British education system to cater for the needs of our multi-racial society. This has included the introduction of teaching programmes dealing with other cultures.

7   Although there are indications that the degree of prejudice and discrimination against black people and other ethnic minorities has declined, there is still much discrimination in our society. Given the growth of unemployment and other economic problems this is likely to continue.
The evidence shows that passing laws is not enough since what is really needed is a change in people's attitudes.

Chapter 9 Work

1   Work is usually paid, not done mainly for pleasure, done under the authority of an employer, takes place in a special place, such as an office or factory, has a productive outcome and is done at particular times

2   (a) a move away from manual towards non-manual work; (b) a move away from primary and manufacturing industries towards service industries; (c) an increase in the numbers of women in the workforce; (d) the growth in unemployment.

3   Workers in the 'core' sector have good working conditions and secure jobs paying better incomes and offering decent conditions of service, whereas workers in the 'peripheral' sector enjoy few benefits, little job security, poor working conditions and low pay; workers in this sector are often part time. The gap between the two sectors is said to be growing and labour involved in the 'peripheral' sector is increasing as a proportion of the work force.

4   Apart from the general benefits of automation, the use of the new microchip technology will result in changes such as the following:
(a) people will be able to order goods and services from their own homes; (b) more people may work from home, using computer keyboards linked to an office or factory; (c) better quality goods of consistently high standard are likely to be produced; (d) information will be more easily stored and available for recall.
There will also be disadvantages, as deskilling and lack of job satisfaction will occur, unemployment will increase while wages

decrease and social mixing will be reduced.

5 Marx defined alienation as a situation where people gained no enjoyment from their work. Its elements include a feeling that a person's work is meaningless, a belief that a worker has no control over his work, increasing conflict between workers and employers since they do not share the same interest in the work, a sense of isolation from others in society, and a loss of personality on the part of the worker.

6 Industrial conflict usually involves poor relations between workers and management and shows itself in the number of strikes and cases of 'working to rule' and 'industrial sabotage', where workers deliberately set out to damage a firm's output.

7 In pre-industrial societies:
(a) Work was not just an economic activity but a social activity too, emphasising the bonds that held people together – working and social lives are unified.
(b) People are likely to have their jobs passed on to them from their parents, a process known as ascription. In industrial societies people choose their occupations.
(c) The concept of work measured in time did not exist. There was less of a tendency to measure work in strict terms and at the same time the notion of there being an appropriate time to go into employment was also less clear.
(d) Work was less likely to be done in a separate workplace away from the home.

8 Some points of difference between Japan and Britain:
(a) Until the mid-nineteenth century, Japan was virtually isolated from the rest of the world and society was rigidly controlled to prevent changes to the economy.
(b) After American involvement and the arrival of US warships the local economy was wiped out and the government inspired a number of radical changes in a relatively short period.
(c) Large firms were developed rather than the small firms characteristic of the British process of industrialisation.
(d) The values of pre-industrial Japan were carried over into the new factories.
(e) The concentration of capital in relatively few hands provided plenty of scope for massive investment in technological development.

9 Work influences family life, community life, health and leisure activities.

Chapter 10 Unemployment

1 Groups more likely to suffer unemployment include: (a) the young and old; (b) members of ethnic minorities; (c) manual workers and the less skilled.

2 (a) The decline in manufacturing industry generally and the wider use of new technology in new manufacturing industries. Service industries have increased, but do not, of course, supply employment opportunities equal to those lost in manufacturing;
(b) Lack of increase in full-time employment during the 1980s;
(c) The effects of automation, new technology, etc;
(d) Increasing foreign competition.

3 Some of the effects of unemployment include:
(a) Government expenditure is diverted from useful projects to employment and other state benefits;
(b) Employers might exploit the situation to pay lower wages and provide poorer conditions for those in work;
(c) Trade unions are weakened;

(d) There is an increasing gap in standards of living between unemployed and those in work;

(e) Increasing poverty in society;

(f) Increasing crime rates;

(g) The possibility of political instability as people feel less confident in the democratic system.

4 Loss of employment causes partial loss of identity for the middle aged and brings serious financial problems. Loneliness results from loss of contact with former workmates and the unemployed feel depressed, bored, useless and frustrated. Family tensions also result from all these factors.

5 Despite the fact that official statistics indicate that women have not been as badly hit by unemployment, the effects upon women are not that different to that of men. Loss of income affects family finances and loneliness and frustration result, as in the case of men. Research indicates that the roles of mother and housewife are not adequate compensation for the loss of work.

Chapter 11 Population

1 It is the study of population, concentrating on changes in its size, the proportions in each age group, geographical distribution and balance of the sexes.

2 The information collected helps the government to plan its future policies by saying how many schools, hospitals, roads and social services are needed. Without the information the government would simply have to guess the extent of needs.

3 The factors that affect the birth rate are:

(a) the use of contraceptives, which allow parents to plan and limit families. Effective birth control methods have been known for about 100 years, but it is much easier to obtain contraceptive advice today than it was 30 years ago.

(b) The financial benefits or costs of having children; if children are seen as an economic asset then there will be a tendency to have large families. Children are useful when there are few social services provided by the state and when there are no pensions. In Britain the provision of pensions to old people has led to children being regarded as more of an economic liability than an asset.

(c) Cultural stress on the 'correct' number of children to have. In each period there are certain attitudes that develop concerning the normal size of family. In Britain at the moment it is two children.

(d) Women's attitudes to child rearing: women's attitudes to the roles of wife and mother changed during the twentieth century. Many women prefer to work than to stay at home as housewives. With the availability of contraception they have chosen to limit the number of children they have.

4 Changes in the death rate have been caused by:

(a) Improvements in sanitation and public hygiene. The result of effective sewers and rubbish disposal has been to eliminate many diseases which previously caused death. Clean water, for example, has eliminated cholera.

(b) Medical advances have ensured that diseases which would have killed a hundred years ago are now controlled by medicine. In particular, vaccination gives us much greater defence against 'killer diseases'.

(c) The rise in the standard of living in Britain has meant that people have better diets and greater home comforts. This has led to better health and a population that is physically stronger.

5 The three factors are the birth rate, the death rate and the level

of migration.

6   An ageing population means that the numbers of old people are increasing in proportion to the rest of the population.

7   The consequences for society are that:
     (a) There is an increase in the 'burden of dependency' which means that the working population has to support an increasing number of non-workers.
     (b) There has to be an increase in the provision of medical services for the elderly.
     (c) There has to be an increase in the provision of social services.
     (d) For individuals there is increasing loneliness.
     (e) The elderly may become an increasing burden on the family.

8   Women on average live longer then men because they are less likely to work in dangerous occupations, less likely to be combatants in wars, less likely to drink or smoke heavily, and because far more men than women are killed in motor vehicle accidents.

9   Emigration: up to the Second World War many people emigrated to the British Commonwealth and Empire. For twenty years after the Second World War the number of emigrants declined as there were so many opportunities in Britain. In the 1970s, the numbers increased again.
     Immigration: levels were low before the Second World War, then they increased significantly in the 1950s and 1960s. There has been a marked decline in the 1980s and 1990s.

Chapter 12 Urbanisation and community

1   Urbanisation is the movement of people from living in rural areas to living in urban areas. De-urbanisation means the movement of people out of the cities to live in outer suburbs and in the countryside. They may still be working in the city, however.

2   Industrialisation led to the growth of towns and cities as we know them in Britain. The development of factories led to the need for large numbers of employees in one place, so that people were drawn to a few industrial centres. Houses were needed and with them shops. Offices developed with the growing complexity of industry (which attracted yet more people).
     De-urbanisation began to occur partly because the factories declined and the employment patterns changed, with the move of offices and the new industries out to the New Towns and countryside. The workers followed.

3   Tonnies distinguished between two types of social life: community and association. Community refers to a society in which people are bound closely together, knowing each other. Generally the society is fairly small. People are judged not just on their behaviour but also on who their parents are and how great their status is. People living in a community tend to identify with it, feeling proud of it and exhibiting a reluctance to move. An association consists of a society of much more formal relationships, usually called 'secondary relationships' by sociologists. A person is measured much more by what he/she does than who he/she is, and there is little identification with the neighbourhood.
     Community is generally connected with life in a rural area and association with city life.

4   Simple contrasts between life in rural and urban societies are sometimes misleading because:
     (a) Some neighbourhoods in towns have strong community links and people have a great sense of belonging, especially if there are many family ties in the area.
     (b) Life in the 'commuter villages' studies by Pahl, which ought

to have had a community life, was deeply divided and there was little sense of community. Williams too has pointed out the myth of the tranquil, happy rural life in his historical studies. The sense of belonging came from what he called the mutuality of the oppressed.

5   Groups living in the inner cities include the 'bohemians', the ethnic minorities, the deprived, the poor and the elderly who are trapped there.

Chapter 13 Poverty and the Welfare State

1   *Absolute poverty* is a term used by those who argue that it is possible to establish a line representing the minimum income people need to keep themselves in a satisfactory standard of health and efficiency. At this standard a person would have a level of food, clothing, and housing which could just be regarded as satisfactory. Anyone with an income below this level would be regarded as being in a state of absolute poverty.
Relative poverty – many sociologists, regarding the definition of poverty already given as being adequate, argue that it is not possible to fix a 'line of poverty', as what is considered poverty varies from time to time and from place to place. It is argued, therefore, that poverty is relative.

2   This line represents the minimum income required to support a person in a satisfactory state of health. It has to be calculated by estimating the minimum costs of food, clothes, housing, etc, required for a person to survive. This line cuts off the poor, who are below it, from the rest of the population.

3   The low paid, the unemployed, the elderly, the sick and disabled, single parents, people living in certain regions of the country (e.g. North of England and Scotland).

4   The poor tend to have fewer medical facilities provided for them and the NHS is proportionally used more by the middle class. The children of the poor often do less well at school. Living in deprived inner city areas the poor often have poorer housing conditions, fewer community facilities and more problems to cope with than in the suburbs. They also have less chance to shop economically. They are less likely to be aware of the state benefits to which they are entitled.

5   Poverty continues to exist despite the Welfare State because:
(a) Rates of benefit are too low.
(b) Benefits are difficult to claim because the system is so complicated.
(c) Some people are too ashamed to claim because they feel there is a stigma attached.
(d) The existence of the 'poverty trap'. People on relatively low pay can actually end up taking home less money because of the way the system works.

6   The Welfare State operates in five main areas: education; social security; community care; health; housing.

7   Advantages of the Welfare State include the following: firstly, it has eliminated the greatest excesses of poverty and deprivation in Britain. Secondly, it aids many people who through no fault of their own would have been reduced to begging. Thirdly, it allows everybody, not just the affluent, to have medical treatment. Fourthly, it gives all children the opportunity to use their talents to the full, because it gives free secondary and higher education. Fifthly, it has allowed people to live in adequate homes, through the development of massive housing developments. Finally, it allows old people some dignity and independence in their retirement by providing a pension.

The disadvantages of the Welfare State, it is claimed, are that it is wasteful of resources and should restrict its benefits to the very poor and seriously disabled, while the rest of society ought to make provision for itself. Secondly, the Welfare State is seen as being too bureaucratic and as having gained too much control over our lives – this takes away people's initiative and also makes the Welfare State too complacent and unaware of our needs. Thirdly, the family is weakened as the state takes over its functions.

8   There is a wide range of services provided by voluntary organisations. These include: (a) marriage guidance counselling; (b) help for those who are physically or mentally handicapped; (c) help for the homeless and the inadequately housed; (d) services for single parents; (e) help for those with drug or alcohol problems. Basically, they fill in the gaps in what the Welfare State provides.

Chapter 14 Politics and power

1   Democracy is the political system where the government of a country is controlled as far as possible by the people themselves. People vote the government into power in regular elections, have a free press and legal system, and the right openly to criticise the government.
Totalitarianism is the political system in which the views of the people are not represented in the creation of the government or its decisions. A small group or individual rules, making all the major decisions and imposing them on the majority.

2   An organisation formed to promote or protect certain interests. Its members aim to persuade political parties or those in power to adopt their views.
The two types of pressure groups are: protective, which try to defend their own interests; and promotional which try to put forward ideas for the benefit of society as they see it. In practice, the two groups overlap and there is no clear distinction between them.

3   The main difference is that a political party tries to gain power in elections; also a political party is concerned with a broad range of issues, the pressure group with only one. Sometimes pressure groups develop into political parties, as the Labour Party developed from the trade union movement.

4   They could persuade people to switch votes in order to block the election of a party they particularly disliked, if the party of their first choice was coming last in the polls. Alternatively, they could make the voters feel so certain that their party was going to win that they might not go out to vote at all – so many people could feel the same way that they could alter the outcome of the election.

5   The mass media do not seem to have a direct influence on voting, as most people select the information they want from the papers. Over periods of time, however they may create images about certain parties.

6   They may not be interested. They may not like the candidate standing for the party of their choice. They may be sure their party is going to win or lose so that there is little point in voting. They may disagree with one aspect of the policy of the party they generally support, but do not want to vote for another party.

7   Geographical location is also linked to voting behaviour. The further north the stronger the allegiance to Labour, with some exceptions. People in inner city areas are more likely to support Labour. The South and the suburbs are Conservative territory, with some exceptions. The Liberal Democrats' main strengths are

the suburbs and small towns. They are strong in Scotland and the South-West.

8   Pluralism is the approach to the study of government which believes that power is not centralised in Britain, but divided in the hands of many groups. It sees pressure groups and political parties reflecting the will of the people and government decisions are simply the outcome of their activities.

Chapter 15 Social control

1   Formal social control is when there are specific organisations set up to ensure that people are behaving correctly – such as the police and the courts. Informal social control is simply the control that is placed upon people by others around them, which is not organised but spontaneous. A person behaving rudely at the table is stared at by others, and comments are made.

2   Socialisation and social control are tied closely together. However, it could be argued that socialisation consists of learning the values of society and social control consists of reinforcing those values and patterns of behaviour.

3   There are many of these. Any from: the family, the peer group, religion, the media, the police, the courts.

4   Religion plays an important role in social control, although it has declined in recent years. The basic values of British society are founded in the Christian religion. In the past the power of religion was much greater and people were frightened of going to Hell, so they would be very likely to obey the clergy. This gave the preachings of the church great weight.

There is some dispute, however, as to whether the preachings of the churches and their interpretations of the New Testament are linked to the interests of the rich and powerful. Marxists argue that the teachings of the churches are used to support the society as it is now and to prevent change.

5   Simple societies rarely have any formal agencies of control like a police force. They rely much more on informal social control, with pressure being brought to bear to enforce conformity, by comments and reactions from others. This can work very well because simple societies generally have few members and so everything that happens is clear to others, and it is difficult to avoid public comment on any deviation from the rules. Also there is the need to rely on others' cooperation in order to survive – if a person is rejected by the others then death is almost certain. To strengthen this, people are held together by very tight bonds of marriage, of age groups and of the 'gift relationships'.

Chapter 16 Crime and deviance

1   Illegal acts are actions that break the law and are punished by the legal system. Illegal acts are formally codified in the law. Anybody accused of breaking the law is judged in the courts. Deviant acts are any acts that are regarded in some way as socially wrong. They may be classified as illegal in certain cases, but this is not necessarily so. A deviant act may be one that is relatively unimportant and usually punished by some informal sanction by other people, not in a court.

2   No, deviant acts are not always defined the same way in every society. They vary according to: (a) time, (b) the society, and (c) who committed the act. Behaviour that was regarded as normal one hundred years ago, might be regarded as deviant today, just as acceptable behaviour in one society may not be acceptable in another. Even within a society, the behaviour of minority groups might be considered deviant by the majority.

3   No. Females commit considerably fewer offences according to the official statistics.
     Explanations for this include: (a) the male gender role can encourage males into criminal activity; (b) females may express anti-social feelings through sexual activity; (c) the official statistics on crime may not reflect the true level of female crime.

4   Labelling is the process whereby we place 'labels' on people, classifying them in certain ways: for example, 'clever', 'thief', 'mad'. As a result of this labelling people are treated differently by others – even if the label is not accurate. The important point is that it is not committing a deviant act that is significant, but being labelled by others as having committed one and therefore to be treated differently.

5   Moral panics are situations in which the police, media and public get extremely concerned with the behaviour of a particular group and over-react, usually clamping down very tightly imposing the full force of the law and order on them. This is part of the process of 'deviancy amplification'. Often members of the group are treated as if they were folk devils!

6   Official statistics only include crimes that are reported to the police. There is much evidence to suggest that many crimes go unreported because people may regard some crimes as insufficiently important or may not want to get involved with the police for various reasons. The police may also be unwilling to treat certain reports of crime seriously enough to record them. The distribution of police, too, can affect the numbers of crimes recorded and the way that they categorise activities influences the final crime figures.

Chapter 17   Media

1   The mass media are one-way systems of communication from a single source to a large number of people who have little or no chance of responding. The mass media involve considerable use of technology and are operated by professionals who communicate the ideas thought important by the owners and controllers of the various media; a profit motive is usually involved. The information and entertainment is organised according to a fixed schedule.

2   The media play an important role in secondary socialisation, reinforcing the basic primary socialisation learned in childhood. They do this because they are the most important source of information about things beyond our personal experience, thus forming our attitudes and opinions about these matters. The media interpret this information, influencing our view of what is normal and what is deviant. Once formed, our views are constantly reinforced by the media.

3   M Ferguson *(Forever Feminine)* studied women's popular magazines and found that although their treatment of women has changed in the years since the 1940s, women's and men's needs are readily accepted as being different. A McRobbie showed the main theme of girl's magazines to be romance and love.
     The study of children's books emphasises the dominance of male characters in the stories and the subordinate roles assigned to females.

4   The media perpetuate the public belief that there is still an immigration problem and give the impression that there are far more blacks and Asians in Britain than there actually are. They also associate 'immigrants' and conflicts in society, and the differences between blacks and whites are constantly referred to

and thus in reality reinforced.

It has also been argued, however, that the media merely reflect racist feelings already held.

5   Some crimes are thought to be of 'greater human interest' than others and are grossly over-reported compared to other crimes. Emphasis in the media on stories of crimes of violence, muggings, cases of indecency, etc, give the public a highly distorted view of the sorts of crimes taking place. This distorted view also affects the law and order policies operating in society.

6   The media label certain individuals and encourage expectations of certain kinds of behaviour from such individuals. This can lead to a panic to introduce measures to deal with such troublesome behaviour and an increase in the amount of actual deviance. (See the media's role in the trouble in certain seaside towns.)

7   Research has produced rather mixed results. Some suggest that the media have little impact in directly encouraging violence, but exposure to violence in the media does make people less likely to be concerned by violence in everyday life; and where other factors encourage aggressive tendencies in individuals, the media can reinforce and further encourage them.

8   In the short term the mass media may only influence the 'floating' voters, but over a long period they may actually bring about a change in party loyalty or cause a change in a person's attitude to certain political issues or events.

9   Compared to quality papers, popular papers have short articles written in extremely simple English.

The information given is very simple and sensationalised, with viewpoints in black and white. There are plenty of photographs, particularly of attractive women.

10 The media are usually influenced by commercial considerations in determining the style of their contents. In particular, advertising revenue is of vital importance and has great influence on media organisations, which therefore need to attract large audiences. The media also set out to win certain types of audience for their publications.

There is evidence that the owners have influence over what is contained in the media and journalists themselves also play a significant role.

Chapter 19
Types of GCSE examination questions

Advice on answering examination questions

When answering examination questions remember that although the *style* may be stimulus response, structured response or whatever, the actual question will be one of only three types, each of which is trying to get you to reply in a particular manner.

Factual questions: those that ask you some points of fact which you have learned in your sociology course, or that are given to you on stimulus material. Here all that is required is that you give the exact information asked for.

Explanatory questions: these usually ads you to explain a particular point or sociological argument you have studied.

Questions of interpretation: these are the ones that ask you to give your evaluation of a particular piece of information, usually given to you in stimulus material.

- When answering a question always look at the number of marks available for it, which will be in brackets beside it.
- The greater the marks, the greater the weight and amount of effort you ought to put into answering it.
- Clearly, if the question is only worth 1 mark, it is pointless writing half a page. Usually there are one or two points to b made and that is all you need to do. on the other hand, a question that is worth 7 or 9 marks for instance, requires greater effort and a full development of a discussion.
- Typically, factual questions are worth less than 4 marks, while explanatory and interpretation questions are worth between 4 and 9.
- Always read the question very carefully and then answer exactly what the examiner is asking you, not what you would like him/her to ask you.
- No marks are ever taken away for mistakes, or relevant information. Examiners will award you marks on what you produce which is relevant to the question. So you can only gain marks, never lose them.
- Try to remain calm and collected in an exam. Work your way at a careful pace through the material. Do not rush: you will have adequate time to write all you wish. The best thing to do is to check the total amount of time available for the complete examination and then divide by the number of questions. You will know then approximately how long you have to spend on each question. It is better to spend an extra half hour and get a higher grade than rush through the examination just because you see others leaving the examination room early.

- If you have worked your way through this book and you have thought about the ideas in it, then I am sure that you will do very well indeed. So be confident!

Multiple-stimulus response questions

These questions have a number of different pieces of information which you must read carefully. There follows a series of questions which are based on the 'stimulus' (the information) provided. Each question refers to a specific source or sources, except for the last question which usually requires you to draw together information you have learned in the course with the information provided in the extracts overall.

Advice on answering the multiple-stimulus questions

- These questions appear very difficult but in reality sae the same as the ordinary stimulus response. It is just that two or more stimulus response questions have been put together.
- Read through all the information provided at a reasonable pace, getting the general idea of the information provided.
- Check through all the sub-questions, working out whether they are of the factual, explanatory or interpretative type.
- Examine the number of marks awarded for each question. Remember the higher the mark awarded the greater the depth or the difficulty of the question. Therefore, give greater weight to the sub-questions awarding the higher marks.
- Take the pace of your answer to fit the time allowed, making sure that you finish at about the time allowed. Do not rush and do not go too slowly.

Stimulus-response questions

Stimulus-response questions are ones in which you are given a piece of information (the stimulus) which may be in the form of a written extract, or a photograph or a diagram, or a statistical table. You are then given A series of questions (about five or six) which generally get progressively harder. The final question or questions usually require more knowledge of society than is given in the stimulus.

Advice on answering the stimulus-response questions

- You normally have a choice of which questions to answer. Go through the questions and examine all the sub-questions that give the highest marks (usually the last two). Base your decision on what stimulus-response questions to answer on whether or not you can answer the sub-questions that award the high marks. (Students often look at the stimulus information and the first couple of sub-questions, which are only worth a few marks. They then decide to do that particular stimulus-response question on the basis of whether or not they can do the low mark sub-questions. When they reach the high-mark sub-questions at the end they find they cannot do them).
- Remember that if the sub-question is only worth 1 or 2 marks, then long explanations are not necessary.

Short-answer/structured-response questions

Short answer questions

These are simple questions that require a fairly limited answer, based ion your knowledge of sociology. They are mainly factual in content and generally require no discussion.

Structured-response questions

These are identical to the stimulus-response style questions, without the stimulus! They follow one these and build up difficulty. The last sub-questions usually require some discussion.

Advice on answering these questions
- Look at the number of marks awarded for the question and base the length and depth of your answer on this.
- Read the question carefully and answer exactly what you have been asked.

Essay-style questions

The final style of question is the essay. There are two types:

The open essay

This is the traditional type of essay question. This asks a relatively open question which you are required to answer with your own ideas and within your own structure.

The guided essay

This is an open question, but the examiners give suggestions as to the subject matter which you ought to include. You can add additional information of your own for which you will be awarded extra marks.

Advice on answering the essay-style questions
- Read the question carefully.
- In the open essay, make a brief plan of what you intend to write.
- All the plan need contain is a number of keywords that remind you of the central points you wish to make.
- In the guided essay there is a form of plan already made for you. Use this, but where possible fit in any additional points you think are useful.
- Even if you disagree within the plan, cover the points suggested by the examiner.
- Keep an eye on the time. Make sure that you use all the time you have available and that you finish all you want to in the time allowed.
- The sociology examination is not a test in English essay writing, but it does help if your work is organised, clear and well written.

Chapter 20
GCSE questions and suggested answers

Stimulus/structured-response and short-answer questions

Question 1

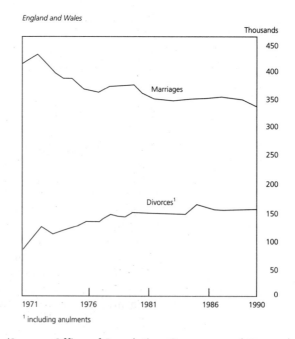

England and Wales

(Source: Office of Population Censuses and Surveys)

(a) (i) In which year was the number of marriages at its highest level? **(1)**

    (ii) Describe the changes in the number of marriages and divorces between 1971 and 1990 shown in the source. **(2)**

(b) 'A high divorce rate cannot be explained by legal changes alone.' How far do you agree with this statement? Give your reasons. **(3)**

(c) Identify and explain **three** consequences of divorce. **(6)**

(MEG)

Answer

- **(a) (i)** 1972
  - **(ii)** The number of marriages has gone down whilst the number of divorces has risen.
- **(b)** There have been several changes in the law which have made it easier for couples to divorce, given financial assistance to those on low incomes wishing to do so, and made it easier for women to get a divorce than previously. This may account for the rise in divorces, but changes in the law often reflect changing attitudes in society, which no longer condemns divorcees. You must also consider that women now have higher expectations of marriage and are less willing to accept the traditional housewife role. Two-thirds of all divorce petitions come from women. People now have higher expectations of marriage, perhaps influenced by the media, and so are more likely to be disappointed than in the past. Also, religion has declined so that divorce is not seen as a sin. Also, as families have become privatised, there is less social pressure and advice put upon partners from the extended family than previously. Finally, people are living longer and have more time to fall out.
- **(c)** Examples:

  More single parent families as couples with children divorce.

  Decline in popularity of marriage has followed from rising divorce rates and led to increase in number of childless couples.

  Emotional disturbance amongst children who suffer the trauma of marital breakdown and the friction of reconstituted families.

Question 2

Study **Items A** and **B**. Then answer **all** parts of the question which follow.

Item A

The Family and Marriage

The 'cereal-packet' family

Only about 5% of all households fit the picture of the 'cereal-packet' family. This is a common name for a household with a working father married to a home-based mother who cares for two small children.

Adapted from *An Introduction to Sociology* by Ken Browne (Blackwell)

Item B

Divorce in England and Wales						
	1961	1971	1976	1981	1986	1990
Number of petitions filed (in thousands)	32	111	145	170	180	192
Divorce rate: number of persons divorcing per thousand married people	2.1	6.0	10.1	11.9	12.9	12.9

Adapted from Social Trends, 1993

(a) Study **Item A**.
  (i) According to the information given, what percentage of households fits the picture of the 'cereal–packet' family? **(1)**
  (ii) According to the information given, what is meant by the term 'cereal–packet' family? **(1)**
(b) Study **Item B**.
  (i) What has been the trend in the number of divorce petitions filed over the period shown in the table? **(1)**
  (ii) What has happened to the divorce rate since 1986? **(1)**
(c) Identify and explain **one** advantage and **one** disadvantage of living in families. **(4)**
(d) Identify **two** changes which have happened in Britain since the 1960s which might explain the trend in the number of divorces. In **each** case, explain why these changes have affected divorce. **(4)**
(e) Identify and fully explain **one** way in which the divorce rate in Britain has affected family life. **(4)**
(f) The length of time children spend in education and training has increased considerably in the last 50 years. Identify and fully explain **one** effect that this has had on family life. **(4)**
(SEG)

Answer

(a) (i) 5%
  (ii) Households in which a working father is married to a home-based mother who cares for two small children.
(b) (i) The number has increased.
  (ii) It has remained the same.
(c) Choose from advantages:
Family educates children and teaches them norms and values – this is good for society.
Provides emotional support for people in an unfriendly world.
Regulates sexual behaviour for society so that conflict over partners is reduced.
Provides a secure place for reproduction to take place so society has safely raised babies.
Choose from disadvantages:
Women may be repressed by the family – some feminists argue women are enslaved into caring for children and serving their husbands.
Family may cause emotional disorder – Laing and Cooper have linked schizophrenia to families.
Much violence occurs within family – there is considerable evidence of physical abuse of women and children that takes place within the family.
(d) Changes and explanations below:
People are having smaller families – there is less need for unhappy couples to stay together if they do not have children at home.
Greater expectations of marriage, particularly from women – people want more from marriage and are more willing to divorce if they do not get it.
Greater life expectancy – people are living together for longer and thus have more time to grow apart.

Legal changes making divorce easier – for instance since 1984 couples only have to wait one year before getting a divorce where previously they had to wait three.

Growing financial independence of women – women may not need to get married to a man in the first place.

Secularisation – the religious importance of marriage has declined, as divorce has become more socially important.

Welfare state – single parents can now claim support from the state rather than stay in an unhappy marriage for the sake of money.

(e) Choose from:

More single parent families as couples with children divorce.

Decline in popularity of marriage has followed from rising divorce rates and led to increase in number of childless couples.

Emotional disturbance amongst children who suffer the trauma of marital breakdown and the friction of reconstituted families.

(f) Choose from:

The family is now no longer responsible for educating children, who spend more time away from the family than previously.

This has weakened the ability for parents to socialise their children in isolation between the years 5–16.

It has reduced the need for supervision of children within the home by mothers who now have more time available for work.

It has lessened the need to rely on the extended family for support and assistance in educating and minding children.

It has reduced the ability for children to contribute money to the household.

Question 3

Study **Items A** and **B**. Then answer **all** parts of the question which follow.

Item A

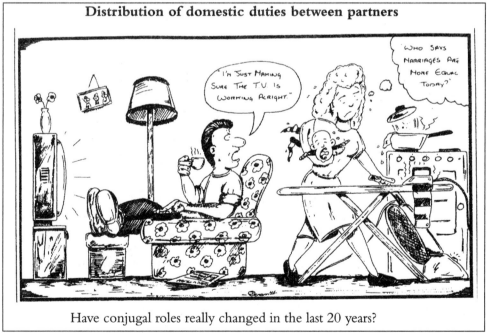

From Ken Browne, *An Introduction to Sociology* (Polity Press)

Item B

> **Sharing home/child duties with spouse**
> Married women managers were asked the question:
> 'How do you share the home/child duties with your husband?'
>
> The table below lists their responses.
>
> | | Percentage giving response |
> |---|---|
> | I do more and it bothers me. | 42 |
> | I do more and it does not bother me. | 16 |
> | We share 50:50. | 39 |
> | He does more. | 3 |

From C. Cooper and M. Davidson, *High Pressure: Working Lives of Women Managers*

(a) According to the information in **Item A**,
  (i) name **one** traditionally female domestic role that the woman is carrying out; **(1)**
  (ii) name the traditionally male domestic role to which the man is referring. **(1)**

(b) According to the information in **Item B**,
  (i) what percentage of women managers said they were bothered that they did more home/child duties than their husbands? **(1)**
  (ii) what percentage of husbands carried out more home/child duties than their manager wives? **(1)**

(c) Name **two** different types of family structure found in Britain today. **(2)**

(d) (i) What is meant by the term, 'segregated conjugal roles'? **(1)**
  (ii) Explain why conjugal role relationships in Britain have changed this century. **(3)**

(e) (i) Identify **one** reason why there are more divorced people in Britain today than there were at the beginning of this century. **(1)**
  (ii) Explain the possible effects of divorce on family life. **(3)**

(SEG)

Answer

(a) (i) Choose from cleaning, ironing, child care, cooking.
  (ii) Repairing things (e.g. the car) etc.

(b) (i) 42
  (ii) 3

(c) Choose from any of the following: nuclear, extended, single parent, modified extended, reconstituted, privatised nuclear.

(d) (i) Where tasks are divided between the wife and the husband in a marriage.
  (ii) The assumed change has occurred due to the improved status and rights of women. This has forced men to accept women as more equal. Also, more women are now working making them less dependent on males, and increasing the need for men to help in the house when women are not there. Another factor is the decline in the pressure from the extended family to keep up traditional roles. Finally, all families are more home centred and so the man is more likely to work around the house.

(e) (i) Lots of reasons, e.g. smaller families meaning less need for unhappy couples to stay together; greater expectations of marriage, particularly from women; greater life expectancy; legal changes making divorce easier; divorce becoming more socially acceptable; decline of religion.
  (ii) Explanations could include detrimental effects on young children and particular difficulties if lone parents remarry. Also, divorce affects the income of the family, particularly if one parent is responsible for child care. Single parent families are more likely to live in poverty. Divorce may affect the attitudes of the family members to marriage, perhaps explaining a decrease in the popularity of marriage.

Question 4

Highest qualification held: by sex, 1984 and 1992

United Kingdom	Percentages			
	Males		Females	
	1984	1992	1984	1992
Degree or equivalent	9	12	4	7
Higher education below degree level	4	6	7	3
GCE A level or equivalent	31	36	12	17
GCSE, grades A–C or equivalent	12	14	20	21
Other qualifications	7	9	11	12

(Source: *Social Trends* 1994)

(a) (i) What percentage of males held a degree or equivalent in 1992? **(1)**
　　(ii) What are **two** of the trends shown in the source? **(2)**
(b) Give **three** reasons why children go to school. **(3)**
(c) Identify and explain **three** ways the school may influence pupils' educational achievement. **(6)**

(MEG)

Answer

(a) (i) 12%

　　(ii) Numbers of people holding degrees has increased. Females are becoming better educated. Rise in other qualifications held by all people. All members of society are becoming better educated.

(b) Reasons include:
To gain skills needed for working life.
To learn about society.
Because they legally have to attend.
To gain qualifications.
To socialise them into the culture of society.

(c) Teacher's attitudes – teachers may think working-class children are less intelligent and therefore put them in lower streams in school.
There may be a culture clash so that working-class children are not used to the middle-class environment they find at school.
Catchment area – schools in deprived areas, where there are many social problems, may have high staff turnover and discipline problems. Pupils who attend these schools will receive an inadequate education.
Michael Rutter in his study *Fifteen thousand hours* found that the way a school was run could have a big impact on the quality of education that pupils get, wherever the school is situated.

Question 5

Joining the Ramblers' Association gives you excellent value for money. It also helps us open up all Britain's footpaths, protect the countryside and campaign for public access to mountain, moorland and woodland.

JOIN THE RAMBLERS TODAY!

(Source: Advertisement from *Heritage* magazine)

(a) (i) Name **one** pressure group apart from the Ramblers' Association. **(1)**
　　(ii) Give **two** ways pressure groups differ from political parties. **(2)**

   (b) Why are some pressure groups less successful than others? **(3)**

   (c) How do pressure groups try to influence decision making in British society? **(6)**

            (MEG)

Answer

  (a) **(i)** Many to choose from, including the Campaign for Nuclear Disarmament (CND), the motoring organisation AA, Shelter, Child Poverty Action Group (CPAG).

     (ii) Pressure groups are concerned with one cause only, and do not seek seats in Parliament.

  (b) Disadvantaged groups in society may lack the resources or education to get their methods heard, whilst those with substantial wealth and education can run more successful campaigns. Also, the Old Boys network means that those in power may only talk to those who are from the same social class. Some pressure groups have more influence and power than others. For example, the Trades Union Congress can threaten strike action.

  (c) Methods – sponsorship of MPs, e.g. by trade unions to get MPs to speak on their behalf.

     Consultancies – many MPs are paid by companies to watch for moves within parliament that might affect their business.

     Payment of funds to political parties to get them to vote in their interests.

     Lobbying MPs and ministers.

     Advertising in the mass media and distributing leaflets.

     Holding public meetings or mass demonstrations.

     Civil disobedience – such as anti-road protesters.

     Organising strikes.

     Providing expertise to government in the knowledge that they will put their message across in doing so.

Question 6

Study **Items A** and **B**. Then answer **all** parts of the question which follow.

Item A

Political Participation

A sample of people in Great Britain were asked about their political activities in the previous two or three years. The figures given are in percentages.

	1982	**1993**
	%	%
Voted in the last election	69	77
Presented their views to the local councillor or MP	13	17
Made a speech before an organised group	14	14
Written a letter to an editor	6	8
Taken an active part in a political campaign	3	4
Stood for public office	1	1

Source: MORI

Adapted from *Social Trends 24* (1994)

Item B

Women make up only a very small proportion of the total number of members of Parliament. In the 1992 general election, women won only 9 per cent of the seats in the House of Commons, so that the UK has only 60 women MPs.

Women hold a very small proportion of other public offices - in 1984 only 19 per cent of those appointed by the Government to public offices were women. There are very few women judges, and very few women on the boards of nationalised industries.

There have never been any women chief constables, and women generally hold low-ranking positions in the armed forces.

Adapted from N. Abercrombie and A. Warde,
Contemporary British Society (Polity Press, 1994)

(a) According to the information in **Item A**,
    (i) what percentage of people asked in 1993 had made their views known to their local councillors or MPs? **(1)**
    (ii) what percentage of those surveyed in 1982 had taken an active part in a political campaign? **(1)**
(b) According to the information in **Item B**,
    (i) state what proportion of MPs elected to the House of Commons in 1992 were women; **(1)**
    (ii) state **one** public office to which women are less likely to be appointed than men. **(1)**
(c) Give **two** reasons why some people in Britain may **not** vote in an election. **(2)**
(d) **(i)** Give an example of an agent of political socialisation. **(1)**
    (ii) Explain carefully how the process of political socialisation occurs. **(3)**
(e) **(i)** Identify **one** type of pressure group. **(1)**
    (ii) Explain **one** way in which a pressure group might try to influence the behaviour of a government. **(3)**
(SEG)

Answer

(a) **(i)** 17
    (ii) 3
(b) **(i)** 9%
    (ii) Chief constable; judge; seat on the board of a nationalised industry; high rank in the armed forces.
(c) Any two from: apathy; unable to get to polling station; no candidate which they support; not eligible; don't support the candidates who are standing.
(d) **(i)** Choose from: friends, family; media, etc.
    (ii) Socialisation is the learning process in society. Political socialisation is the way in which people learn political beliefs and values. For example, people learn in Britain that the best political process is democracy. They may be influenced in their beliefs by their family, their friends, the media and by their social class, just like with other values.
(e) **(i)** Choose from: promotional, protectional, single issue, national, local.
    (ii) By lobbying – meeting with MPs to persuade them to act in a certain way. This may be supported by letter writing, leafleting, newspaper campaigns, mass demonstrations, financial contributions to political parties. All of these methods are designed to show the strength of feeling about an issue so that an MP believes it is worth the government's attention.

Question 7

'...The working class is really, in a sense, nearly all of us. Our society is a capitalist one – a society in which the ownership and control of industry, property and trade belongs to a relatively small number of individuals. These capitalist owners are the really dominant class in our society – the "upper class". Compared to them the rest of us are all "workers" in the sense that all of us have to sell whatever labour power we have in return for a wage or salary.

'But, whilst the vast majority of people are actually employed in producing things to make profits for the owners, there is a largish group engaged in managing this process on behalf of the owners and controllers making day-to-day decisions, studying and organising technology, looking after health, culture, entertainment and legal problems and, not the least important, running the education system at its different levels. This is the well-known middle class. Although it tends to be a little fuzzy at the edges, its way of life is sufficiently different from that of either the ruling class or the working class to form a distinct group.'

  (a) What does the term 'capitalist society' mean according to the above passage **(1)**
  (b) Name any **three** tasks performed by the middle class on behalf of the owners, according to the passage. **(3)**
  (c) Which **three** social classes does the passage identify? **(3)**
  (d) Explain the meaning of the terms: (i) white collar worker, and (ii) semi-skilled manual worker. **(3)**
  (e) Give **four** examples of social class influencing our lives. **(4)**
  (f) What major differences can you identify between manual and professional workers? **(4)**

Answers

  (a) A capitalist society is one in which 'the ownership and control of industry, property and trade belongs to a relatively small number of individuals'.
  (b) There are quite a number of tasks mentioned. You should have chosen three from:
   (i) making day-to-day decisions; (ii) studying and organising technology; (iii) looking after health, culture, entertainment and legal problems; (iv)running the education system.
  (c) (i) the upper class or ruling class; (ii) the middle class; (iii) the working class.
  (d) **(i)** a white collar worker: an office or shop worker, or similar, who has a job that requires relatively little skill and carries no great managerial responsibility; **(ii)** a semi-skilled manual worker: a person who is engaged in physical labour that requires a moderate level of skill.
  (e) Your answer could cover any example of the relationship between social class and: (i) socialisation/the family; (ii) education; (iii) politics; (iv) job prospects; (v) standards of infant care; (vi) crime and deviance; (vii) politics.
  (f) (i – conditions): (1) salary and fringe benefits/piece rates, hourly pay; (2) comfort and safety at work; (3) status; (4) authority and autonomy; (5) hours worked each week.
   (ii – leisure): (1) social status; (2) difference in the values and social/political views of the two groups; (3) educational differences.

Question 8

Newspaper readership and voting intentions, UK 1992 (percentages)							
	Con	**Lab**	**Lib**		**Con**	**Lab**	**Lib**
Daily Telegraph	71	13	15	The Sun	39	48	10
Daily Mail	66	17	15	Independent	31	40	26
Daily Express	66	19	13	The Star	23	64	9
The Times	61	18	17	Daily Mirror	19	59	10
Financial Times	50	27	18	The Guardian	12	59	22
Today	48	35	14				

(Adapted from *The Sunday Times,* February 1992)

(a) What is meant by the term 'mass media'? **(3)**

(b) To what extent does the political view of a person influence their choice of newspaper? **(3)**

(c) How do the mass media help to create awareness of issues amongst the general public? **(6)**

(MEG)

Answer

(a) All forms of communication which are directed to a very large audience from a small number of producers with no personal contact, e.g. TV, newspapers, radio, cinema, advertising.

(b) Most people choose their newspaper for a reason other than its political content. Also, over 70% of the newspapers shown in the table support the Conservative Party, yet at General Elections the Conservative Party draws only around 40% of the overall vote. Clearly, many people must be choosing a newspaper that does not reflect their political choices. The table points out that 48% of *Sun* readers (a Conservative supporting newspaper in 1992) were Labour supporters. However, there is a loose link between the newspapers that support the Labour Party *(Daily Mirror* and the *Guardian* in 1992) and higher levels of support for that party.

(c) The mass media have many stories that they could possibly transmit to the public, but they only choose to run some of them. This is the practice of agenda setting. The mass media lay down the list of events that they will show and that people will discuss. People can only form opinions about things they have been told about, and most people get their information from the mass media.

Some issues may not be discussed in public because the media do not choose even to cover them. This is called gatekeeping. The media may try to protect the interests of certain groups by refusing to cover certain stories. For example, they may choose to report strikes but not industrial injuries, when the latter cause the loss of more working days than strikes.

Question 9

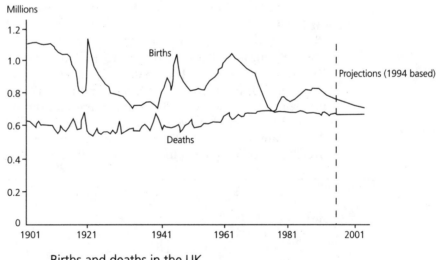

Births and deaths in the UK
(Source: *Social Trends 27,* 1997)

(a) What does the term 'natural increase' refer to in the table? **(1)**

(b) From the table, identify two period in which births did not exceed deaths. **(2)**

(c) What factor other than birth and death rates affects the population growth? **(2)**

(d) Identify and explain the changes in the birth rate shown in the table. **(6)**

(e) What social consequences arise from such changes in the birth rate? **(9)**

Answers

(a) The excess of births over deaths in a given year.

(b) 1916–18, 1939–40, or 1976–77.

(c) New migration – the difference between immigration and emigration.

(d) Falling birth rate; world wars, 1930's economic depression; use of contraceptives; rising cost of children; growth in women's employment (1960–70s)/
Rising birth rate; post-war booms, generational effects – when one baby boom 'breads' another (early 1940s, early 1960s); rising prosperity rate (late 1950s, early 1960s).

(e) Changes in population structure, especially on ageing population; move towards child centres families; women free to go out to work; shifting demands for state services like education and health care from younger age groups to older.

Question 10

Study **Items A** and **B**. Then answer **all** parts of the question which follow.

Item A

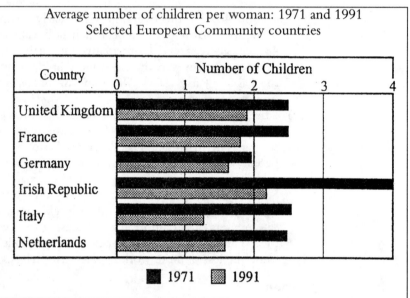

Adapted from *Social Trends*, 1993

Item B

Over 900 thousand people moved to live in a different region of the United Kingdom during 1991. The South East had the largest net loss (42 thousand) to other regions. In other words, 42 thousand more people moved out of the South East region than moved in; 16 thousand moved from the South East to the South West; 32 thousand moved from the South East to East Anglia but only 23 thousand moved from East Anglia to the South East. Northern Ireland gained an overall total of 3 thousand from mainland Britain.

Adapted from *Social Trends*, 1993

(a) Study **Item A**.
  (i) According to the chart, what was the trend in the numbers of children born to women in selected European Community countries? **(1)**
  (ii) According to the chart, which country has had the biggest fall in the numbers of children per woman? **(1)**

(b) Read **Item B**.
  (i) According to the information given, did Northern Ireland have a net gain or a net loss? **(1)**
  (ii) According to the information given, how many people moved to East Anglia from the South East during 1991? **(1)**

(c) Identify **two** reasons why women today are likely to have fewer children than their grandmothers did. In **each** case explain why this has led to a smaller family size. **(4)**

(d) Identify and explain **two** factors which have led to Britain having a healthier population now than 150 years ago. **(4)**

(e) Identify and fully explain **one** social consequence of Britain having an ageing population. **(4)**

(f) Identify and fully explain **one** reason why many people are moving out of the towns and cities to live in rural areas. **(4)**

(SEG)

Answer

(a) (i) Numbers went down.
(ii) Irish Republic.

(b) (i) Net gain.
(ii) 32000

(c) Choose from:
Compulsory education of children has meant that children are an economic burden for longer as they are unlikely to find work before the age of 18.
Women have less incentive to have children.
Changing role of women has meant that women have greater employment opportunities and so are putting off getting married and having children.
Declining infant mortality rate means that women fully expect their children to be around to look after them when they are older. They therefore need fewer children as insurance.
Improved contraception has meant that it is now easier for women to delay having children.
The Welfare State now looks after people when they are older – parents have less need to have large families to look after them.

(d) Reasons for healthier population:
Improved hygiene, sanitation and medicine – this has meant that people are living longer and staying healthier for longer.
Higher living standards – better housing, heating, and importantly better diet due to cheaper and more widely available food have all led to the population becoming healthier for a longer period of time.
Public health and welfare – the NHS provides free health care and particularly ante-natal care which has improved life expectancy and health of population.
Health education – has informed people of need for food hygiene and importance of diet.
Improved working conditions – fewer industrial accidents and diseases caused by work, greater leisure time and earlier retirement have all added to the amount of healthy life that a person enjoys.

(e) Best examples are:
An increased burden of dependency. The working population have to pay more taxes for higher levels of government spending on welfare benefits, social and health services.
More poverty. Older people often fall below the poverty line as they do not have the income from employment to support them.
Unemployment may rise. More people are living until retirement age and doing jobs for longer. This restricts jobs for youngsters.
Other possible consequences are increased emotional strain on the family forced to look after elderly relatives, assistance from elderly relatives with child care and baby-sitting. Also, for the individual, greater leisure time and loss of status derived from work.

(f) Reasons for de-urbanisation:
Better transport links have made it possible for people to commute to work from outside urban areas, and for firms to locate outside of towns and cities.
Industrial firms have moved out of cities because the cost of land, rent and rates is cheaper in rural areas.
Better environment and cheaper housing. City areas have high house prices. Often in rural areas there are more open spaces, less noise and less pollution, and the cost of living is lower.
Government policy. Recent governments have sponsored rehousing schemes which have taken people away from inner city areas on to new housing estates. Also, incentives have been offered to firms to locate on 'greenfield' sites.

Question 11

Study **Items A** and **B**. Then answer all parts of the question which follow.

Item A

> The level of poverty in a district can be measured by using the Material Deprivation Index. This is worked out by combining the following four factors:
> more than one person per room;
> households with no car;
> households lacking basic amenities;
> households with no central heating.
> The maximum score is 4. The highest scoring districts are inner and outer London boroughs and the cities of Liverpool, Birmingham and Hull.

Adapted from Ray Forrest and Dave Gordon, *People and Places* (School for Advanced Urban Studies 1993)

Item B

Number of people entirely dependent on Income Support per thousand people of working age, 1992

	Number per thousand
North	141
Yorkshire and Humberside	119
East Midlands	104
East Anglia	83
South East	114
South West	100
West Midlands	123
North West	147
United Kingdom	119

In **1989** the rate for the United Kingdom was 91 per thousand.

Adapted from *Regional Trends* (1994)

(a) According to the information in **Item A**,
   (i) state which cities are amongst the highest scoring districts; **(1)**
   (ii) state one of the four factors used in the Material Deprivation Index. **(1)**
(b) According to the information in **Item B**,
   (i) which region of the United Kingdom had the lowest rate of people entirely dependent on Income Support in 1992? **(1)**
   (ii) what change in the number of people entirely dependent on Income Support occurred in the United Kingdom between 1989 and 1992? **(1)**
(c) Give **two** examples of services provided by the Welfare State. **(2)**
(d) (i) What is meant by 'universal welfare benefit'? **(1)**
   (ii) Explain why a government might decide against using universal welfare benefits when considering ways of fighting poverty. **(3)**
(e) (i) Give **one** reason why an individual might be living in poverty. **(1)**
   (ii) Explain why people might find it difficult to move out of poverty. **(3)**
(SEG)

Answer

(a) (i) Liverpool, Birmingham, Hull and outer London.
   (ii) One of the following: more than one person per room; households with no car; households lacking basic amenities; households with no central heating.
(b) (i) East Anglia
   (ii) The number went up.

(c) There are many possible including any one of the following: free state education; subsidised housing; unemployment services; social security payments; free NHS treatment.

(d) (i) The benefits are available to all regardless of income.

    (ii) They do not target the poor because everyone gets them. They are more costly because they apply to everyone. People on high incomes can receive the benefits when they have no need for them. They are very expensive and encourage demand for the benefits rather than reduce it.

(e) (i) Many possible reasons including: born into a culture of poverty; lack of education; failure of the Welfare State; effects of capitalist society; personal inadequacy; ill health.

    (ii) Because of the cycle of deprivation – the idea that the poor endure poor housing and poor living conditions and receive a poorer education and are therefore unable to get a better job. This is one reason why they cannot move out of poverty. Another important reason to mention is the Marxist argument. Marxists argue society needs lots of people in poverty to do the menial jobs and to stop those in work demanding higher wages. There is therefore not the opportunity to move out of poverty because the owners of society's wealth do not want this to happen.

Question 12

(Source: J. Paxman, *Daily Mail* 13/8/94)

(a) (i) What is social mobility? **(2)**

    (ii) Apart from education give **one** other way a person may experience social mobility. **(1)**

(b) Why is it difficult to measure social mobility? **(3)**

(c) What factors restrict social mobility in the U.K? **(6)**

(MEG)

Answer

(a) (i) The ability to move up or down between social classes.

    (ii) Choose from: promotion; marriage to a male partner in a higher class; ability.

(b) Reasons:

The status of occupations changes over time, e.g. clerical workers.

At what point do you measure a person's class position – from when they get their first job? or their second? etc.

Many people get promoted within occupations but social mobility studies don't take account of this.

The Registrar General's scale excludes half the population – it does not include women.

(c) Obstacles to social mobility:

Sexism may restrict women's progress.

Racism may restrict the progress of some ethnic minorities.

Elite self-recruitment – the top jobs go to people from boys public schools. This stops working-class children moving up the scale.

Working-class children don't get the same education as the middle class, and may have more obstacles in their way (e.g. lack of books at home) and so can't rise up the scale.

Question 13

Study **Items A** and **B**. Then answer **all** parts of the question which follow.

Item A

Distribution of employees in types of industry, Great Britain (percentages)			
	1986	**1991**	**1993**
Manufacturing	25	21	20
Service	66	71	73
Other	9	8	7

From *Social Trends 24*

Item B

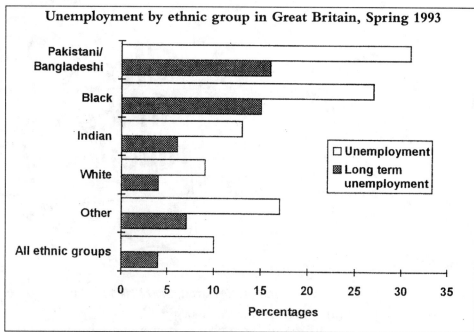

Adapted from *Social Trends 24*

(a) According to the information in **Item A**,
   (i) what was the employment trend in manufacturing industry from 1986 to 1993? **(1)**
   (ii) what percentage of employees worked in the service industries in 1993? **(1)**
(b) According to the information in **Item B**,
   (i) from which ethnic group were people most likely to be unemployed in 1993? **(1)**
   (ii) which ethnic group had a long term unemployment rate of 15%? **(1)**
(c) Give **two** reasons why unemployment occurs. **(2)**
(d) (i) What is meant by the phrase, 'core labour force'? **(1)**
   (ii) Explain why some social groups may **not** be part of the core labour force. **(3)**
(e) (i) Identify **one** factor which affects the level of an individual's job satisfaction. **(1)**
   (ii) Explain how the level of job satisfaction experienced by an employee might be increased. **(3)**

Answer

- **(a)** **(i)** Downwards.
  - **(ii)** 73%.
- **(b)** **(i)** Pakistani/Bangladeshi.
  - **(ii)** Black.
- **(c)** Choose from any two of: recession, seasonal demand for workers, government policy, lack of qualifications or skills, benefit levels higher than paid work.
- **(d)** **(i)** Those people in secure, full-time employment.
  - **(ii)** Because they lack the necessary skills and qualifications, some workers may be part of the peripheral or secondary sector. This means they are likely to be in part-time or low paid work, with little job security. They are likely to be employed on a temporary basis and dropped out of the market when not required.
- **(e)** **(i)** Many possible answers including: the amount of money a person receives, the degree of autonomy (freedom), the amount of skill used, rank in company.
  - **(ii)** Teamworking – people work together in groups to accomplish particular tasks that create a feeling of belonging and achievement. Job rotation involves allowing people to do different jobs at different times, reducing boredom so people take more pride in their work. Job enlargement means making each particular job cover a wider range of activities, which gives the worker more responsibility and thus more satisfaction.

(SEG)

Question 14

'Many jobs are dreary and unsatisfying, repetitive and exhausting. The most that can be said for them is that they provide an income. It is jobs such as these, on the assembly line, or in unpleasant and dangerous conditions, that are likely to be automated.'

(Source: K. Ruthven, *Society and the New Technology*)

- **(a)** Give **three** reasons why people work. **(3)**
- **(b)** To what extent does automation reduce repetitive and unsatisfying work? **(3)**
- **(c)** In what ways do workers respond to dreary and unsatisfying jobs? Explain your answer. **(6)**

(MEG)

Answer

- **(a)** Many possible answers including:
  - To earn money (extrinsic reason).
  - For the interest and enjoyment of the job (intrinsic reason).
  - To get friendship.
  - To get status.
  - To get a sense of identity.
- **(b)** Automation may eliminate repetitive tasks and reduce hours of work, and reduce dangerous work. It may also require more highly skilled workers to work complex machinery. However, it may cut people off from each other as fewer workers are needed. People may be deskilled – computers and machines make it easier for anyone to do previously difficult jobs, and wages may decrease. Automation may well reduce boring and unsatisfying work because it reduces work altogether and increases unemployment.
- **(c)** Responses to dreary and repetitive jobs (also called alienation):
  - Producing poor quality goods and limiting output.
  - Absenteeism – going on the sick.
  - Leaving the job – many boring jobs have a high turnover of staff.
  - Strikes and non cooperation with management, perhaps directed through the unions.
  - Sabotage – deliberately damaging machinery or goods to halt production for a change in boring work.

Question 15

'Burglaries are so common that, statistically, someone's home is broken into every 24 seconds of the year, and insurers are paying out £2 million a day.'

(Mr Tony Blair, speaking as Labour Party Home Affairs Spokesman in February 1993.)

(a) What is meant by the term 'deviance'? **(3)**

(b) 'Young working class men commit the most crime.' To what extent is this statement true? **(3)**

(c) Why do police records underestimate the true extent of crime committed in Britain? **(6)**

(MEG)

Answer

(a) Deviance is any behaviour which is disapproved of by society.

(b) Young people commit most crime because they may lack status in society and the police stereotype them. Working-class people may commit more crime because they suffer more poverty and unemployment and have more opportunity to commit crimes. Males may commit more crime because they are socialised differently and are expected to behave differently. However, the police may stereotype working-class males. Also, working-class males commit more detectable crimes. In addition, there is more criminal opportunity in urban areas where the working class live. This may affect the figures.

(c) Two broad reasons:

Non-reporting of crime: the victim may be too scared , embarrassed or not bothered to report the crime to the police. The victims of crime may themselves be in trouble with police, or may feel they will deal with the situation themselves. Victims may not be aware a crime has been committed.

Non-recording of crime: the police may not record the offence because they regard it as too trivial, a waste of time, may distrust the witness, or regard an incident as nothing to do with them.

Question 16

Study **Items A** and **B**. Then answer **all** parts of the question which follow.

Item A

'It is very difficult to estimate how much crime there is in society. We can see the amount of crime rather like an iceberg. The amount above the waterline represents the official figures about the amount of recorded crime. The amount below the waterline represents the unrecorded amount we do not know about officially, and is called the "dark figure of crime".'

Item B

	All	Men	Women	16 – 24	25 – 54	55 +	White	Black
PUBLIC CONFIDENCE IN THE POLICE COMPARED TO THREE YEARS AGO (percentages)								
More confident about the police	7	6	9	6	6	12	8	5
Same confidence	46	52	40	41	44	54	46	48
Less confidence in the police	31	26	36	38	34	18	32	25

Adapted from *Sociology Review*, April 1992 (Philip Allan)

    (a) Read **Item A**.

        (i) According to the passage, what is represented by the 'amount above the waterline'? **(1)**

        (ii) According to the passage, why is it difficult to estimate the real amount of crime in society? **(1)**

    (b) Study **Item B**.

        (i) According to the table, in which group was there the greatest fall in confidence in the police in the previous three years? **(1)**

        (ii) According to the table, what percentage of females had more confidence in the police in 1992? **(1)**

    (c) Identify and explain **two** reasons why the official figures for the number of crimes are likely to be different from those actually committed. **(4)**

    (d) Identify **two** methods used by the police and the courts to encourage most people to conform to the law. In *each* case, explain how these methods may lead to conformity. **(4)**

    (e) Identify and fully explain **one** way in which the mass media influence people's view of the amount of crime in society. **(4)**

    (f) Identify and fully explain **one** way in which the mass media create stereotypes of the role of men in society. **(4)**

    (SEG)

Answer

    (a) (i) The official amount of recorded crime.

        (ii) Because it is difficult to tell how much crime has not been recorded.

    (b) (i) People aged 16–24.

        (ii) 9%

    (c) Two broad reasons:

    Non-reporting of crime: the victim may be too scared, embarrassed or not bothered to report the crime to the police. The victims of crime may themselves be in trouble with the police, or may feel they will deal with the situation themselves. Victims may not be aware a crime has been committed.

    Non-recording of crime: the police may not record the offence because they regard it as too trivial, a waste of time, may distrust the witness, or regard an incident as nothing to do with them.

    (d) Choose from formal methods of social control:

    Arresting people suspected of crimes – this deters people from breaking the law in the first place.

    Fining people found guilty of crimes – this costs people money and is intended to act as a deterrent to future misdemeanours.

    Imprisonment – this is also a deterrent as it makes the offender think twice before committing another crime, but also discourages others in society from committing crimes.

    (e) The mass media may create a moral panic – an over-reaction to the amount of a particular type of crime (e.g. mugging) in society. This leads many people, in particular the police, the judiciary and politicians, to see this particular type of crime as more common than it really is.

    The mass media tend to be very selective in their coverage of crime. In particular, they focus on violent crime because it's more dramatic. This leads people to fear crime more than they normally would. This particularly affects vulnerable groups in society like the elderly.

    (f) The mass media usually portray women in the media as sex-objects (for example the page 3 girl in tabloid newspapers) who are there because they look pretty, not because they have some special talent. Alternatively, the media portray women in the role of housewife/mother, whose main concern is bringing up children or the domestic arrangement in the house, for example in soap operas. Men, on the other hand, appear in a variety of roles which are usually more challenging. On the other hand, men are rarely shown in the caring role given to women. This is very evident in advertising.

Essay-style questions and answers

The degree of depth and length in which these essay-style questions should be answered varies with the Examination Groups.

Questions

Chapter 1 Socialisation
(a) What is meant by the term socialisation? Explain how people come to be socialised.
(b) Human beings are made, not born.
Explain what you think is meant by this statement. Your answer could include reference to the following:
- the nature–nurture debate;
- the process of socialisation;
- how the main agencies of socialisation operate.

Credit will be given for any other relevant information,

Chapter 2 Research methods
(a) Describe and explain the uses and limitations of participant observation as a method of sociological research.
(b) A local authority in an area with a population of over 100 000 people of different ages has decided to improve the local leisure facilities. Before deciding how to spend money, however, the authority wishes to find out what kind of leisure activities local people would like.
(i) Describe the methods that could be used to discover the opinions and needs of the local people, remembering the size of the population.
(ii) Suggest ways to present the results of the investigation.

Chapter 3 The family
(a) In what ways has industrialisation affected the family?
(b) (i) How do sociologists explain the increase in divorce that has taken place this century?
(ii) Does this indicate a breakdown in marriage and the family?
(c) Describe and explain the changing relationships between members of the family over the last 100 years.
(d) Describe and explain the changes that have taken place in the family and marriage in the last 40 years.
Your answer might include some of the following:
- changing relationships between parents and children;
- changing relationships between husbands and wives;
- female employment and its effects;
- the growth of alternative family types.

Chapter 4 Education
(a) What explanations can you offer for the fact that children from some ethnic minorities do not do as well at school as the majority of children?
(b) In what ways do influences outside the school influence a child's educational achievement?
Your answer could include reference to the following:
- family income and class;
- attitudes of parents towards education;
- the peer group and the neighbourhood influences;
- the language of the home
(c) It is often said that the school plays a very important part in forming the career choices of males and females. Suggest why this is so.
(d) There are many factors which influence how well pupils do at school. Describe and explain some of these factors.

(NEAB)

(e) To what extent can changes in education in the last twenty years be said to have increased educational opportunities in Britain?

(SEG)

Chapter 5   Social stratification

(a) What is meant by social mobility? What are the reasons for a person's mobility in British society?

(b) To what extent has social mobility become more common in Britain during the last 50 years?

(NEAB)

(c) Describe and explain the importance of social class influencing people's lives.

(d) (i) What are some of the problems associated with defining 'wealth' and 'poverty'?

    (ii) How might wealth and poverty affect the status and the life chances of individuals in society?

    (iii) Explain some of the other factors which might affect the status and life chances of groups in society.

(NEAB)

Chapter 6   Gender

(a) 'Women are still treated as second-class citizens in Britain today.' Explain and discuss.

(b) By nature girls are submissive and domesticated. This is true in all societies. Explain these statements and discuss them using sociological evidence.

Chapter 7   Age

'What did sociologists mean by 'youth culture'? Is there a distinctive youth culture in Britain today which most young people share?

Chapter 8   Race, ethnicity and migration

Explain the sorts of problems that people in ethnic minorities experience in Britain. Can you suggest why this is so?

Chapter 9   Work

(a) What is the relationship between technology and work satisfaction?

(b) What is automation? Describe and explain the possible consequences of automation.

(c) There have been many changes in the patterns of employment for adults. Describe and explain some of these changes.

(NEAB)

Chapter 10   Unemployment

What are the consequences for people's lives when they are made unemployed?

Chapter 11   Population

(a) Describe and explain the changing pattern of births in the twentieth century.

(b) There is a greater proportion of the population over the age of 65 than ever before. Explain this and discuss what the consequences are.

Chapter 12   Urbanisation and community

(a) Discuss the extent to which there are differences between living in urban and rural communities.

(b) What problems are facing people in inner cities today? What explanations can you suggest?

Chapter 13   Poverty and the Welfare State

(a) Some people suggest that poverty is the state when people are so poor that they cannot buy enough to eat; others claim that poverty is not having what others in the same society normally expect to have.

Discuss the problems in measuring the extent of poverty. What are the consequences for social policy of the different definitions?

(b) Why do the poor generally tend to remain poor?

(c) Why has it been suggested that 'the Welfare State is in crisis'? What solutions have been suggested?

Chapter 14 Power and politics

(a) What methods do pressure groups use to influence political decisions and public opinion?

(NEAB)

(b) How far is the voting system used in a general election in the United Kingdom fair and democratic?

(NEAB)

(c) Explain some of the factors which might affect voting behaviour.

(NEAB)

Chapter 15 Social control

Conformity to the rules of society occur partly as a result of social control. Explain the meaning of 'social control' and how it operates.

Chapter 16 Crime and deviance

(a) (i) What is meant by the term 'deviance'?
    (ii) Why are some deviant acts criminal and others not?
(b) (i) Are official statistics on crime a good guide to the true level of criminal activity? Explain the reasons for your answer.
    (ii) What influence on policing and the activities of courts does 'labelling' have?

Chapter 17 Media

(a) Using examples, discuss how the mass media influence people's attitudes.
(b) What do journalists mean when they speak of 'news'? Explain why the contents and presentation of newspapers vary.
(c) How far can it be argued that the mass media contribute significantly towards gender socialisation?

(SEG)

Answers

1 (a) Socialisation equals learning the values and expectations of society, through informal and formal processes. You need to discuss the role of the family, school, peer group, etc, and give examples; a good one would be the way gender roles are learned.

   (b) The outline information is listed for you here and you should broaden the points given. Nature-nurture means the debate over the extent to which behaviour is natural or learned. Socialisation needs discussing and you should cover the activities of the family, school and the peer group.

2 (a) The uses of participant observation are generally in situations: (i) where the researcher wishes to study people as they are acting naturally; (ii) in order to achieve greater depth of understanding; (iii) where there is no sample frame or it would be inappropriate to give a questionnaire – as with a deviant group.

   Its limitations are that the researcher may lose his/her objectivity, may influence the group, and that no one else can repeat the check on it.

   (b) (i) Probably a mail questionnaire, sent to a sample survey of people on the local register of electors.
       (ii) They could be presented in the form of a set of clear pie charts and stating what proportion of the population favoured which option. Alternatively, there could simply be a series of tables. However, a wide variety of answers is acceptable.

3 (a) You would want to base your answer on three areas of discussion: changing structure of the family – the extended/nuclear discussion; the changing relationships in the family, with emphasis on the role of the mother; the decline in functions.

   (b) Changing values concerning marriage, the changing role of women; the changes in the law; the decline in the importance of the church; the weakening of the family; the fact that people from a wide variety of backgrounds marry; the high expectations of marriage.

It does not necessarily indicate a breakdown as people remarry and 90% of people still marry. Divorce rates reflect more the legal availability of divorce.

(c) You need to look at the changing husband/wife relationship; the parent/child relationship and the elderly/younger generation division. Points to stress include the greater degree of equality in the family, the role of the woman especially; the way children are asserting themselves more; the fact that old people are geographically more distant from their children. You need to discuss the concepts of symmetrical family and privatised family life, geographical mobility, smaller families and child-centredness, etc. Do not forget to point out that women are still the ones with most domestic responsibilities.

(d) This is a general question that requires a full debate on the decline of the extended family among the working class (Bethnal Green) and the increase in the modern symmetrical family. You should point out that there is greater home-centredness and males have lost their clear role as head of the household, but the woman still is responsible for the home. Discuss the older generation in this context. Point out the increase in divorce, remarriage and the growth of single-parent family life, etc.

4 **(a)** Mention some facts of different achievement. Point out that not all ethnic minorities do badly – East African Asians and Jews, for example. Main reasons are direct racism, different family structures and expectations, the deprivations of the neighbourhood, language differences, 'hidden curriculum'.

(b) The outline of the answer is already given. You need to fill these out in some detail. Try if possible to mention some studies. Do not forget to include race and gender differences, not just social class.

(c) This essay is designed to get you to write about the way that schools treat children differently according to their gender. You should talk about the differences in the subjects that males and females take and why this is so (boys – maths, girls – secretarial and domestic subjects). Go on to discuss the 'hidden curriculum' of teachers' expectations. It might be worth arguing that you cannot separate the influence of school from the wider gender roles of society.

(d) There are five key groups of explanations which influence how well pupils do at school. These explanations are:
- poverty and deprivation in the home;
- family socialisation;
- cultural explanations;
- structural explanations;
- the school as an institution.

Many children suffer great poverty in their homelife and this can seriously affect how well they do at school. The National Child Development Study found that one in sixteen children suffered from 'multiple deprivation' which included such things as low income, poor housing, poor diet – all of which impact on the educational chances of children. Of course, many children from poor backgrounds do succeed in the education system so this cannot be the full answer.

A second form of explanation, based on family socialisation stresses the degree of interest and support shown by the parents. In one national study by Douglas, this was found to be the single most important factor in a child's success.

Also, language development is crucial, as Bernstein has pointed out. Middle-class families were more likely to bring up their children to use language forms which developed 'conceptual' thoughts and the ability to express oneself.

Cultural explanations point out the differences between the various groups in society in terms of their access to what are considered the mainstream values of the society. This lack of culture can influence children's ability to benefit from school, as the work there does not reinforce knowledge learned in the home.

Those who come from the appropriate backgrounds have a very great advantage in that their home and educational values mutually support one another. Bourdieu calls this advantage of the middle and upper classes *cultural capital*. Cultural explanations may help us to understand the school 'failure' of Bangladeshi and Pakistani children.

Structural explanations look to the much wider economic and social structure of society to understand the reasons for school failure. They include the functionalist writers who argue that schools act as sieves grading out higher ability children and Marxist writers who argue that educational failure ensures the majority of people accept that the upper class are cleverer.

The final set of arguments stresses the importance of the school – how it is organised and the quality of the teaching. The higher the quality according to Rutter, the better the success rate of the pupils from all backgrounds.

Secondly, researchers point to the influence of the views of both teachers and of other pupils (the peer group). It would seem that the higher the expectations of the teachers and the peer group, the greater the level of achievement at school. These factors are especially important for females and for those from certain ethnic minorities.

(e) The key changes are:

The 1988 Education Act.

The introduction of the National Curriculum – core subjects, and fixed programmes of study plus attainment targets. Increasing educational opportunities? Good points – allows an increasingly mobile population to move schools without hindering children's progress; has made it easier to monitor what is being taught. Bad points – has decreased the flexibility of schools to provide courses appropriate to the needs of their children.

Local management of schools – schools now control their own affairs and finances and can opt out of local authority control. Good points – schools are more responsive to the needs of the community which should increase opportunities. But, grant maintained schools in practice get more money than local authority schools – so not everyone benefits.

Greater parental choice and involvement. Parents can now decide where they send children. This will allow good schools to grow and bad ones to fail, thus driving up standards. But, what about children in the 'sink' schools that aren't popular?

Making schools more aware of industry. Through things like work experience, CPVE and TVEI schools are supposed to be more work related. This has raised opportunities within education for children to be prepared for work, but has not increased their overall chances of finding employment.

5 **(a)** Mobility is the movement up and down the class structure. Reasons include the person's ability, gender, own class background, education, the changing economic structure of society, the reproductive patterns of those in the higher classes.

(b) The answer to this question must include arguments for and against a free and open society in Britain.

The *changing occupational structure* has meant there is more room at the top than at the bottom. But, the status of many clerical jobs has been eroded, so this may not be real mobility.

Manual classes have more *children* than non-manual classes. Therefore, there has been upward social mobility to fill the newly created non-manual jobs. However, there is still a high degree of *self-recruitment*, and the amount of self-recruitment is greater in non-manual classes than manual.

Educational change has given greater opportunity to working-class children, so that today a quarter of all professionals are recruited from the working class. But, in the last 10 years there has been a reduction in the numbers of working-class children going to university.

Evidence from the Oxford Mobility Study found that for all groups the chances of upward social mobility had increased. However, the relative chances of upward mobility have not significantly changed over time.

Functionalists argue that society is a meritocracy, so any increase in social mobility means that society is becoming fairer. Marxists argue that even if social mobility exists, it involves only small changes in income. The real division is between the owners and the rest of society and very few people become owners from humble beginnings. Social mobility hides the real divisions in society by making people feel free and in control of their own destiny, whereas in reality it is the owners who are in control.

(c) This covers a whole range of influences including family size, health, length of life, chances at school, type of job, living standards, accents, leisure patterns, etc.

(d) (i) Wealth refers to the amount of property an individual owns which can be turned into cash for the benefit of the owner, and the amount of money that person possesses.

Sociologists have identified two different types of wealth. The ownership of things that people use, such as cars and houses (called wealth used for consumption) is not 'spare' wealth. Wealth that is used for production, such as money invested in land and shares to make a profit, is regarded as 'spare' wealth, and possession of this wealth is seen to be a more important sign of a person's status in society. However, the official figures do not distinguish between the first type of wealth used above and the second form of wealth used to finance production.

It is difficult to obtain figures on wealth since the wealthy in society tend to be secretive about it. Also, are we to include occupational pensions as wealth? For many people pensions are an important source of wealth, but they cannot be turned into cash and so do not fit the definition given above.

It is difficult to decide when a person is wealthy because any judgement is likely to be biased. It is difficult to say at what point one person becomes wealthy when another does not. Also, people may not appear wealthy because they don't spend lots of money on themselves, but in fact may have a considerable sum invested in stocks and shares.

Poverty is difficult to define because:

Some sociologists, such as Rowntree, argue that absolute poverty should be used as a guide. This is based upon a reckoning of the resources people need to survive physically (food, shelter, heating, etc). The problem with this is that the needs people have depend upon the type of job they do (does a bank clerk need as much food as a miner?), and where they live (in the desert? at the North Pole?). Also what is considered a subsistence diet changes over time.

It is also difficult to decide what adequate shelter consists of. It is not clear at which point a person's type of shelter becomes a serious threat to their life. It is possible that people can survive on the streets, for instance, though this increases the chances of them dying. Where should the line be drawn?

Other sociologists, such as Townsend, argue that relative poverty should be used as a measure of poverty. This argument states that you cannot isolate what is regarded as poverty or wealth from the general expectation and living standards of society. What was a luxury for past societies may now be seen as necessity, for example central heating. Sociologists who use this definition tend to draw up a list of items that they believe is essential. Anyone who lacks a number of these things is said to be in poverty.

The problems with this are:

Who is to decide what things are necessities? For example, does not possessing a TV mean that you are in poverty?

It is difficult to draw the line between poverty and non-poverty.

There may be some people who choose to spend all their money on alcohol yet have no central heating. These people may show up as being in poverty when in reality they have enough money to enjoy a better lifestyle. What constitutes poverty will vary greatly from time to time and from society to society, making comparisons of poverty rates difficult.

(ii) Living in poverty may have the following effects:

Poor people tend to live in inner city areas and are more likely to suffer from and take part in crime. Also, there are fewer doctor's surgeries in inner city areas, and worse schools. Studies show that poor children do worse than others at school. Housing conditions are lower, there are less community facilities, more pollution. Also, supermarkets are increasingly located out of town so that poorer people are forced to buy from more expensive small shops and can't afford to purchase cheap fresh fruit and vegetables.

Greater homelessness.

Less secure and less safe employment, with lower pay.

More isolation and stress and less self-esteem are associated with the poor.

Obviously, those who possess wealth will be able to enjoy a lifestyle opposite to the one described above. Also, they may be able to directly increase their status and life chances because wealthy people are the most powerful in society. They are in control of government and business and can make the rules to favour themselves. Those who possess greater wealth are given higher status by society. Their views are taken into account more often in the mass media. Those in poverty may be accorded lower status because they are seen either as failures or as social security scroungers.

(iii) Factors include:

Social class (occupation) – the higher the social class you are in, the better your life chances in the areas of income, health care, schooling, crime, housing and lifestyle. The higher a person's social class, the higher their social standing.

Gender – females are still expected to have a different status to men. They are expected to be mothers and housewives, though their status is changing. Females are more likely to do unpaid work (domestic work) and receive less pay at work. Thus, they are more likely to be dependent upon others. They are more likely to do part-time jobs and break their careers to have children. Thus, they are more likely to end up in poverty, and less likely to succeed in careers than men. They are concentrated in a narrow range of jobs like care work and clerical work, and so have fewer opportunities in life than men.

Ethnicity – certain ethnic minority groups, particularly Afro-Caribbean, Pakistanis and Bangladeshis are more likely to be unemployed and denied the best jobs. Thus, they get lower status and worse life chances than whites. These groups also tend to live in inferior housing. Many of the black population are working class, and so face more of the problems associated with class outlined above. The status of black people in society is lowered by racism in society, and by the attitude of the police to black people – black people are more likely to be convicted of crime for example.

Age – older people face worsened life chances due to loss of income from work, loss of status held through work, deterioration in health, and loss of social contacts. Elderly people may be viewed as a social burden and so have lower status.

6 **(a)** This refers to the fact that women are discriminated against in education and employment; that they are still expected to look after the home and the children; that they are still the object of harassment, both physical and sexual. These points need to be developed. However, point out the advances made by women legally and culturally, mainly as a result of the feminist movement.

(b) The point of this question is to discuss the way that women are socialised into their roles in our society. Examine the role of the family, the peer group, the media and the school, You should then compare this with examples of female roles in other societies.

7 Youth culture means the distinctive set of values held by younger people. There is not a single youth culture. Instead there is a variety of youth cultures, based upon the class, gender and ethnic divisions in our society. Your essay should take various examples of this from skinheads to New Age Travellers. Use your own special knowledge of contemporary youth for examples.

8 You should raise the issues of prejudice and discrimination. Examples of these could include the problems over housing, employment, treatment by the police and the mass media. It is useful here actually to know some specific examples. The various explanations for prejudice ought to be covered – authoritarian personality, stereotyping, scapegoating.

9 **(a)** People tend to get satisfaction from jobs that give them control over their actions, that are interesting, and are varied. It would seem that craft work is most interesting, while machine minding and assembly line work is the least rewarding. In white-collar jobs the routine work on computers and word processors is least interesting. Opinions vary over the use of automation. A good answer would raise issues about alienation and whether it was just the type of technology that caused work satisfaction.

(b) Automation is the control of the complete work process by machines. There are basically two arguments – the optimistic and the pessimistic. The first sees people being liberated from dull, boring work and allowing them greater leisure and freedom. The second see machines replacing people, so causing high levels of unemployment with all the attendant political, social and economic problems.

(c) The occupational structure has changed.

There has been a shift from the primary sector (agriculture and fishing) to the secondary sector (manufacturing industries) to the tertiary sector (services). Nowadays, over two-thirds of Britain's workforce are employed in the service industries. This has led to an increase in the number of people doing non-manual work, as service jobs require non-manual workers. There has been a corresponding drop in the numbers involved in manual work traditionally associated with manufacturing. As the traditional industries of shipbuilding, mining and manufacturing have declined, many unskilled and semi-skilled jobs have vanished. Also, changing technology has meant that machinery has replaced the work traditionally done by workers, and new skilled workers are required to look after the new machines.

There has been a growing number of women employed in work since the start of century.

Women now make up 46% of the working population, and this figure is set to rise. Women are more likely to work in non-manual work and be employed in the service sector of the economy, although they are concentrated in lower paid jobs within the service sector. The biggest increase in the numbers of women working has come amongst married women. This has let to many families having two incomes, whilst other families have none. Nearly half of all women workers work part time.

There has been an increase in part-time work.

Two out of three of all new jobs created are part time. Part-time work often benefits employers who do not have to pay National Insurance or give the same employee benefits. Many workers prefer part-time work because it gives them flexibility. Changes in employment law to give part-time workers more rights may reverse the trend towards part-time work.

Changing technology.

Society has changed the way it produces goods. Previously, craft production gave the worker full control over the product made, usually because the worker worked by hand. This was replaced by mechanisation where people were required simply to operate machinery. Jobs were split down into simple, repetitive tasks, but this increased division of labour led to a decrease in job satisfaction. Now, automation is increasingly occurring in industry, whereby machinery is used over practically all the manufacturing process, displacing manual workers from employment, and requiring only a small number of highly skilled employees to supervise the manufacturing process. Thus, automation has increased job satisfaction amongst those in work, but increased unemployment. It has also led to the need for a more highly skilled workforce.

Growing unemployment

Since the 1970s there has been an increase in the numbers of people unemployed to around the three million figure. This may have been due to a number of factors. Three million extra female workers have entered the workforce since the war, and people are living longer decreasing unemployment vacancies. Foreign competition has led to redundancies, as has a depression in the economy and the unwillingness of the government to tackle unemployment through job creation schemes. There may also exist a skills gap as employers lack the skills required to fill high-tech jobs. Some people have pointed out that there is a growing difference between workers in secure, well-paid work with decent conditions of service and high job security, and those who work in part-time, low-paid work with little job security, poor working conditions and few employment rights. This is called the growing importance of the split between core workers and peripheral workers.

10 The point here is first of all to stress that unemployment is bad and that there is a myth of the unemployed scrounger living a high life on social security. Then you should go on to point out how unemployment hits people very differently. Young people and middle-aged people are faced with very different problems, while women may be forced back to the domestic role. In other words the consequences vary according to age, gender and financial resources.

11 (a) You need to explain the overall decline in the birthrate – contraception, the desire for a higher standard of living, changes in female attitudes to their role; also the increase after the Second World War, the affluent years of the early 1960s.

(b) People are living longer because they have a higher standard of living and housing and they receive higher standards of medical care.

The consequences of this are the ageing of society; the shifting demands for welfare and health services; the influence on consumer industries; the burden of dependency; a decline in the status of the elderly. The numbers of women living longer might be worth mentioning.

12 (a) There are clear differences between life in an urban and in a rural community. Life in urban communities tends to be more superficial; people less often have multiple roles; less sense of community; the people tend to move and do not identify with the neighbourhood. However, you ought to point out that there are strong arguments against this simple division – refer to Pahl's studies. Answers about traffic and pollution are not really comparing 'communities' and would score low marks.

(b) The problems consist of poverty, urban decay, racial tension, drugs, poor housing. Explanations would centre on the move away from the city of the 'stable' working class and the middle class to the suburbs and the new towns. Industry has declined and the new industries are likely to relocate in out-of-town locations. Lack of housing provision for single people often makes them sleep rough. Inner city areas are therefore deprived.

13 (a) This is a debate on the relative definitions of poverty – remember that there are a number of these, and the absolute one by Rowntree. The point here is that depending on where you draw the poverty line, the numbers of people in poverty increases or decreases. This would imply that respectively more or less resources and help should be given. Also the relative definitions of poverty go beyond discussions of money and also talk about resources.

(b) This is a reference to the cycle of poverty and the culture of poverty. Both these concepts ought to be discussed and they could be compared to a Marxist explanation. You should stress that poverty is not just lack of money, but resources in general.

(c) This question refers to the fact that there are major problems of finance facing the health and social security services. The people who founded the Welfare State never expected this level of social problems to continue so long. There are solutions from both the left and the right of the political spectrum. Those on the left suggest that more money ought to be spent, but that the problems arise out of our economic system, which needs reforming. On the other hand, those on the right talk about cutting back and encouraging people to take out private health insurance policies. They compare the universalistic policies of the NHS with the idea of helping the poor – in effect a two-tier system.

14 **(a)** Methods – sponsorship of MPs, e.g. by trade unions to get MPs to speak on their behalf.

Consultancies – many MPs are paid by companies to watch for moves within parliament that might affect their business.

Payment of funds to political parties to get them to vote in their interests.

Lobbying MPs and ministers.

Advertising in the mass media and distributing leaflets.

Holding public meetings or mass demonstrations.

Civil disobedience – such as anti-road protesters.

Organising strikes.

Providing expertise to government in the knowledge that they will put their message across in doing so.

(b) Arguments for:

It makes sure that important government decisions are made by the party that gets the most votes. Proportional representation often puts crucial decisions in the hands of small groups who hold the balance of power.

It maintains strong local links between an MP and his/her constituency. This is fair because people can directly appeal to someone who looks after everyone in one area, and not just those who vote for them.

The current 'first past the post' system is simple to use and everyone understands it.

It has worked well for many years so why change it.

Arguments against:

The winning party rarely gains a majority of the votes (this has happened only twice the twentieth century). This does not seem democratic because it is likely that most of the population voted against the government.

Most votes are wasted. If you vote for a candidate who does not get elected, or if you vote for a candidate who gets a big majority, your vote may be seen to be useless because it has made no difference to the outcome. If all the votes polled were counted up nationally and then seats in Parliament divided up equally amongst the parties, your vote would have meant something.

The outcome of general elections is generally decided by the outcome of a small number of marginal constituencies. Most of the seats up for grabs at an election are 'safe' – one party is sure to win. So, the parties rely on a small number of voters making their minds up in areas where the result is in the balance.

The MP for one area will be unable to represent everyone in that area because many people will not agree with him/her.

(c) Social class: most working-class people are Labour supporters. Most middle-class people support the Conservatives. However, some middle-class people, especially those employed by the government, support the Labour Party. Also, the Conservative Party could not get elected without the help of working-class voters.

Party images: few people know what policies the parties really stand for. Rather, they are influenced by a general 'image' that the party puts across in its election broadcasts and advertising.

Family: many people share the beliefs of their parents.

Geographical area: those in the North, in Scotland and Wales, and those in the inner cities are more likely to vote Labour. Those in the South and rural areas are more likely to vote Conservative.

Ethnic origin: black and Asian people are more likely to vote Labour because Labour has more sympathetic policies, and more black and Asian MPs than the other parties.

Religion: this is more important in Ireland. In Britain, Catholics are more likely to be working class and therefore Labour supporters than Anglicans.

Mass media: this may have an effect, either by reinforcing people's ideas or by actively changing them.

Gender: in the past women were more likely to vote Conservative, though in recent elections this has not been the case.

15 Social control is the way that people are persuaded to follow the rules and expectations of society. It operates in two main ways – formally and informally. The main agencies include the family, the peer groups, school, religion, the mass media and the police. Take some of these and look at them in some detail.

16 (a) (i) Not confirming to expected patterns of behaviour.

     (ii) The reasons suggested include reflecting the majority view; the results of moral crusades; and reflecting the interests of the powerful. These should be discussed using examples to illustrate your point. You could also raise the issues of the variation in what is considered deviant/illegal across society and time.

  (b) (i) They are only rough guides, little else. The main problems occur with the uneven reporting of crime to the police and the way these reports are subsequently categorised by the police. You should develop the reasons why people report crime or not, and then go on to look at policing practices which also influence the statistics. You might find it useful to refer to the British Crime Survey.

     (ii) You should examine the influence of labelling and the role of the media in creating moral panics, which can influence the acts of the police and judges. You could use the example of Stan Cohen, Jock Young or Stuart Hall. You could go beyond this and comment on the attitudes of the police and courts to female offenders and show why they treat them differently as a result of the label produced by the gender role.

17 (a) This is a wide ranging question. The simplest way to tackle it would be to take a few areas of social life, such as women, politics or crime, and then see how they influence cultural attitudes. You could then go beyond this and look at the way they influence us, either directly through the 'hypodermic syringe' type model, or through the 'cultural approach'. Labelling, stereotyping, moral panics, etc, would all be acceptable here.

  (b) The point here is that there is no such thing as news, merely what journalists define as news. They look for the sort of things that would interest the presumed readership of their papers. You must discuss the concept of news values and how they vary according to the paper. You might want to raise the issues of ownership and control.

  (c) Gender socialisation refers to the culturally created differences between men and women that are learnt from society.

Ways in which the media may affect gender socialisation:

Daily newspapers include pictures of semi-naked women encouraging people to see women as sex objects.

Women's magazines present accepted roles – that women should look attractive, be good mothers and good wives. This may encourage women to learn these roles.

Angela McRobbie studied *Jackie* magazine and found that this magazine encouraged girls to be passive and romantic, whilst men were shown to be independent.

Early reading books were heavily stereotyped with boys and girls doing gender separate activities.

On television, men are portrayed in more active roles than women, so that both men and women learn to accept that women are passive.

However, the media are a form of secondary socialisation. There are many other influences on people that have an important effect, such as the family and peer group.

The influence of the media may be limited because the audience can select what they want to read and watch. The media may simply be reflecting the ideas of society about gender roles, not shaping them. Viewers have minds of their own and are not simply fed a diet of stereotypical images.

Nowadays, women are shown on TV and in magazines in a variety of roles. The mass media are using men as sex objects in advertisements.

Chapter 21
Coursework

Projects and how to go about them

Each of the Examining Groups has devised a different format for the coursework, though they all share certain basic requirements. Each Examining Group requires that you demonstrate the following:
- knowledge and understanding of your chosen topic;
- a sensible method of going about the investigation;
- an understanding of the alternative methods chosen;
- use of appropriate sources;
- analysis of results
- evaluation of what your project shows and its effectiveness.

Set out below is a useful guide to completing your coursework, a summary of which is given in Fig. 21.1. It will enable you to organise your work in a way that will help you to achieve high marks. You may decide to use the headings below in your own research. However, you should check with your Examining Group to see if it has any specific coursework requirements not dealt with below.

Introduction to the research

Title

Your title should be short and concise. Keep your title simple and well defined to show the examiner that you have a clear picture of the area you wish to investigate. Some of the best titles take the form of a short question that can be answered by your study, for example:

'Does school influence boys and girls to choose different careers?'

'It could be you! The effect of the National Lottery on spending habits.'

'Racist attitudes in school: a case study.'

You should check with your teacher or the Examining Group to see if your title is acceptable before you go ahead with any research – for some Groups this is a requirement. Also, your teacher will have a bank of previously acceptable titles that you can use. Finally, do not worry too much about the title, it can always be changed at a later date.

The topics chosen to investigate and the reasons for choosing the investigation

In this section you should aim to give a brief introduction to your coursework. This is your chance to show that you have considered your project in detail. You should put in some background information about your topic and why it is really worth studying. Try to show a personal interest in the topic at this stage, and briefly mention how your project is linked to areas of sociology that you have studied, such as gender, social class and ethnicity.

Choosing the right topic is essential. You should aim to choose an area that is easy to investigate, that interests you and that is linked to a subject you have studied on your course. Do not be too ambitious. The best coursework submissions are invariably those that are straightforward, well defined and relevant to your course. For example, a study into 'The social importance of pets' is unlikely to be linked to your syllabus directly. Similarly, a study entitled 'The Social History of England' is likely to be too big for a small study, and again is not a straightforward sociology topic.

Examiners tend to award higher marks to candidates who have chosen topics that they are interested in or are linked to their personal circumstances. This is because if you are interested in a topic you are more likely to put more effort into it. Also, if you choose a topic you are familiar with, it may take you less time to research. Finally, those projects that deal with problem areas such as smoking, drugs and alcohol are often difficult to investigate and often produce poor results as a result.

The hypothesis to be tested

This is a very important part of the study. A **hypothesis** is a statement that predicts something – it is a guess about something that has not yet been tested. The following is a good example of a hypothesis:
'School influences girls to choose different careers to boys.'

It may not be true to say that school makes girls choose different careers to boys; the purpose of your coursework is to find out if this guess is right.

You must be able to prove your hypothesis right or wrong. So, 'How do teenagers spend their money?' is not a hypothesis, it is a question. Some of the best projects prove their hypothesis to be incorrect. If your results prove your initial hypothesis incorrect, you will gain credit for explaining why. You can, if you wish, have more than one hypothesis.

When choosing a hypothesis it is important to be very careful with words like 'increasing' or 'nowadays'. These words are difficult to define and mean different things to different people, i.e. 'Truancy amongst schoolchildren is increasing'. Where will you find information about truancy in the past, and will you be able to compare it with the information that you intend to collect? Similarly, the hypothesis 'There is a lot of crime about nowadays' is difficult to test. What do you mean by 'a lot'? Will everybody agree with your idea of what a lot of crime represents? Also, the term 'nowadays' implies that some change has occurred over time. Could you measure this easily?

Primary evidence

Remember that **primary evidence** is that which you have collected yourself.

Every study has a **survey population**. This means all the people whom you might investigate who are relevant to your study. Usually, the survey population is too large to deal with, so you will be expected to chose a smaller cross-section of people to investigate. This is called a **representative sample**.

You must explain in your project why you have chosen the type of representative sample that you will be using. Usually, you should choose one of the following:
- simple random sampling;
- systematic sampling;
- quota sampling;
- stratified random sampling.

In this section, you should discuss the good points and bad points of the method of sampling you have chosen.

The methods used to collect evidence

In this section you must write about the **method** of collecting information you intend to use. You should write about why you have chosen one method and not another, and the possible drawbacks of each. Have you chosen to use interviews instead of questionnaires?

Your choice of method should be one that allows you to investigate your subject in a way that will give you a good set of results. You must also show that you understand the alternative methods that sociologists use, and explain why you have chosen not to use them. Your coursework may use any of the following methods:

- questionnaires;
- interviews (closed or open-ended);
- observation.

It is vital that you compare and analyse each of the methods open to you, and that you choose a method suitable for your study. For example, if the title of your study is 'Male and female attitudes towards marriage', it may not be suitable to use the technique of observation.

Avoid using too many methods – it takes longer and can become complicated.

Secondary evidence

Successful projects demonstrate an awareness of the current issues in sociology. At this stage you should include a plan of the steps you will take to obtain secondary evidence – where do you intend to look and how will you go about it?

For any area you choose to investigate, there should be a supply of background information available. Look in textbooks, in *Social Trends* (a book of statistics available in all libraries, in the reference section) and in newspaper and magazine articles to find any information that is relevant to the title of your study. Don't forget to use a CD-ROM, either at home or in your local library.

Conducting the research

The pilot study

A pilot study is like a test run. You should conduct a pilot study to see if your chosen methods work. You will be able to see if you are likely to get a decent set of results, and to overcome any potential problems before you do the actual project. It is essential to try out your methods before you do them, and to keep a record of any improvements. This is rewarded by examiners, and prevents you from making crucial mistakes later.

You should keep a record of your pilot study and explain how and why you have improved it. For example, you may find that respondents will not answer an interview question because they find it embarrassing.

The main survey

The sample

In this section, you should describe the final sample you have chosen. What does the sample consist of – how many people do you have? Also, what types of people in terms of age, sex, ethnic grouping and social class make up your group? Try to construct a table showing the different characteristics of the people you have chosen – their age, sex, ethnic group and social class, etc.

You should say how you chose the sample, how you contacted people, how many responded and how many refused to take part.

Collection of data

You should include a copy of your questionnaire or interview schedule. Include one completed questionnaire as an example.

Explain what information you were trying to obtain from the sample and how your questions helped you to do this.

Describe how you physically obtained the information from the people in the sample. For example: where did you interview them, how did you record the interviews, how did you distribute and collect the questionnaires?

Research findings

Here, you should display your information in a readable form. If you have used a questionnaire, you should try to display your information in the form of a table.

You should go through each question in turn, and if possible display the results in the form of a graph or a table. If you have used interviews you should include a brief summary of any trends you have found in your research, and supplement this with direct quotations. If you have used observation as a technique, you should write a brief summary of what you have observed. If you use a graph, you must comment upon it, though you do not need to analyse your findings at this point.

Secondary evidence

Here you should include any secondary data you have collected which helps you investigate your hypothesis. For example. you may have discovered a table about the leisure pursuits of people in Britain from *Social Trends*, or a magazine article about arranged marriages.

You must not just include masses of leaflets and articles. This is a waste of time and looks as though you are padding out your project with very little thought. For every piece of secondary evidence you include you should write a brief paragraph answering the following questions:

- Why have you selected it and included it?
- Who produced it and why was it produced?
- Where did you get it from?
- Can the evidence it provides be relied upon?
- What does the evidence say about the topic you are researching?

Analysis

Summary and discussion of results

Write down the original hypothesis again. Next, list your main findings. Say whether or not your findings – obtained from your primary and secondary sources – have supported or contradicted your hypothesis.

You should point out any interesting patterns you have found, or any unusual findings that either contradict your hypothesis or go against any sociological ideas you have encountered.

Which parts of your research agree or disagree with your hypothesis? Is your information reliable? Think of some reasons why it might not be.

It is very important to link your findings to different areas of the syllabus. For example, if your project title is 'Male and female attitudes to marriage', you may be able to link your findings to work on the family, social class, work, gender, ethnicity and religion.

The best candidates consider the links between the work they have done and the work of others.

Evaluation

Discussion of research methods

This is a very important part of your project.

You should point out what went right, and what went wrong with your research methods. Include here whether you are pleased with the samples you selected. Did your respondents take the questions seriously? Did your observation have any effect on those you were observing? What was the response to your questionnaire? Did you find any useful secondary sources? Did you have any ethical problems with the research?

It is likely that you will have experienced some problems with the methods used. Your questions may have been poorly designed, the response small, or the sample unrepresentative. Many researchers experience difficulty with this. Providing you show the examiner that you are aware of the difficulties and limitations of your research, you will be rewarded. Consider:

- With hindsight, would another method have been more suitable?
- Was your sample representative?
- Were your research methods reliable?
- Should you have asked different questions?
- If you were starting again now, what would you do?

Discussion of project findings

- Do you think your research has been useful?
- Have you managed to collect some useful new evidence that perhaps challenges some of the sociological assumptions that you had before?
- Have you had enough evidence to test thoroughly your hypothesis?
- Do you think your data are valid?
- Are there any gaps in your evidence? Consider whether more qualitative or quantitative approaches might have added to your findings.

Finally, in what ways have you improved your skills as a researcher? You should indicate to the examiner that you are more aware of the problems of doing research. End on a personal note – have you enjoyed doing the project?

Bibliography

Write down in alphabetical order of author all the books you have used.

Appendix

This could include copies of any letters you have written or received, or any tables you have mentioned that were not suitable for inclusion in the main project. Resist the temptation to pad out this section with unnecessary magazine articles.

Also include in this section a diary. This should indicate the different steps you have taken in doing the research, who you have spoken to about the project and when, and the date of any consultations you may have had with your teacher. The Examining Groups give credit for evidence of planning and recording.

Finally, *do not copy work from books, newspapers, magazines, etc without saying where it comes from*. If you ignore this advice, you may well be disqualified from your course.

Index